Liberating Cu

Most people think of the museum and the preservation of valued objects as a distinctly modern, western invention. But nearly all cultures keep objects of special value, and many have created elaborate structures for storing and displaying them as well as methods for their care and preservation. *Liberating Culture* looks at non-western models of museums and curatorial practices, and uses them to challenge many of the basic assumptions on which western museology is grounded.

With examples from Indonesia, the Pacific, Africa, and Native North America, Christina Kreps explores the similarities and differences between western and non-western approaches to objects, museums, and curation, revealing that what is culturally appropriate in one context may not be so in another. Further case studies from the USA, Canada, and New Zealand illustrate how a growing recognition of indigenous curation and concepts of cultural heritage preservation is now transforming conventional western museum practice.

This volume offers both students and practitioners a study in comparative and critical museology that poses a new paradigm for museological thought, discourse, and action. It advocates the liberation of culture – its collection, curation, interpretation, and preservation – from the management regimes of Euro-centric museology, and the restoration of people's rights to the control and management of their own cultural heritage.

Christina F. Kreps is Director of Museum Studies and Assistant Professor of Anthropology at the University of Denver.

Museum Meanings

Series editors
Eilean Hooper-Greenhill
Flora Kaplan

The museum has been constructed as a symbol in western society since the Renaissance. This symbol is both complex and multi-layered, acting as a sign for domination and liberation, learning, and leisure. As sites for exposition, through their collections, displays, and buildings, museums mediate many of society's basic values. But these mediations are subject to contestation, and the museum can also be seen as a site for cultural politics. In post-colonial societies, museums have changed radically, reinventing themselves under pressure from many forces, which include new roles and functions for museums, economic rationalism, and moves towards greater democratic access.

Museum Meanings analyzes and explores the relationships between museums and their publics. "Museums" are understood very broadly, to include art galleries, historic sites, and historic houses. "Relationships with publics" is also understood very broadly, including interactions with artefacts, exhibitions, and architecture, which may be analyzed from a range of theoretical perspectives. These include material culture studies, mass communication and media studies, learning theories, and cultural studies. The analysis of the relationship of the museum to its publics shifts the emphasis from the museum as text, to studies grounded in the relationships of bodies and sites, identities, and communities.

Also in this series:

Liberating Culture

Cross-Cultural Perspectives on Museums, Curation, and Heritage Preservation

Christina F. Kreps

Routledge
Taylor & Francis Group

LONDON AND NEW YORK

First published 2003
by Routledge
11 New Fetter Lane, London EC4P 4EE

Simultaneously published in the USA and Canada
by Routledge
29 West 35th Street, New York, NY 10001

Routledge is an imprint of the Taylor & Francis Group

© 2003 Christina F. Kreps

Typeset in Sabon by
Florence Production Ltd, Stoodleigh, Devon
Printed and bound in Great Britain by
TJ International, Padstow, Cornwall

British Library Cataloguing in Publication Data
A catalogue record for this book is available from the British Library

Library of Congress Cataloging in Publication Data
Kreps, Christina F. (Christina Faye), 1956–
Liberating culture: cross-cultural perspectives on museums, curation,
and heritage preservation/Christina F. Kreps.
p. cm. – (Museum meanings)
Includes bibliographical references and index.
1. Museums – Philosophy.   2. Museums – Social aspects.   3. Ethnological
museums and collections – History.   4. Museum curators – History.   5. Cultural
property – Protection.   6. Material culture – Conservation and restoration.
7. Indigenous peoples – Cross-cultural studies.   8. Eurocentrism.
I. Title.   II. Series.
AM7.K74 2003
2002031776   069′.01–dc21

ISBN 0–415–25025–0 (hbk)
ISBN 0–415–25026–9 (pbk)

Contents

Figures

Preface

In 1990, I set off to Indonesia to explore the possibility of doing research on the role of museums in national development, as well as on how the museum concept was interpreted in a non-western cultural context. I had become interested in Indonesian museums after spending time in the Netherlands conducting research on the historical development of Dutch museums and their colonial ties. I went to Indonesia thinking, rather naively, that I would find museums that were somehow distinctly "Indonesian." Instead, I found that Indonesian museums were remarkably similar to western-style anthropology museums, at least those officially recognized as "museums" by the government. I had traveled halfway around the world in search of "difference" only to be confronted with what appeared to be yet another example of western cultural imperialism and an ever-advancing, global cultural homogenization.

A year later, I returned to Indonesia to begin a study that was eventually to become my doctoral dissertation in anthropology. My field site was the Provincial Museum of Central Kalimantan, Museum Balanga, located in the interior of Indonesian Borneo. Several months into my research, I came across the following inscription in Museum Balanga's Visitor Comment Book: "A small Royal Tropical Institute museum in Kalimantan. *Bagus*! [very good]." Written by two Dutch tourists, the comment struck me as an uncanny twist of fate. It was precisely because of my previous research on the Royal Tropical Institute Museum in Amsterdam that I had ended up in Central Kalimantan. But the inscription also hit a nerve because it seemed to confirm my initial impression of the museum as a mere reproduction of the western museum model. What better evidence could there be for this impression than the fact that here in the heart of Indonesian Borneo two Dutch tourists had encountered a replica of one of their country's most famous ethnographic museums? Perhaps they too had come in search of "difference" only to find a testimony to their own colonial legacy in Indonesia.

It was not until much later that I discovered that I needed to look beneath the surface of Museum Balanga to find the difference I was searching for. I had failed to see the museum's distinctive qualities because of my own entrenched preconceptions of what constitutes a museum and museological behavior. In addition,

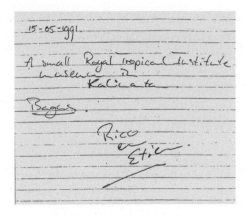

Figure 0.1 Inscription in the Provincial Museum of Central Kalimantan, Museum Balanga's Visitor Comment Book that reads: "A small Royal Tropical Institute museum in Kalimantan. *Bagus!* [very good]." Author's own photocopy.

I found myself caught in the web of the "cult of the expert." In other words, my Indonesian colleagues considered me a "museum expert," there to advise them on how to run their museum in a more "professional" manner. I was so busy instructing my colleagues in "standard" museum practices that I overlooked how their work reflected local values, traditions, and practices related to the curation of indigenous cultural materials. Despite my training in anthropology, I was blind to thinly veiled cultural differences.

Only gradually did I begin to see how much I had been shaped by what Indonesian museum professionals interestingly call "museum-mindedness," or, a particular way of thinking about museums and their purposes. This museum-mindedness, not coincidentally, is largely based on the western museum model. Because of the pervasiveness of the western museum model most of us have difficulty imagining museums or museological behavior in any other forms.

This book is, in part, about liberating our thinking from Eurocentric notions of what constitutes the museum and museological behavior so we might recognize these phenomena in varied forms. I provide examples of non-western models of museums and curatorial practices to show that while the western museum has become the predominant museum model throughout the world, museological behavior is a cross-cultural phenomenon with great historical depth. I examine the similarities and differences between non-western and western museological behavior, and show, through cross-cultural comparison, how differences exist not in the extremes, as we might expect, but fall along a continuum of variation.

Although much of what is presented in this book was inspired by my research in Indonesia, its genesis lies in my study of Dutch anthropology museums. In 1987, I went to the Netherlands to explore why Dutch ethnographic museums, and specifically the Royal Tropical Museum in Amsterdam, seemed so different from American anthropology museums in their approach to the representation of non-western cultures. For example, the Tropical Museum, in contrast to most American anthropology museums at the time, did not just focus on "culture areas." Instead, it dealt with actual nation states and political constructs like the "Third World," in which people were not just experiencing culture change but confronting concrete development issues and problems. Concepts such as the "Third World" and "development" were not typical subjects in American anthropology museums.

Here again, I went in search of difference, or more precisely, the source of difference. I was curious to find out what accounted for the differences between Dutch and American anthropology museums in light of the fact they share a number of similarities. For instance, both are products of western culture and owe their existence largely to western expansion and the development of anthropology as a discipline in the late nineteenth century. Additionally, Dutch and American museum professionals are part of an international, professional museum network in which a great deal of information is exchanged on museum theory and practice. My anthropological training told me that I needed to delve into the historical background of Dutch museums and examine them within their own particular socio-cultural context to find the answers to my questions.

Dutch anthropology museums developed within the context of Dutch colonialism. In many respects, they were products and tools of the colonial enterprise. For example, the Royal Tropical Museum was first established as the Colonial Museum in Haarlem in 1864 by the Society to Stimulate Trade and Industry. The purpose of the Society was to promote commercial interest in the Dutch colonies. The Colonial Museum was designed to give the Dutch public a view of life in the colonies (such as the Dutch East Indies, now the Republic of Indonesia) and the "great achievements of the Kingdom." In 1910, the Museum was moved to Amsterdam and incorporated into the Colonial Institute.

Museum exhibitions included displays of export products such as coffee, sugar, spices, rubber, textiles, and so forth. Dioramas of plantations and factories informed visitors about how these products were produced as well as the people who produced them. The Museum's ethnographic displays consisted of various examples of native material culture such as textiles, models of vernacular architecture, tools, weapons, and crafts. Exhibits were designed to highlight the contrast between the native people's "simple" technology and the more "sophisticated" and "developed" technology of the west. The ideology behind the exhibitions was clear: colonialism could be justified on the basis of how it was bringing "progress" to the colonies and thus part of the west's "civilizing mission." In short, how and why non-western people's cultures were exhibited in the museum directly reflected these colonial interests.

After World War II and the loss of Dutch colonial territories, the Colonial Museum had to reorient its purposes and activities because its former mandate was no longer relevant. Relations between the colonizers and the colonized had changed and the museum began to mirror these changes. The Colonial Institute changed its name to the Royal Tropical Institute and the Colonial Museum was renamed the Tropical Museum. The Dutch government stepped in to replace the private business interests that supported the museum during the colonial era, becoming its primary sponsor. The Museum also expanded its geographical focus to cover all tropical regions, not just those of former colonial territories.

During the 1960s, the Dutch government was contributing greater resources to development projects in the so-called "Third World." Museum visitors were also becoming more aware of the economic, social, and political realities of people living in developing areas through television and other media. Furthermore, many of the people who were formerly represented in the museum as colonial subjects were no longer living in faraway places. They were now members of Dutch society. Consequently, the Tropical Museum was pressured to present a more realistic picture of people living in the Third World, and began to develop exhibits that took an "emancipatory" or "consciousness-raising" approach. Exhibits were dedicated to creating greater public awareness of the disparities between "developed" and "developing" countries.

From 1975 to 1979, the Tropical Museum closed its doors to the public in order to renovate its exhibitions and create a new Tropical Museum, or, "a center where visitors are welcome to meet and become involved in the Third World." The mission of the new museum was to enrich the public's appreciation of development issues and to show how the Netherlands and countries of the Third World "share in one another's fate." The Tropical Museum was transformed from being a product and tool of Dutch colonialism, upholding the values of western superiority and dominance over non-western people, into an institution concerned with promoting greater cross-cultural awareness and international cooperation. In essence, it had undergone a process of decolonization.

Part of what I learned from my research in the Netherlands was that differences between the representational strategies of Dutch and American museums largely could be attributed to differences in their societies' respective interactions with and relations to non-western peoples. Larger imperial and colonial projects had influenced each country's museums, but such projects varied in their respective philosophical underpinnings, time frames, geography, and outcomes. For instance, while the Netherlands was forced out of many of its colonial territories after World War II, Euroamericans and other immigrants settled in what was to become the United States. As a "settler" nation the United States developed its own brand of colonialism, which, from the viewpoint of Native Americans, could be seen as internal colonialism. Exactly how this "style" of colonialism affected museums and their representation of Native American cultures is part of the subject matter of this book.

In general, my study of Dutch museums showed how museums are products of their own particular historical and cultural contexts, and how museums also do not exist as isolated entities in society. Rather, they evolve along with other social transformations in a dialectical process. The Tropical Museum, for example, reflected the changes that were taking place in Dutch society as well as the changing nature of its relationship to non-western societies. But it was not simply reflecting these changes; it was also helping shape them. I saw how museums, as ideological instruments, can be used either to consciously indoctrinate or to enlighten and liberate.

At the end of my research period in the Netherlands, I presented my findings at an International Committee on Museums of Ethnography (a subcommittee of the International Council of Museums) conference. The conference was held at the Royal Ethnographic Museum in Leiden. After my presentation, two Indonesian participants, Drs. Bambang Sumadio and Drs. Suwati Kartiwa of the Indonesian Directorate of Museums, approached me. Having found my paper provocative, they urged me to come to Indonesia to examine museums in a post-colonial context, and to study how museums functioned in the process of national development. As citizens of a former Dutch colony, they saw the connections between my study on museums during the colonial era and the development of their own museums. Four years later, I arrived in Indonesia to begin my research.

This book is the outcome of these and many other cross-cultural encounters. It is also the product of a series of revelations, which ultimately concern the implications behind the hegemony of Eurocentric museology: a hegemony that has worked not only to mask diverse approaches, but also to undermine the rights of other people to exercise control over the management and care of their own cultural heritage. In this respect, the book is about liberating culture – its collection, curation, interpretation, and preservation – from the management regimes of Eurocentric museology. The aim is to open the field to include multiple voices, which represent a wide range of experiences and perspectives. By giving credence to bodies of knowledge and practices that have been historically overlooked or devalued, the book suggests that those who have been marginalized as "the other" are central to the formulation of new museological paradigms. The book demonstrates how there is not one universal museology, but a world full of museologies. On the one hand, the study is about recognizing and respecting diversity. But on the other hand, it also concerns finding points of convergence or sites for the creation of more collaborative and mutually beneficial cross-cultural interactions. In this regard, the book explores the changing nature of relationships between anthropology museums and the people that historically have been their subjects.

Acknowledgements

Every book has its own story of how it came into being. This book is the product of some fifteen years of research and travel. Thus, I have many individuals and institutions to thank for their assistance and contributions.

Much of the material presented in this book is based on my research on museums in the Republic of Indonesia carried out over a period of ten years. I am greatly indebted to all my colleagues and friends at the Provincial Museum of Central Kalimantan, Museum Balanga, which was my initial field site from January 1991 to August 1992. Each contributed to my work in one form or another. I thank them for their endless patience and uncommon goodwill. I am especially grateful to Drs. Dium Rangin, Director of the Museum, for his hospitality and willingness to allow a prying anthropologist to snoop around his museum for a year and a half. Drs. Sri Utami Pasquet kindly served as my research assistant, but became so much more than that title can convey. Her companionship and generous spirit saw me through more than one daunting moment, and the devotion she showed toward her work was a constant inspiration. I also want to thank staff members Drs. Mohammed Yadi, Yulita, and Markorius Agau for their many efforts taken on my behalf. A special note of gratitude is extended to the Directorate of Museums in Jakarta, which served as an institutional sponsor of my research, and to all those staff members who graciously shared their time and expertise on Indonesian cultural policy and museum development. The late Drs. Bambang Sumadio, former Director of the Directorate, took special interest in my project and helped guide me through its various stages. His wisdom and foresight echo throughout the book. As a leader in the Indonesian museum community and visionary, he is sincerely missed. A special thankyou to Drs. Puspita Wibisono, former Director of the Textile Museum in Jakarta, who made my many trips to Jakarta more pleasurable by sharing her home and family with me. I am also grateful to the Indonesian Institute of Sciences for granting me permission to conduct research in Indonesia. Funding for this period of research in Indonesia was supported by a Fulbright Hays Dissertation Research Award. I want to thank the staff members of the American Indonesian Exchange Foundation for their hard work in assisting grantees, and helping us stay out of trouble.

My research on Indonesian museums began while I was a graduate student in the Department of Anthropology at the University of Oregon. Although many years have passed since I finished my doctoral studies in 1994, I remain indebted to my dissertation committee members, Mel Aikens, Nancy Lutz, and Anita Weiss, for their intellectual guidance and support. As an additional member of my dissertation committee, Clifford Sather offered his considerable expertise on Borneo ethnography. Heartfelt thanks go to Aletta Biersack, my doctoral advisor and academic mentor, for always pushing me to think harder and to have confidence in my own ideas.

Much of my graduate work was made possible through National Resource Foreign Language Area Studies Fellowships administered through the University of Oregon Southeast Asian Studies Program and Northwest Regional Consortium on Southeast Asian Studies. I am grateful to these programs for their assistance and for other awards that helped fund various phases of my dissertation project. I was very fortunate to receive a Doctoral Dissertation Award through the University of Oregon Graduate School, which allowed me to devote full time to writing during my final year. Additional support from the Oregon Humanities Center for Graduate Research Fellowships Program was also much appreciated.

Subsequent research was carried out in Indonesia in 1996 and 1997 while I worked as a consultant on the Kayan Mentarang Culture and Conservation Project sponsored by the World Wide Fund for Nature Indonesia Programme and the Ford Foundation. I want to extend a special thank you to Bernard Sellato who invited me to work on the project, and who has continued to generously share his extensive knowledge on Borneo over the years. I also appreciated Cristina Eghenter's collegiality while working on the project. Jennifer Lindsay, Cultural Program Officer at the Ford Foundation in Jakarta and her predecessor, Alan Feinstein, were also very helpful. During this period I also received a grant from the Asian Cultural Council to conduct further research on indigenous curation in Kalimantan. Many thanks to the Council for this support, and especially to Sarah Bradley for her ongoing efforts to help advance museological studies in Indonesia.

In conjunction with my work on the Kayan Mentarang Conservation Project, I was awarded a Smithsonian Fellowship in Museum Practice in 1997. The fellowship allowed me to spend six months at the Smithsonian exploring "participatory approaches" to museum development and taking advantage of its vast resources. Nancy Fuller of the Center for Education and Museum Studies deserves a special note of gratitude for her encouragement and abiding interest in my work. Her vision and leadership continue to move us in new directions. I also benefited from stimulating conversations with Stephen Weil, Emeritus Senior Scholar at the Center. Paul Taylor, Curator of Asian Ethnology of the Department of Anthropology of the National Museum of Natural History played a critical role in my project by providing additional funding, a space to work, and above all, the opportunity to exchange perspectives and engage in lively debates. As an Indonesian specialist, I gained much from Dr Taylor's knowledge and insights accumulated from many years of working in Indonesia. While at the Smithsonian, I also had the privilege of observing the work of the Center for Folklife Programs and Cultural Studies. I want to thank the staff members of the Center, especially Richard Kurin and Richard Kennedy, for sharing their time and knowledge and for allowing me to sit in on planning meetings for the 1997 Festival of American Folklife. This experience was highly rewarding.

I would like to acknowledge my colleagues in the Netherlands, Paul Berghuis, Gosiwijn van Beek, and Peter van Mensch, who played a pivotal role in my museological training on both theoretical and practical levels. Harrie Leyten and Wilhelmina Kal of the Tropical Museum in Amsterdam kindly shared their knowledge of the museum's rich history and transformation over the years. I thank them all for their guidance and assistance while I was a Research Associate at the Reinwardt Academy in Leiden in 1987, and for subsequent opportunities to exchange ideas. It was through my research and contacts in the Netherlands that I became interested in Indonesian museum development. Paul Berghuis deserves a special note of thanks for introducing me to the Reinwardt's work in Indonesia, and for many hours of engaging conversation over Bir Bintang.

Many of my ideas on cross-cultural approaches to curation were first presented at the session "Indigenous Curation: Alternative Perspectives on Preservation, Collecting, and Presentation" during the 1994 Annual Meeting of the American Anthropological Association. I owe an intellectual debt to Philip (Minthorn) Cash Cash who helped conceive the idea of the session and to other panel participants, Nelson Graburn, Alice Horner, Molly Lee, Lisa Mibach, Tom Miller, Nancy Rosoff, Patrick Tafoya, and Margaret Hardin (discussant), whose contributions helped advance this new field of study. Revised versions of my paper, as well as those by Graburn, Lee, and Rosoff, were later published in a special issue of *Museum Anthropology* (1998). I am thankful to Susan Bean, editor of the journal at that time, for inviting us to submit the papers and ushering the project along.

Although I have been compiling material for the book for more than a decade, the process of actually writing it began after I joined the faculty of the Department of Anthropology of the University of Denver in 1998. I want to express my gratitude to the University for the institutional support I have received, and to my colleagues who have helped make its completion possible. A Faculty Research Award and a grant from the Office of Internationalization funded further field research in Indonesia in August 2000. Assistance from the Walter Rosenberry Fund helped cover costs related to illustrations. The Arts, Humanities, and Social Sciences Division granted me time off from teaching to work on the book. My colleagues in the Department of Anthropology, Larry Conyers, Tracy Ehlers, Richard Clemmer-Smith, Sarah Nelson, and Dean Saitta, have been supportive by passing on important references, listening and responding to my ideas, and in general, by creating an encouraging atmosphere in which to work. I also owe a great deal to my students who constantly remind me of the point of it all.

I am especially grateful to Jan Bernstein and Cynthia Sheldon of the University of Denver Museum of Anthropology for educating me in the complexities of implementing the Native American Graves Protection and Repatriation Act (NAGPRA). The opportunity to participate in the consultative process with tribal representatives has provided a deeper understanding of the significance of the law and its impact on Native people. I would also like to thank Joyce Herold in the Department of Anthropology at the Denver Museum of Nature and Science for sharing her insights gained from many years of collaborating with Native communities on NAGPRA and other projects. I feel fortunate to have been able to work with her and others at the museum over the past few years. My experiences there have reacquainted me with the realities of what it means to put theory into practice.

I am very much indebted to my colleague and friend Ann Dobyns, of the Department of English at the University of Denver, for taking the time to read through the entire manuscript and make helpful suggestions. I also want to thank Jan Bernstein, Miriam Clavir, and Tracy Ehlers for reading and commenting on various parts of the manuscript. I especially appreciate the efforts of Eilean Hooper Greenhill and Flora Kaplan, editors of the series "Museum Meanings," who provided constructive comments and encouragement as the book progressed. I am particularly grateful to Flora Kaplan for her initial help in preparing the book proposal and seeing it through the review process. Many thanks to Julene Barnes and Catherine Bousfield at Routledge for bringing the book to print and making the process seem less formidable. Finally, much gratitude goes to my family and friends for helping me stay the course.

1

Introduction: liberating culture

The museum idea and the practice of collecting and preserving valued objects are generally considered distinctly western cultural inventions and preoccupations (Ames 1992, Cannon-Brookes 1984, Clifford 1988, Pearce 1992). But nearly all cultures keep objects of special value and meaning, and many have developed elaborate structures for storing and displaying them as well as methods for their care and preservation. In many respects, these practices are similar to those of western museums and curatorship. As Moira Simpson has pointed out in her groundbreaking book, *Making Representations: Museums in the Post-Colonial Era* (1996):

> This impression of museums as a purely western concept is not entirely accurate. Museum-like models have existed traditionally in other cultures for many years, and some facets of conventional museum practice conform to these indigenous models.
>
> (1996:107)

Yet until recently, non-western models of museums and curatorial practices escaped the attention of western scholars and museologists. This lack of attention can be seen as not only a reflection of an ideology that views the museum and museological behavior as uniquely western, but also a belief in the superiority of western, scientifically based museology and systems of cultural heritage preservation. In short, this ideology has blinded us from seeing other cultures' models of museums and methods of treating cultural materials as diverse forms of museological behavior.

The growing recognition of non-western museum models and curatorial methods can be attributed to several developments that have taken place in the museum world over the past fifty years or more. One is the sheer proliferation of museums across the globe. The worldwide growth of museums has largely occurred since the end of World War II (UNESCO 1995:185). No longer confined to metropolitan centers and designed to cater to an urban elite, today museums of all sizes and forms can be found in some of the most out-of-the-way places. Museums have become part of global cultural networks, and, as Appadurai and Breckenridge have suggested, "are part of a transnational order of cultural forms that has emerged in the last two centuries and now unites much of the world" (1992:35). As western scholars have begun to investigate the forms museums take in diverse national and cultural settings, they have observed how the museum has been transformed to take on local cultural characteristics (Hudson 1987, Kaplan 1994, Taylor 1994). While some have been concerned with the "indigenization" of the western museum concept, others have begun to explore non-western people's own models of museums and curatorial practices (Clavir 2002, Clifford 1997, Simpson 1996, Stanley 1998, Rosoff 1998, Schild-krout 1999).

The growing awareness of non-western models of museums and curatorial prac-tices is also one of the many outcomes of the scholarly critique of museums that has emerged over the past two decades. The literature on this topic is now exten-sive (Ames 1992, Bennett 1994, Clifford 1988 and 1997, Haas 1996, Hooper-Greenhill 1992, Jones 1993, Karp and Lavine 1991, Macdonald and Fyfe 1996, Stocking 1985, Vergo 1989, Walsh 1992). The new critical theory of museums problematicizes the museum and museum practices, illuminating their Euro-centric, epistemological biases and assumptions. Museums have come to be seen as "hegemonic devices of cultural elites or states" (Durrans 1992:1), and "technologies of classification" (Macdonald 1996:7) that have helped construct particular ways of categorizing and viewing people, cultures, and things. As a result, "the museum's position is no longer seen as transcendent. Rather, it is implicated in the distribution in wealth, power, knowledge and taste shaped by a larger social order" (Harris 1990:142). In general, museums are now viewed as "contested terrain" where diverse communities debate what culture is, how it should be represented, and who holds the power to represent culture (Karp and Lavine 1991).

Critical analyses have also revealed how museums and objects are a "potent force in forging self-consciousness" (Kaplan 1994:1), and play important roles in the construction and expression of national, regional, and local ethnic iden-tities. The museum's capacity to function in these processes lies in its position as an instrument of education, or "purveyor of ideology" (Kaplan 1994:3), as well as custodian of objects loaded with symbolic capital. As products and agents of social and political change, museums are now viewed as sites for the struggle over and assertion of identity (Boswell and Evans 1999, Clifford 1997, Foster 1991, Handler 1988, Kaplan *et al.* 1994, Karp *et al.* 1992, Simpson 1996).

Criticism of anthropology museums, or those housing ethnographic collections, has been particularly strong, emanating not only from the scholarly community but also from the people whose cultures have been historically represented in these museums, i.e. non-western, indigenous, or Native peoples. As these communities have increasingly begun to demand a greater voice in how their cultures are presented in museums, they have also challenged conventional, museological paradigms of cultural representation and preservation. At issue are questions of power and authority concerning who has the right to speak for and represent whom. Museums are now challenged with confronting the historical imbalances of power that have marked their relationships with indigenous people, and are forced to redefine their strategies, roles, policies, and programs as they affect people and their cultural heritage. Today, museums are urged to establish "on-going dialogue and partnership with indigenous communities and to define a framework for respectful collaboration in the restoration of that inherent human right – the right to be the custodian of your own culture" (Arinze and Cummins 1996:7).

The assertion of Native peoples that they should be the custodians of their own culture has invariably led to debates over the rightful ownership of cultural property[1] (as well as human remains) in museums and the issue of repatriation. In Simpson's words, "one of the most difficult issues seeking resolution by museums in the post-colonial era is that of repatriation" (Simpson 1996:171). The demands of indigenous communities regarding these issues are bringing about dramatic changes in museum policy and practice:

> Curatorial staff are re-examining museological practices and the legitimacy of their possession of materials which previously were held and displayed without question to property rights, authority or wishes of those from whom they were taken. They have to address questions of ownership, care, display, and interpretation.
>
> (Simpson 1996·171)

Repatriation campaigns also have brought attention to the ethics of the owner-ship, curation, and display of sacred objects, or objects of religious, spiritual, or ceremonial value (see Simpson 1996:191–214, Clavir 2002).

Of particular importance to this study is how changing attitudes toward cultural property ownership and its curation are mirroring the changing nature of rela-tionships between anthropology museums and Native peoples. In the United States, for example, the anthropological museum world has been undergoing profound transformations as a result of the passage of the Native American Graves Protection and Repatriation Act (NAGPRA) by the United States Con-gress in 1990. In addition to protecting Native American burial sites, the Act required all federally funded museums to make inventories of Native American and Hawaiian human remains, funerary, sacred, and ceremonial objects and provide these inventories to federally recognized tribes. It also granted tribes the legal right to request repatriation of these materials. The implementation of NAGPRA has brought about a dramatic shift in the power relations between Native Americans and the museum and scientific communities. It has also influ-enced curatorial practices in mainstream museums. One of the many outcomes of NAGPRA is an increasing presence of Native American curators, traditional scholars, and advisors in museums. This presence is challenging the hegemony of western, scientifically based museological paradigms as Native perspectives and methods of "traditional care" have begun to be integrated into mainstream museums. "The 'Native point of view,' and voice, is increasingly being heard, and the attitudes and policies of anthropologists and museums are changing as a result" (Ames 1992:79).

Although NAGPRA has met resistance in some quarters, in others it has been embraced as an exciting opportunity to establish collaborative relations with Native American communities, to gain a deeper understanding of the mean-ings and values of certain classes of objects, and to expand our knowledge of

3

alternative methods of curation. The establishment of museums and cultural centers on the part of Native American communities themselves has also added to our awareness of the diversity of curatorial approaches, showing us that what is appropriate in one context may not be in another. Such changes are occurring not only in the United States, but in other countries as well.

> Today most self-respecting anthropology museums in the United States, Canada, Europe, Australia and New Zealand rally around the same set of principles and practices of including native advisors, advisory boards, community councils, task forces, etc. A few have even moved beyond mere consultation and have established greater equality at the decision-making level by hiring native co-curators or native museum directors.
>
> (Kahn 2000:58)

Consequently, cooperation, collaboration, and participation have become key-words in the vocabulary of the professional museum community.

Acknowledging the value of indigenous curation should not diminish the role of professional curatorship in museums. Certainly, it would be shortsighted and irresponsible to suggest, for example, that professional conservation techniques are categorically unsuitable for the protection of non-western cultural materials. Rather, recognition opens up possibilities for dialogue and the exchange of information, knowledge, and expertise. The point is to give credence to bodies of knowledge and practices that have been historically overlooked, or devalued. The recognition of indigenous curatorial practices and museum models is another step toward the decolonization and democratization of museums and museum practices. It reminds us that while museums are as diverse as the communities they represent, so too are the ways in which people care for and preserve their cultural heritage.

A critical theory of museum ideology and practice

This book is an inquiry into cross-cultural perspectives on the museum, curation, and cultural heritage preservation. In its cross-cultural approach, it can be broadly characterized as a study in "comparative museology," or rather the systematic study and comparison of museological forms and behavior in diverse cultural settings. Its aim is to show that although the museum is generally construed as a modern western cultural form, museological-type behavior is a long-standing, cross-cultural phenomenon. The book provides examples of non-western museums and indigenous curatorial practices, in particular, from Indonesia, the Pacific, Africa, and Native North America, to demonstrate how these are cultural expressions that deserve recognition, study, and preservation in their own right as examples of cultural diversity. It also shows how non-western forms of curation and concepts of cultural conservation are being integrated into mainstream museums, for example, in the United States, New Zealand, and Canada. This trend exemplifies how museums are increasingly moving toward the development of more cross-culturally oriented approaches to the management, care, and interpretation of their collections.

In general, the book is intended to further the liberation of culture from the hegemony of the management regimes of Eurocentric museology. As such, it is meant to contribute to the continual reappraisal of museums and museological practice. Throughout the book museology is understood as the study of the philosophy, purposes, and organization of museums (Burcaw 1975:12) as well as museum activities such as the collection, care, presentation, preservation, and interpretation of collections. Curation, or curatorship, refers to any activity or body of practice specifically devoted to the care and treatment of objects and their protection.

In the broadest sense, the book is an anthropology of museums and curatorial practices grounded in critical theory. By this I mean it looks at the museum and curatorial practices as cultural artifacts in themselves, or rather, as cultural constructs located in specific social, political, economic, and historical contexts. It also means that anthropology itself is implicated in the study since the discipline has contributed heavily to the construction of museological paradigms, especially as they relate to the collection, interpretation, and preservation of non-western cultural materials (see Bouquet 2001). Of particular importance are how the discipline of anthropology has contributed to the formation of ethnographic collections in museums, and the historical and political conditions under which collections have been acquired. Ethnographic objects did not come to be in museums by historical accident. But rather,

> their placement in museums . . . [is] the outcome of large-scale historical processes . . . The historical processes that led to the collection of . . . objects in museums have to do on the one hand with the forces of economic development and nationalism that transformed Europe in the nineteenth century and on the other hand, with those of imperial domination.
>
> (Stocking 1985:4)

The post-colonial critique of anthropology has uncovered the discipline's historical location of power in relation to its subjects, and its complicity, at times, in the subjugation of colonized peoples (Asad 1973, Said 1978). In response to such critiques, anthropology, in recent decades, has subjected itself to a much-needed self-scrutiny, resulting in a "reflexive turn" whereby anthropology has become in itself an object of critical inquiry (Clifford 1988, Fabian 1983, Huizer and Mannheim 1979, Hymes 1972, Marcus and Fischer 1986, Rosaldo 1989, Stocking 1985). Thus, a critical theory of museum ideology and practice informed by anthropology must interrogate both museology and anthropology as its subjects.

The book is also anthropological in its application of research methods typical of sociocultural anthropology, in particular, those of ethnography and comparison. Ethnography is a research process "in which the anthropologist observes, records, and engages in the daily life of a culture . . . and then writes accounts of this culture" (Marcus and Fischer 1986:18) or some aspect of that culture. The value of the ethnographic method lies in its reliance on "participant observation," or, the collection of data through first-hand observation. The culture in question, in this case, is that of museums and museological behavior observed in a wide range of national and cultural contexts.

I use the comparative method to explore the ways in which non-western and western models of museums and curatorial practices are both similar and different. While this approach implies that the units of comparison are of like kind, i.e. the museum and curatorial methods, each tradition is examined on its own terms and in the context of its own cultural settings. The use of the comparative method also implies that my understanding of non-western museums and curatorial methods is ostensibly influenced by the cultural logic of western museums and museological practices. However, rather than taking this logic for granted and as the referent to which all other forms are compared, the objective is to indicate how an understanding of one cultural form is extended by placing it into critical and dialectical relation to another (Kapferer 1988:xii). The aim is to show how vital dimensions of western museums and practices are thrown into general significance through the lens of other cultures and vice versa. As is true in the deconstruction of any paradigm, we begin to unravel its biases, assumptions, meanings, and implications when we place it in critical and dialectical relationship to other forms of thought and practice. By deconstructing the western museum concept and museology, we can see how exotic its constitution of reality has been. As Michael Ames, an anthropologist and former Director of the Anthropology Museum of the University of British Columbia, has urged, "We need to study ourselves, our own exotic customs and traditions, like we study others; view ourselves as 'the Natives'" (1992:10).

Keeping Ames' suggestion in mind as well as the "reflexive turn" in anthropology and museology, the book reflects my own viewpoints and vested interests as both an anthropologist and museum professional. I have been investigating the museum and the museum profession as a cultural phenomenon for some fifteen years, conducting ethnographic research on museums in the Netherlands, the United States, and the Republic of Indonesia. Much of the data presented in the book is derived from these studies. I have also had the opportunity to work in several museums in the United States in a variety of positions over a period of some twenty years. This dual position of both scholar and museum worker has given me a wide range of insights, perspectives, and experiences from which to draw. This position has allowed me to see how theory does or does not play out in real practice. Thus, my task has been not only to deconstruct museums and museum practices, but also to attempt to construct new and alternative approaches. In this respect, I concur with Ames' following remarks regarding the limitations of scholarly, detached critical analysis and the need to examine our work within the context of real-life situations.

> It is easy enough to criticize museums for being what they are or for failing to be what one thinks they should be, and to judge from one's own moral perspective the actions and inactions of others. It is more difficult to propose changes that are feasible, and to ground both criticism and reform in an understanding of the situation, economic foundations, and socio-political formations of the museums to be gauged . . . Useful criticism needs to combine assessment with the empirical examination of real situations, recognizing the complexity and intermingling of interests involved, as well

as relations between the individual and the social, and the conditions within which they operate.

(Ames 1992:4)

My outlook on museums and curatorial practices also has been shaped by theoretical frameworks and methods of analysis that take a decidedly critical stance, such as Marxist, postmodernist, and deconstructionist approaches as well as post-colonial critiques of western forms of cultural representation. Central to these approaches are issues of power and authority, and attempts to illuminate the contradictions embedded in dominant ideological structures. It has also been influenced by trends in several fields such as cultural studies, international development, as well as those of the "new museology."

Discourse analysis has become a popular tool for interrogating the biases and assumptions embedded in dominant ideological structures and forms of practice. The work of Foucault on the dynamics of discourse and power in the production of knowledge and representation of social reality has been especially important. "It is in discourse that power and knowledge are joined together" (Foucault quoted in Alasuutari 1995:115). The concept of discourse refers to

> the way in which a certain phenomenon thematizes knowledge, deliberation, action and institutionalized practices as an object of discussion. It includes what is taken for granted in that discussion and how disagreements on the issue occur. In this definition discourse also includes silences. The question as to who is expected to remain silent or which topics are not to be spoken about forms an integral part of the discourse, just as does the question of how it is appropriate to address the topic.

> (Alasuutari 1995:137)

Applied to museology, discourse analysis can be instrumental in unveiling the mechanisms by which western museology has produced certain ways of thinking and talking about museums and curatorial practices, while disqualifying and even making others impossible to see. As an analytical tool, discourse analysis creates the possibility of "standing detached from [museological discourse], bracketing its familiarity in order to analyze the theoretical and practical context with which it has been associated" (Foucault quoted in Escobar 1995:6). By viewing western museology as a discursive field, or historically constructed domain of thought and action, we can see how it has become an apparatus for producing knowledge about and exercising power over the curation and preservation of cultural materials.

Until recently, museology has relied almost exclusively on one knowledge system, namely the modern, western one. This knowledge system has dictated the ways in which cultural materials have been viewed and curated, systematically organizing and transforming them according to European constructs of culture, art, history, and heritage. Western models have been both the context and referent for our practice. Because of the hegemony of western museology, most people have difficulty thinking and talking about museums, curation, and heritage preservation in terms other than those provided by western museological discourse. Consequently, "the goal of the analysis is to contribute to the liberation of the discursive field so that the task of imagining alternatives can be commenced" (Escobar 1995:15). At a time when museology is under critical reappraisal and renewal, we have the opportunity to reimagine museological discourse, taking it in new directions and creating new spaces for the inclusion of multiples voices and perspectives.

In response to the need to be more inclusive of multiple voices and perspectives as well as new paradigms of thought and action, scholars have been giving greater attention to "indigenous knowledge," or the local knowledge that is unique to a given culture or society. Indigenous knowledge reflects and constructs people's ways of ordering and communicating about their world, and serves as the information base of a society. Local knowledge contrasts with international knowledge systems, which are largely based on western scientific knowledge. International knowledge systems are generated through a global network of universities, research institutes, government agencies and professional bodies (Warren *et al.* 1995:XV).

The recognition and use of indigenous knowledge have been particularly important in the field of international community development as development workers have come to realize that western models and practices are not always effective for use in non-western cultural contexts. Furthermore, many now see that international knowledge systems do not hold all the answers. As a result, development workers have begun more and more to rely on and integrate indigenous or local knowledge into community development projects, for example, related to agriculture, healthcare, and environmental conservation. But the approach also has relevance to museology. Throughout the book, I consider indigenous curation and concepts of cultural heritage preservation as a form of indigenous knowledge. I suggest that just as development workers are looking to indigenous knowledge systems for guidance, museologists may also find inspiration in indigenous knowledge concerning the care and treatment of cultural materials and concepts of cultural heritage protection.

The indigenous knowledge approach is especially relevant to museum development projects in so-called "developing countries," where projects are often conceived by outside "experts" and imposed on local communities. I examine this problem within the context of discussions on museum development in Indonesia and several African nations. I describe how indigenous approaches to cultural resource management can be incorporated into such projects to make them more compatible to local cultural contexts to better meet the needs and interests of particular communities. The approach is also suggested as a means of countering the negative effects of what has been identified as "normal professionalism."

Robert Chambers, in his book *Challenging the Professions: Frontiers for Rural Development* (1993), characterizes normal professionalism as the thinking, values, methods, and practices prevailing in professions and disciplines that reflect the biases and interests of international knowledge systems and centers of power. To Chambers, normal professionalism is reproduced through teaching and training, and defended on the grounds of specialization. Normal professionalism is also linked to structures of power and knowledge. Challenging the authority of "experts" and "specialists," Chambers calls for a "new professionalism" that entails reversing the flow of power and sources of knowledge from "top-down" to "bottom-up" approaches. The new professionalism stresses the decentralization of power through the empowerment of local people and support of their own initiatives. In general, the new professionalism in development studies emphasizes diversity and multiple approaches (Chambers 1993).

Much of what Chambers writes about normal professionalism in development studies is applicable to the western museum profession with its increasing emphasis on specialization and professionalism. We can help museum workers carry out their tasks more effectively and aid in the protection of valuable cultural resources by providing professional training and skills. But we should also consider how the imposition of professional standards and techniques could inadvertently undermine local or indigenous curatorial practices as well as a museum's long-term goal of cultural heritage preservation. Indigenous curatorial knowledge and practices have much to contribute to our understanding of museological behavior cross-culturally, or rather, how people in varying cultural contexts perceive, value, care for, and preserve cultural resources. These concepts and practices are worthy of preservation in their own right as they form part of people's cultural heritage and identity.

The "new museology" movement that has gained popularity in the international museum community over the past several decades embodies many features akin to the indigenous knowledge approach and new professionalism in development studies. The movement has its roots in the social movements of the 1960s and 1970s and the appearance of community-based museum initiatives. It reflected a widespread dissatisfaction with conventional interpretations of the museum and its functions (Davis 1999, Maynard 1985, Vergo 1989).

The new museology movement emerged from a series of round tables, International Council of Museums (ICOM) general conferences, and discussions within ICOM committees, and, in particular, the International Committee on Museology (ICOFOM) beginning in the 1970s. The movement's basic philosophy and principles were expressed in the "Declaration of Quebec" of 1984. According to the Declaration, the new museology is primarily concerned with community development and social progress. It reaffirms the social mission of the museum as a new point of departure and the primacy of this function over traditional museum functions (Maynard 1985). One of the aims of the movement has been to challenge conventional notions of museum definition and practice, and to widen the museum concept to embrace a variety of forms and meanings. It represents a transformation in what are seen as the aims of museology as well as a shift in the attitudes and thinking of museologists.

The "new" museum of the new museology is a democratic, educational institution in the service of social development. The new museum differs from the traditional museum not only in the recognition of the museum's educational potential, but also in its potential for promoting social change. Conventional museums are seen as object-centered whereas the new museum is people-centered and action-oriented.

The new museology is fundamentally concerned with the democratization of museum practices and bottom-up, participatory approaches. It stresses the importance of community or public participation in museums, not only as visitors, but also as participants in all aspects of museum work. The idea of museum democratization also suggests that the knowledge, skills, and experiences of the people for whom museums exist hold as much value as those of museum experts or professionals. The new museologists strive to bridge the gap between professionals and non-professionals by working with community members, utilizing the people's own knowledge, experiences, and resources. Rene Rivard, a museum theorist and leading figure in the new museology movement, describes this form of museum work as "people's museography." According to Rivard, people's museography is "a body of techniques and practices applied by a population to the conservation and enhancement, in a museum or otherwise, of the collective heritage of the community and its territory" (1984:84).

Community and identity are central, organizing concepts in the new museology. The notion of community is not necessarily decided in spatial terms, but rather, is made up of persons with a similar socio-economic and cultural background who share common interests and needs. The "new" museum is an educational institution directed toward making a population aware of its identity, strengthening that identity, and instilling confidence in a population's potential for development. Identity is seen as the totality of images that a group has of itself, its past, present, and future. The role of the museum is to put a population in a position to visualize, be aware of, and name these images, which are manifested at the material and non-material levels of everyday life. By identifying and naming the material and non-material elements that constitute their environment, people realize their right to their own local and regional identity, taking possession of their world and gaining control over it. New museologists also strive to help people cope with everyday life by pointing out problems and solutions to them. To achieve these goals, a museum must orient itself to local conditions and the specific interests and needs of a given population (Hauenschild 1988:5–6). A museum is said to be something that grows out of a community and expresses its own identity, challenging the assumption that there can be a set model or single blueprint for museums (Walsh 1992). The work of cultural documentation, curation, and conservation is thought to be an organic and dynamic process that is part of how a changing community defines itself (Lavine 1992:155). Local communities determine the nature and purposes of museum tasks in the process of defining themselves (Fuller 1992).

The new museology movement is largely about giving people control over their cultural heritage and its preservation as part of how they maintain, reinforce, or construct their identity. The approach acknowledges the importance of preserving not only resources that represent a community's past, but also vital elements of its living culture and its continuing development. Cultural heritage consists of people's material culture as well as their collective memory, oral traditions, personal histories, and everyday experiences. These aspects of culture are also the object of collection, documentation, study, and preservation. As a people-centered, bottom-up approach to cultural heritage preservation, the new museology promotes the idea that "each society needs to assess the nature and precariousness of its heritage resources in its own terms and determine contemporary uses it wishes to make of them, not in a spirit of nostalgia but in the spirit of development" (UNESCO 1995:176).

The new museology's dynamic approach to heritage preservation stands in contrast to more conventional preservation paradigms, which have tended to fix cultures in time and space and focus on the past. This perspective denies the fluid and flexible nature of culture in addition to its creative capacity for change. Ironically, preservation paradigms that privilege the past are often steeped in futurist rhetoric. Preservation discourse is replete with phrases such as "we need to save the past for the future" or "our future lies in the past." While such dictums may be useful for garnering support for preservation legislation and promoting heritage awareness, they divert attention from what lies between the past and the future, that is, the present and the value of living culture and the forces that sustain it. In the words of Raymond Williams, "a culture can never be reduced to its artifacts while it is being lived" (1960:343). Living culture defies preservation if preservation means fixing it in time and space and reducing it to object or artifact. As many authors have noted, cultural preservation does not just entail the collection, conservation, and display of objects through the development of better technical and evaluative methods, but also support of knowledge, customs, traditions, and values associated with objects (Handler 1992, Kaeppler 1994, Cruikshank 1995).

Cultural conservation: a new paradigm for cultural heritage preservation

Cultural conservation is a relatively new term that has emerged in recent decades to reflect alternative approaches to and new ways of thinking about heritage protection. It is a new paradigm because it embodies an integrated view of heritage that, like the new museology, emphasizes local involvement in heritage protection efforts. In the United States, the concept of cultural conservation grew out of a critical rethinking of the national system of heritage preservation in the early 1980s. What emerged was a "new discourse on heritage," in addition to a radical shift in the way policy was to be conceived and implemented (Hufford 1994).

The new paradigm was intended to redress problems that arose out of heritage protection legislative measures of the 1960s and 1970s, which designated three arenas of action: "1) nature (natural species and ecosystems); 2) the built environment (historic and prehistoric artifacts, buildings, sites and districts); and 3) folklife/culture (living artistic expressions and traditional communities and processes). Each arena had its professionals, legislative mandates, public and private supporters, and assorted goals and visions" (Hufford 1994:2). These arenas tended to mirror the divisions of the world maintained in academies and

11

other cultural and scientific institutions. However, those responsible for carrying out policy discovered that these divisions hindered comprehensive, coordinated planning and implementation. For example, to many, distinctions made between "nature" and "culture" and divisions between "tangible" and "intangible" resources obscured the complex interdependencies of culture and the environment. Problems were also encountered when representatives of national interests tried to impose external standards on local communities and sites that spanned a broad cultural spectrum. Many acknowledged that determining the significance and integrity of resources is a highly subjective undertaking, based on local cultural values and historical experiences. "The tendency of earlier heritage planning to authenticate past cultures and environments reduced the power of contemporary communities to manage the environments on which their dynamic cultures depended" (Hufford 1994:3).

In an attempt to address these problems, the United States Department of the Interior and American Folklife Center of the Smithsonian Institution conducted a study on policy, published in 1983. The study recommended that the term "cultural conservation" be adopted as a "concept for organizing the profusion of public and private efforts that deal with traditional community life" (Hufford 1994:3). Cultural conservation was suggested as an alternative to preservation because the term "conservation" more adequately reflects the dynamism of cultural resources, implying that, like natural phenomena, cultural phenomena inevitably change. Cultural conservation offers an overarching framework for the protection of cultural heritage with wide-ranging policy implications. In effect, the study proposed moving away from a fragmented approach to heritage protection, dominated by elite and professional constituencies, to an integrated approach based on grass-roots cultural concerns.

Cultural conservation is said to be interdisciplinary and action-oriented, encompassing a broad range of fields and professionals including folklorists, anthropologists, archeologists, historic preservationists, environmental planners, and scientists engaged in both environmental and cultural conservation activities. "The term 'conservationist' unites professionals in the applied sciences and humanities as advocates who bring their views of culture and ecology to bear on threatened facets of the world" (Hufford 1994:4). It connotes a concern for the conservation of both biological and cultural diversity.

"A central task of cultural conservation is to discover the full range of resources people use to construct and sustain their cultures" (Hufford 1994:4). For instance, there are many ways of determining what constitutes a "resource," and of assigning significance to an object, custom, practice, belief, site, or natural feature. Consequently, the identification of a resource should be guided as much as possible by those who ascribe significance to it. Understanding the context, or "vernacular systems" in which a resource makes sense, is also necessary because there can be a great difference between the "insider" (native or vernacular) views and those of the "outsider" (scholarly, official, professional, or elite). Accordingly, insider and outsider views need to be reconciled. As a case in point, a traditional society's myths, legends, and beliefs may appear quaint, unscientific, and not grounded in "objective reality" from the perspectives of elite or scientific systems (Hufford 1994:6). But these modes of expressions can become essential resources for planning and carrying out projects if seen as aspects of vernacular systems. The investigation of vernacular systems of history making is seen as particularly significant since a people's history contributes to their sense of identity. Vernacular histories can be stored in myths, artifacts, festivals, ceremonies, or landscapes, and are vital resources for the ongoing construction and maintenance of places as well as social identities dependent on them (Hufford 1994:6). Vernacular systems of natural resource management are also important objects for conservation since traditional systems of knowledge can form a basis for managing culture and the environment as a whole.

The Smithsonian Institution Center for Folklife Programs and Cultural Studies applies a concept of cultural conservation that clearly manifests the above ideas. To the Center, "cultural conservation is a scientific and humanistic concern for the continued survival of the world's traditional cultures" (Hunt and Seitel 1985:38). The concept has grown out of several related insights gained from humanistic and scientific studies over the past twenty years or more. Of particular importance is the concept of the ecosystem, derived from studies in biology and environmental conservation. Just as the idea of environmental conservation suggests that natural species exist in webs of interrelationships, the concept of cultural conservation acknowledges that living individuals and groups are part of larger economic, political, and social systems. Similarly, as strategies have been devised to protect the threatened environments on which endangered species depend, seeing traditional cultures in larger contexts allows planning for their continued vitality.

Many now recognize that when cultures die, because practitioners die or are forced to give up their culture, great resources of knowledge and understanding are lost. "We lose evidence of the variety of human cultural possibilities" (Hunt and Seitel 1985:38). Lost also is people's knowledge of their environment, acquired through observations accumulated over generations. Complex and meaningful aesthetic systems may also perish or leave artifacts devoid of their original meanings. But perhaps more importantly, when people lose their cultures or when they are devalued, the people lose a fundamental human tool for comprehending and coping with the world, for understanding and integrating their lives, and for orienting and raising their children. The effects of this loss are immeasurable, but may manifest themselves in social dysfunction and alienation that endures for generations (Hunt and Seitel 1985:38).

Both cultural and environmental conservation are now seen not only as feasible but also as necessary for human survival, and an integral part of the development process. When culture is integrated into development, it can enable the bearers of traditional culture to adapt their ideas and actions to a changing environment within the context of their own cultures and on their own terms (Hunt and Seitel 1985:38).

Museums are key arenas for the kind of dynamic cultural work described above because they are grounded in a conservation ethic. Yet too often museums are strictly devoted to the preservation of material culture, and are preoccupied with the past. If museums are to contribute to cultural conservation understood as "a concern for the continued survival of traditional societies," there needs to be further movement away from static notions of conservation that have been embedded in salvaging and rescuing paradigms. While "rescuing may become the only means of helping a given community record their endangered and dis-integrating cultural history" (Sharma 1999:54), museums should also strive to support and conserve the living knowledge, customs, and traditions associated with material culture. This is critical because "the maintenance of traditional practices in many communities is in part an assertion of cultural identity" (Sharma 1999:56). Conservation that focuses on the people and culture behind objects helps sustain living culture rather than fossilize it in museums. As a strategy, cultural conservation suggests that museums conserve cultures while they live rather than wait to collect their remnants after they die (Kurin 1989:14).[2]

Throughout the book, I continue to use the term "preservation" rather than "conservation" when referring to concepts and approaches to the protection of cultural resources. I do so to avoid confusion with the museological under-standing of conservation as measures taken to prevent the deterioration or destruction of cultural materials. In subsequent chapters, I show how the new paradigms for cultural heritage preservation discussed above can inform and be applied to actual practice.

Cultural hybridization: rethinking cultural interaction and exchange

The notion of cultural hybridization (or hybridity) has emerged in recent years as a way of reconceptualizing cross-cultural interactions and exchange, as well as explaining processes involved in the generation of new or alternative cultural forms. The concept is useful for understanding the forms museums and museological practices take in varying national and cultural settings, and how the integration of non-western curatorial methods into mainstream museums can lead to the creation of new forms or approaches to curation.

The notion of hybrid or creolized cultural forms developed in the 1980s as anthropologists and other social scientists began studying processes of global-ization and the conditions of modernity (Canclini 1995, Clifford 1997, Featherstone *et al.* 1995). The concept arose largely in response to previous tendencies to set traditional culture in opposition to modern culture, denying how elements of traditional and modern life can be intertwined. But the idea of hybrid cultural forms does not imply a belief in the simple combination of discrete elements of traditional and modern culture, nor fixed identities (Escobar 1995). Rather, cultural hybridization is about cultural creation (UNESCO 1995:79). "Hybridity can be understood as the ongoing condition of all human cultures, which contain no zones of purity because they undergo continuous processes of transculturation (two-way borrowing and lending between cultures)" (Rosaldo quoted in Canclini 1995:xv).

In the study of cultural interactions and transnational cultural flows, increasing attention has been given to the fluidity of culture, seeing it as adaptable, flexible, and ever-evolving rather than fixed and bounded. Research is now often focused on sites of cultural confrontation and interaction or "intercultural zones" (Sahlins 1994) where the complexities of cultural interaction and exchange can be investigated, and where cultural meaning is contested, negotiated, and constructed on multiple levels (Barth 1989, Marcus 1995). This idea of cultural hybridization serves as an antidote to essentialist and fixed notions of culture and identity as well as theoretical frameworks concerned with drawing boundaries and demarcations among cultural phenomena (Nederveen Pieterse 1995:55). Cultural hybridization is about cultural creation and re-creation as people actively accommodate and resist hegemonic forces that emanate from multiple sources (Marcus 1995). Hybrid cultural forms can be seen as sites where culture is generative and innovative, offering possibilities for change and continuity, not merely the replication of either old or new cultural forms.

Some have argued that the transnational flow of cultural forms is leading to global cultural homogenization, while others assert that the cultural flows evident in the world today are producing hybrid forms, which in themselves can be seen as unique cultural products (Hannerz 1989). The creation of hybrid forms demonstrates local communities' capacities for reshaping and redefining cultural forms to meet their own interests and purposes. To borrow from Appadurai and Breckenridge, "every society appears to bring to these forms its own specific history and traditions, its own cultural stamp, its own quirks and idiosyncracies" (1988:5). Thus, the world system can work toward cultural heterogeneity as much as it can lead to homogeneity (Hannerz 1989:207, Friedman 1990).

The notion of cultural hybridization can be seen as a more dynamic and even empowering approach to understanding contemporary processes of culture contact and exchange. However, it is necessary to consider the terms and conditions under which mixing occurs because relations of power and hegemony can be inscribed and reproduced within the context of hybridization (Nederveen Pieterse 1995:57). Implied in the notion of hybridization are relations of mutual give and take. But "hybrid culture can result from the imposition of values of one community on to another" (Sharma 1999:56). What needs to be kept in mind are historical relationships of power, or, that not all groups have been or are in a position to be equally creative and responsive. For some people, especially oppressed minorities, hybridization can also been seen as forced assimilation and acculturation (Sharma 1999:57). As Sharma warns us:

> We cannot simply celebrate hybridity without considering the power differentials between First and Third World nations [or dominant and subaltern groups]. Hybrid cultures can occur as a result of a number of factors including mutual give and take, past and present influences, and the Zeitgeist. It can also result from mass coercion, oppression and imposition.
>
> (1999:59)

The concept of cultural hybridization has its pitfalls, and, as with all models, we must guard against applying it too generally for "the idea of hybridity . . . threatens to mask particularity for the sake of an oversimplifying generality" (MacClancy 1997:15). Nevertheless, the concept can aid in liberating our thinking about processes of cultural contact and exchange, and help move both theory and practice in new directions.

The book provides examples of processes of cultural hybridization at work in the museum world. These processes become especially evident in following discussions on the global expansion of the western museum model and how it is both reproduced and transformed in non-western cultural contexts.

Chapter summaries

In the above sections, I presented the main arguments and concepts of the book. I argue that although the museum and associated practices are generally construed as modern, western cultural constructs, museological behavior is a cross-cultural phenomenon. To substantiate this claim, I provide numerous examples of non-western museological behavior throughout the book. Such examples also serve to refute the assertion that non-western people are not concerned with the care and preservation of their material cultural heritage. In addition, these data provide the foundation for a comparative study of museums, museological practices, and concepts of cultural heritage preservation.

In this introduction, I also outlined the parameters of a critical theory of museum ideology and practice and described movements in several fields that have informed this study. In subsequent chapters, I show how this theoretical framework can be applied to the analysis of particular museological practices, as well as current trends in the museum field.

In Chapter 2, I examine the implications behind the global spread of the western museum model and how narratives of museum history (as an essentially modern and western cultural product) have been appropriated into the discourse on museum development in the Republic of Indonesia. The Provincial Museum of Central Kalimantan, Museum Balanga, serves as a case study to demonstrate how the western museum model is interpreted as well as transformed in a non-western cultural context. In this respect, I examine how Museum Balanga is a site of cultural hybridization where local approaches to the interpretation and representation of cultural materials are mixed with those of a wider, international museum culture. I also highlight points of disjuncture in the mixing of these cultures. Here I describe how the museum's curatorial methods and modes of cultural representation mimic those commonly found in western, ethnographic-style museums, and the incongruity of these methods in a context where much of the culture on display is still being lived. A description of practices associated with the collection and curation of heirloom jars among the Dayak underscores the point that while the museum may be a modern institution in

Indonesia, museological behavior has a long history in Kalimantan. The chapter stresses how a particular ideology of museum development not only masks indigenous approaches to the care and treatment of objects, but also undermines a museum's long-term goal of cultural heritage preservation through the imposition of outside methods.

Chapter 3 provides examples of indigenous models of museums, curation, and concepts of cultural heritage preservation from Indonesia, the Pacific, and Africa. These examples serve to further refute the claim that the practice of collecting, storing, caring for, and conserving objects in places like museums is a uniquely western cultural phenomenon. They also challenge the assertion that non-western peoples are not concerned with the care and preservation of their cultural property. This argument is of particular significance since it has often been used to justify the collection and retention of non-western people's cultural property in museums. I demonstrate how many cultures have developed elaborate means for protecting their cultural property, and how this property is essential for the transmission of culture from one generation to the next. In this respect, the chapter emphasizes the critical role material culture plays in cultural heritage preservation, which I define simply as the transmission of culture through time.

Chapter 4 focuses on developments that have been taking place in the United States since the passage of the Native American Graves Protection and Repatriation Act (NAGPRA) in 1990. NAGPRA is seen as human rights legislation, and part of a set of laws that have been passed since the 1960s to redress wrongs committed against Native peoples. The overarching framework for the discussion is the issue of cultural restitution, and the rights of indigenous people to regain control over the management and care of their cultural property. Restitution is a process in which the historical conditions under which objects were acquired are acknowledged and rectified through concrete actions.

> In restitution, we can look at the process by which the objects were initially acquired, the kinds and ways the objects have become embedded in museums and the ways in which they can, in turn, be liberated. That is not an issue of just simply putting things in a box and sending them off through the post. It is really a significant issue that requires all parties to look very seriously at what happened, how it happened and what the program for the future represents.
>
> (Stanley 1998:24)

The chapter provides examples of how mainstream American museums are changing their policies and practices to accommodate Native American concerns, especially regarding the care and treatment of human remains, and "culturally sensitive" objects. Of particular importance is how Native American methods of traditional care are being integrated into mainstream museums. Such developments illustrate not only the changing nature of relationships between Native Americans and the museum and scientific community, but also changes in the attitudes of American society in general toward Native peoples. The chapter also covers developments taking place within the Native American museum community such as the creation of the National Museum of the American Indian as well as tribal museums and cultural centers.

Chapter 5 shifts the focus from the United States to museums in so-called developing countries, and the important role museums can play in the development process. I address how museums in developing areas differ from their counterparts in the "developed" world, functioning, in many cases, as instruments of social change and development. In such contexts, museums must be socially relevant and expand their functions to address socio-economic problems and needs.

The chapter begins with a discussion of the relationships between culture and development. Culture is seen as foundational to the development process and an essential point of reference since development is intertwined with and affects a people's whole way of life. I examine how greater recognition of the "cultural dimension of development" is leading to more integrated, holistic approaches to community development, which place local people and their culture at the center of development work. Culture-based approaches to community development are by definition "bottom-up," grass-roots approaches, which build on local people's knowledge, skills, and resources. Critical to the approach are the participation of local people in all phases of a project, and the use of "appropriate technology." Appropriate technology is defined as technology that is appropriate to a given situation and need, using mostly local or easily obtainable materials and skills. The chapter draws attention to how these trends in the field of international development can be applied to museum development projects.

My work on the Kayan Mentarang People's Museum Development Program in East Kalimantan, Indonesia serves both as a case study in culture-based approaches to community development and as a model of how museum development projects can be approached to better meet the needs and interests of local communities. I suggest that just as international development work has shown the need to use "appropriate technologies" in diverse settings, museum development projects should also be shaped to fit a particular cultural context, building on people's own concepts and systems of cultural heritage preservation. I also show how the concept of cultural conservation discussed in a previous section can be fruitfully applied in museum development projects directed toward both cultural and environmental conservation.

The chapter concludes with a description of traditional conservation methods in museums and community-based conservation projects. I suggest how these approaches can serve as an alternative means of addressing conservation problems on the local level as well as preserving indigenous knowledge and skills. A unifying theme throughout the chapter is the importance of cultural heritage preservation efforts in the preservation of global cultural diversity. As a source of different ways of knowing and being in the world as well as creativity and imagination, cultural diversity is fundamental to human survival and well-being, which theoretically is the goal of development.

The final chapter considers the implications of the study for the liberation of culture from the management regimes of Eurocentric museology. The liberation of culture is not only about giving back or restoring a people's right to control the management of their own cultural heritage. It is also about liberating our thinking from a Eurocentric view of what constitutes a museum and museological practice. The liberation of culture allows for the emergence of a new museological discourse in which points of reference are no longer solely determined and defined by the west. The aim is to open the field to multiple voices and perspectives in the spirit of inclusiveness.

I also discuss how comparative museology provides a conceptual framework for exploring the differences and similarities between museological forms and practices, and for drawing some general conclusions about museological phenomena. Comparative museology is also suggested as a framework for the development of more inclusive, cross-cultural approaches to cultural heritage management. Several examples of cross-cultural heritage management strategies are presented as well as suggestions for their further elaboration. In this respect, I am concerned with showing how the theoretical insights gained from comparative analysis can be translated into practice.

The chapter concludes with a discussion of how critical analysis is imperative to the further development of comparative museology and cross-cultural heritage management strategies because it is only through sustained critique and reflexivity that practice can be continually transformed. The aim is to problematicize the museum and museological practices across cultures, time, and space, rather than take them for granted or accept them uncritically. Here I caution against succumbing to extreme cultural relativism in efforts to recognize and show greater respect for diverse museological forms and practices. The challenge is to reconcile the need to respect diversity with the need to respect principles of equality and cultural democracy.

2

The Eurocentric museum model in the non-European world

The idea that the museum is a distinctly western and modern cultural product is deeply embedded in museological discourse and narratives of museum history. The literature on the history of the museum concept is now extensive (Ames 1992, Bazin 1967, Bennett 1995, Duncan 1995, Hudson 1977, Pearce 1992, Walsh 1992), and with rare exception (Simpson 1996), the museum's western origins and modern character are generally taken for granted. Bazin, in his often cited book *The Museum Age* (1967), notes that Chinese emperors were making collections of paintings and calligraphies as early as the third century BC. According to Bazin, the Shoso-in located in the Todaiji Monastery at Nara, near Kyoto, Japan is the oldest museum in the world (1967:27–29). However, outside a few examples, the text is almost exclusively devoted to the historical development of European or western museums.

Pearce, in *Museums, Objects, and Collections* (1992), also mentions how material has been assembled and displayed in many other parts of the world, but, nevertheless, situates the museum's birthplace firmly in Europe and the modern era. "Museums are a characteristic part of the cultural pattern of modern Europe, and of the European influenced world" (1992:1). According to Pearce, as well as to several other authors, the museum is an invention of European modernity, embodying and reflecting the metanarratives of modernity – scientific objectivism, an emphasis on reason and rationality, and notions of time based on the idea of progress and evolutionary stage models of social and cultural development (Pearce 1992, Ames 1992, Bazin 1967, Walsh 1992). While these narratives of museum history may be grounded in historical fact, we might also consider how they have helped construct a Eurocentric museum ideology and contribute to the reproduction of the western museum model worldwide.

The global expansion of the museum concept

The past half-century has seen an extraordinary growth of museums throughout the world. According to a UNESCO (the United Nations Educational, Scientific, and Cultural Organization) report of 1995, 90 percent of the total number of the world's museums have been created since the formation of UNESCO and the International Council of Museums (ICOM) in 1946 (1995:184). An exact count is difficult to establish, but Van Beek noted that "in 1984 there were 34,987 museums all over the world and the number was increasing at an estimated rate of 10 percent every five years" (1990:26).

On a worldwide scale, ICOM is probably one of the most prominent purveyors of the museum idea. ICOM is an international, non-governmental organization of professional museum workers dedicated to the improvement and advancement of the world's museums, the museum profession, and museological interests. It is the largest professional museum body in the world with some 12,000 individual members and 106 National Committees (Boylan 1996:50). ICOM's headquarters are in Paris, France where it operates under the auspices of UNESCO.

Since its inception, ICOM has formulated a number of museum definitions. The definition currently in use defines a museum as a "non-profit making, permanent institution in service to society and its development, and open to the public which acquires, conserves, researches, communicates and exhibits, for purposes of study, education and enjoyment, material evidence of people and their environment" (ICOM Statutes 2001). This definition is intended to encompass a wide range of institutions and facilities, such as zoos, aquaria, botanical gardens, and nature reserves; science centers and planetaria; galleries, cultural centers, conservation institutes, and so forth. In fact, to some, the definition is so far-ranging that it has become increasingly difficult to define precisely what a museum is or is not. But to others, museum definition remains necessary because it can

> describe, direct, or enforce the way in which a museum interacts with its cultural setting. Definition arises from the need to establish common ground to facilitate general or discipline-specific communication. When expressed within the discipline of museology, it both reflects and directs institutional behavior. However, a definition can have a prescriptive function or even an enforcement role when it is used outside the discipline.
>
> (Robb 1992:28)

Museum definition can also serve as a model and standard for the professionalization of museums. "The agreement of an official body of national or international museum workers on a definition of a museum creates a prototype" (Robb 1992:28).

The phenomenal growth of museums (and the museum profession) worldwide prompted Hudson, in his book *Museums of Influence* (1987), to ponder why "a characteristically western institution" has spread over the world in the course of two centuries. Hudson writes:

> The fact that museums have spread and multiplied is an obvious enough fact ... I have asked myself the reasons for this extraordinary phenomenon, extraordinary, because in so many instances it defies economic logic and common sense. All five continents appear to be chronically

21

afflicted by serious financial and political problems, but the number of museums continues inexorably to increase. Why should this be so, and, in particular, why should even the world's poorest countries . . . feel that their self-respect demands museums?

(1987:3)

Hudson points out that even though the museum has become a global phenomenon, the western museum model is not monolithic and reproduced worldwide without alteration. But rather:

Museums take on the colouring of the society in which the activity takes place. A church in the United States is not the same as a church in Denmark or South Africa . . . A museum in China does not operate in the same social and political context as a museum in Egypt or Bulgaria.

(1987:3)

Yet, despite this tendency, Hudson goes on to say that museums possess a particular "quality" or "essence" that makes it possible for us to differentiate museums from other institutions and for an "international traffic in museology" to occur.

Just as there is something one might term the essence of a church, so one can identify without too much difficulty the essence of a museum, a central quality which makes it possible to organise bodies like . . . the International Council of Museums . . . A museum in France has more in common with a museum in Finland than it has with a petrol station or a printing works in its own country. The international traffic in museology is necessarily different from the country to country movement of ideas and innovations in printing technology. Yet the ways in which thoughts, improvements and habits are transmitted from one region of the world to another has been studied in only rudimentary fashion.

(1987:3)

This chapter explores how and why this "characteristically western institution" has been "transmitted from one region of the world to another," as well as the implications of this movement, through an examination of museum development in the Republic of Indonesia and, specifically, the case of the Provincial Museum of Central Kalimantan, Museum Balanga.[1]

Becoming "museum-minded" and Indonesian museum development[2]

On the surface, Indonesian museums strongly resemble western-style museums in their functions and methods of cultural representation. The explanation for this is rather straightforward. First, Indonesia, like many other post-colonial nations, inherited the museum idea from their colonial past. Indonesia was colonized by the Dutch, beginning in the seventeenth century, and was known as the Netherlands East Indies prior to its independence in 1949. What is now the National Museum in Jakarta (the nation's capital) was founded in 1778 by the *Bataviaasch Genootschap van Kunsten Westenschappen* (Batavia Society for Arts and Sciences). Second, most leading museum professionals responsible for planning and developing Indonesian museums received their training in western countries or from western museum specialists.[3] Indonesians also adopted the International Council of Museum's museum definition and have attempted to follow standard museological methods formulated by the international museum community. Finally, Indonesia has been the recipient of technical and monetary assistance from UNESCO and other foreign agencies involved in cultural work. In short, Indonesian museum professionals have been part of the "international traffic in museology" for several decades, and each conveyor in this traffic has left its mark.

A former director of the Indonesian Directorate of Museums, in response to an interview question on why the western museum model was used in Indonesia, stated:

> If you have to decide to do something and you see that something is already well established, you tend to take it. It is the same in other things. Why do Malaysian soldiers march like the British? They have not created their own way of marching because the British army's name and glories are known everywhere. I think that is a good moral. ICOM has developed this international congress [of museum professionals]. In the first phase [of museum development] people in Indonesia try to follow ICOM standards as a base. Later on they might develop their own.[4]

On my first visit to Indonesia in 1990, several government museum officials related to me how Indonesians are "*belum* [not yet] museum-minded." These officials asserted that because the museum is not an Indonesian cultural product the museum remains a foreign concept in the minds of most Indonesians. I found the phrase intriguing not only because of the usage of English, i.e. "museum-minded," but also because it implied that a state of museum-mindedness actually exists or that some people are *already* museum-minded.

A perceived absence of museum-mindedness was also said to account for the public's lack of interest in museums, and in general, was thought to be one of the main obstacles to the successful integration of museums into Indonesian society. Museum leaders stressed that it is one thing to build a museum infrastructure, that is, buildings and other "hardware," but quite another to create a mentality or "software" to go along with it (Directorate Permuseuman 1989:10). Accordingly, museum leaders and workers were responsible for cultivating a sense of museum-mindedness in the public, or rather, a particular way of thinking about museums and their purposes. Making Indonesian people museum-minded was seen as a process, but with a predetermined outcome based on their own preconceptions of what it means to be museum-minded. In this light, what Appadurai and Breckenridge say about Indian museums and their publics can also be applied to Indonesia: "museums need not worry so much about finding their publics as about making them" (1992:36).

A lack of museum-mindedness was also attributed to the country's stage of socio-economic development. Indonesia is considered a "developing" nation

Figure 2.1 Sign posted at the entrance to the Provincial Museum of Central Kalimantan, Museum Balanga. The sign informs visitors of a museum's functions and purposes defined by the International Council of Museums (ICOM).
Photograph by Christina Kreps, 1991.

undergoing a process of modernization. Becoming "developed" and "modern" was an overriding theme of former President Suharto's administration. Consequently, all resources in society, including museums, were mobilized to further development and modernization. Museums, in the eyes of government officials, are a feature of modern and developed nations. "Museums are known to play a role in the modern world and museum development is evidence of a developed country" (Departemen Pendidikan dan Kebudayaan 1987:7). Thus, museums are seen as both a symbol of modernity and a tool of modernization, and becoming museum-minded is largely about becoming and being modern.[5]

Prior to independence in 1949, museums in Indonesia were set up and run by the Dutch colonial government. They were established to support scientific research and further the political, economic, and cultural interests of the colonists. Museums in post-colonial Indonesia, however, were not to be elite institutions serving the interests of a few, but instead, were to exist for "the people" and their development. "The role of the museum in the free Republic of Indonesia has a different role from the museum in the Dutch East Indies. The orientation for museums is that they are to function to develop the people" (Departemen Pendidikan dan Kebudayaan 1987:7).[6]

Indonesian museum development did not really gain momentum until the 1970s when the government began instituting a nationwide museum system under the direction of the Directorate of Museums (*Direktorat Permuseuman*). The Directorate, based in Jakarta, was established in 1975 by presidential decree and became the main government agency responsible for overseeing the development of all museums in Indonesia, both publicly and privately owned (Sutaarga 1987:4). The Directorate operated under the auspices of the National Department of Education and Culture until this department was dissolved in 1999. In 2001, it was placed under the newly formed Directorate General for History and Archaeology, Department of Culture and Tourism.

As of 2000, some 262 museums existed in Indonesia, belonging to various government agencies and private foundations. The Directorate reached its goal of setting up provincial museums in each of the country's twenty-seven provinces with the establishment of the Provincial Museum of East Timor in April 1995 (Directorate of Museums 1999).[7]

The Directorate of Museums has been the primary agency responsible for planning, administering, and developing the nation's provincial museums. In 2000, however, greater power was beginning to be given to provincial museums and provincial-level government agencies, in keeping with the government's movement toward greater provincial autonomy in the post-Suharto era. The Directorate has provided technical assistance, sponsored training programs for museum workers, and produced programmatic statements on museum functions as well as detailed instructions on how to carry out museum tasks (Taylor 1994). Thus, the Directorate has created standard procedures for all provincial museums to follow. It also has been a member of the International Council of Museums since 1970, and leading Indonesian museum professionals have actively participated in international museum conferences and programs. The Directorate has attempted to promote standard methods and practices formulated by the international professional museum community, and has seen professional museum training as essential to the further development of provincial museums.[8]

According to a 1987 government decree, provincial museums collect, conserve, preserve, and present objects that have cultural and scientific value; carry out research, disseminate works on the collections, and provide educational guidance on objects and matters of cultural and scientific value characteristic of a region. Provincial museums are considered general museums with collections pertaining to regional natural history, archeology, history, and ethnography. They are said to be educational institutions first and foremost, but are also to serve as recreational outlets for the public. Provincial museums are also to play a role in the nation's development and modernization. They function in this capacity primarily as educational institutions, and by promoting modern ways of thinking based on science and the use of modern technologies (Sumadio 1987:5).

Even though provincial museums are to focus on regional culture and history, they are also supposed to promote the idea of national culture and aid in the government's program for national integration. This is theoretically accomplished by showing how regional cultures contribute to national culture, underscoring the nation's motto "Unity in Diversity." As stated in one Department of Education and Culture publication: "Museums should cultivate national cultural values, which strengthen national pride and a spirit of national unity" (Departemen Pendidikan dan Kebudayaan 1986:1).

Museum Balanga as a site of cultural hybridization

The Provincial Museum of Central Kalimantan, Museum Balanga, is located in the provincial capital of Palangka Raya. The town, with a population of approximately 100,000, is a "frontier" community carved out of the once thick forests of Central Kalimantan.[9] It is the commercial and government center of the province, situated some 80 miles (or 130 kilometers) from the Java Sea. The primary means of accessing Palangka Raya is by boat or airplane since few roads exist in the province that are navigable year round. In the eyes of some, Palangka Raya's remote location makes it an unlikely place to find a museum. As one Australian visitor wrote in Museum Balanga's comment book: "I hardly expected to find a museum in Palangka Raya or in all of Borneo, for that matter." This visitor's comment reflected not only the prevalent image of Borneo as a wild and "uncivilized" land, but also popular attitudes regarding the context in which one expects to find a museum.

Museum Balanga was first established as a regional museum (*museum daerah*) in 1973. According to a former director of Museum Balanga, the idea to create a museum in Palangka Raya originally came from an Australian dignitary who visited the town back in the early 1970s. Several leading community members who were concerned about the preservation of Central Kalimantan's cultural heritage decided to follow through with the idea. As stated in one of the museum's publications:

> For a long time the people of Central Kalimantan longed for a museum which would give a picture of the various aspects of life of the people of Central Kalimantan and its natural environment. This desire led to the establishment of a museum in Palangka Raya.
>
> (Mihing 1989:3)

In 1989, Museum Balanga was officially designated a provincial museum (*museum negeri*), which placed it under the purview of the Directorate of Museums and the central government. In an interview with the Director of Museum Balanga in 1991, I was told that before the museum was incorporated into the national museum system it was not a "real" museum. By this he meant that previously the museum was not being managed in line with the state bureaucracy and according to professional museum standards as dictated by the Directorate of Museums.

Museum Balanga functions to collect, preserve, document, study, display, and disseminate information on the cultural and natural history of the province. The

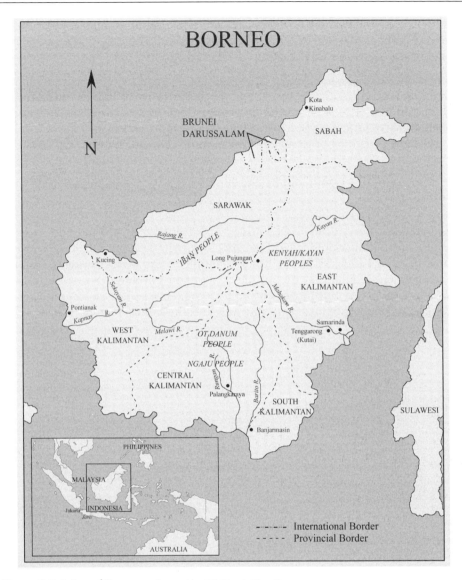

Figure 2.2 Map of Borneo. Created by W. Derek Hamilton.

museum is primarily devoted to the collection and representation of Dayak culture, although the province is ethnically diverse and home to immigrants from other Indonesian islands. The name "Dayak" is a generic term that refers to the non-Malay, non-Chinese indigenous inhabitants of Indonesian Borneo. A number of different Dayak groups exist in Central Kalimantan who possess their own names, languages, and cultural traditions. Despite this diversity, even among the Dayaks, Museum Balanga mostly concentrates on Ngaju-Dayak culture. This is partly due to the fact that the Ngaju are the most numerous Dayak group in the province. In 1994, it was estimated that there were between

27

500,000 to 800,000 Ngaju-speakers in a province with a total population of some 1.5 million (Schiller 1997:14). The Ngaju are also the most politically and economically powerful Dayak group in Central Kalimantan.

Historically, Dayaks have lived in villages along the banks of Kalimantan's many rivers. Their livelihood has rested on the cultivation of rice in addition to hunting, fishing, and gathering forest products for trade such as rattan, resins, rubber, and aromatic woods. Most Dayaks today are also engaged in some form of wage labor, working in timber camps, mining operations, or as civil servants.

In keeping with the Directorate of Museum's assertion that Indonesians are "not yet" museum-minded, Museum Balanga appeared to be a foreign idea in the eyes of the local community. Outside of visiting government officials and dignitaries, school groups, and occasional tourists, few people visited the museum on a regular basis. Many local people surveyed did not know the museum existed despite its formidable presence on the edge of town. (Museum Balanga consists of nine buildings enclosed in a 3-hectare complex. The word "museum" is also inscribed in large letters on the façade of its main building.) For some, it was just a place to "keep old things," while for others it was just another cluster of government buildings whose real purposes and functions were unknown.

The museum idea was also alien to many of the individuals who worked in Museum Balanga. Museum workers were civil servants who, for the most part,

Figure 2.3 The Provincial Museum of Central Kalimantan, Museum Balanga.
Photograph by Christina Kreps, 1991.

had had no formal museological training before coming to work at the museum. The majority of Museum Balanga workers were also Dayaks, who retained, to varying degrees, ties to their traditional culture. They received their training on the job and under the guidance of the Directorate of Museums.[10] Consequently, the Directorate was charged with instilling a sense of museum-mindedness not just in the public, but also in the people working in provincial museums.

Bearing on the museum staff's lack of museum-mindedness, I was interested in how museological tasks were performed in Museum Balanga in comparison with work in European and American museums. Museum Balanga resembles western ethnographic museums in its functions and exhibition style. However, the ways in which museum work was actually carried out often reflected local values, beliefs, and perceptions on the uses and treatment of objects, which at times, appeared to conflict with those of professional, western museum culture.

Western museum culture operates with a particular set of standards, practices, and value systems regarding the collection, care, interpretation, and representation of objects. Within this museum culture objects are made museum pieces or "special" by meeting criteria established by anthropologists, art historians, scientists, curators, and collectors. Standard criteria for evaluating an object's value may be its provenience, or where and when it was made; its formal aesthetic properties; its rarity, uniqueness, or authenticity; its monetary value as determined by an art or antique market; and its scientific value as evidence of natural or cultural phenomena (Clavir 2002, Clifford 1988, Kirschenblatt-Gimblett 1991).

Most of the objects in Museum Balanga's collection are classified as "ethnographic," representing various aspects of Dayak culture. According to the Directorate of Museum's classification system, an ethnographic object is anything made by local people and still in use. For the most part, objects are displayed using an exhibition style similar to western ethnographic museums' whereby objects are grouped thematically and shown in a reconstructed cultural context. For example, one exhibition leads visitors through the stages of life by showing objects used in rituals related to birth, courting, marriage, and death. This "life-cycle" exhibit is a standard feature of nearly all provincial museums in Indonesia and was originally designed and installed by Directorate staff from Jakarta. A life-size diorama features a house on the river complete with canoes, hunting and fishing gear such as traps, weirs, blowpipes, spears, and nets. Other displays include implements used in traditional gold mining and agriculture as well as tools and materials used in the production of basketry and bark cloth. Also on display are ritual paraphernalia and objects associated with Kaharingan ceremonies. Kaharingan is the traditional religion of the Ngaju and other Dayaks of Central Kalimantan. What actually constitutes Dayak culture is a matter of debate, but to many, Kaharingan is the basis of Ngaju-Dayak culture and provides the inspiration for much of its unique cultural expressions (Schiller 1997).

Many of the objects on display in the museum are examples of things still being used in everyday life, and found in people's homes, in the market, or in villages.

Not surprisingly then, objects such as baskets, fishing and hunting gear, and tools were seen as ordinary by the staff and local people. This quotidian perception of objects was reflected in the way staff members handled objects and managed the collection, which, from the perspective of a professional curator, might be considered careless or improper. The perceived ordinariness of the objects was also the reason why many local people did not visit the museum. They saw no point in visiting a place to view objects they had in their homes and used on an almost daily basis.

Conventionally, in western museums, once an object enters the museum it takes on a new life and usually does not leave the museum except for purposes deemed acceptable by the curators. Museum workers are obliged to safeguard objects so their museum value is preserved. Rarely are objects used for the same purposes they were originally made. However, in Museum Balanga, objects were often borrowed by local people for use in ceremonies, performances, and for community events such as festivals, official ceremonies, and festivities related to the observance of national holidays. The following incident is a case in point.

One day I arrived at the Museum in time to see the staff preparing a float for a parade commemorating Indonesian Independence Day, August 17, 1945. Staff members were busily carting objects out of the museum to create a display on the back of a truck. The display was designed to represent a traditional Dayak mortuary ceremony known as a *tiwah*. Large brass gongs had been arranged on the bed of the truck along with 5-foot-tall wooden figures known as *sapundu*. An antique ceremonial cloth was being nailed onto the side of the truck while two other workers were giving the only masks in the museum's collection a new coat of paint.

Observing these actions, I was confronted with the dilemma of whether or not to intervene in the staff's activities. As a person trained in "proper" and "professional" museum practices, I felt compelled to inform the workers about the potentially damaging effects of their actions on the objects. When I expressed my concerns to one staff member, who was wrestling a *sapundu* onto the truck, he turned to me with a perplexed look and said: "Oh, it doesn't matter. There are lots of them in the villages." Obviously, this approach to the objects challenged my own sense of museum-mindedness and the idea that the carvings, masks, and other objects were "special" by virtue of the fact they were in the museum. It also underscored the differences between my views of and relationship to the objects and those of the staff. To this man, as well as to many other members of the museum staff, they were objects still embedded in Dayak living culture. But to me, they were "ethnographic specimens" whose value rested on their status as examples of Dayak "material culture."

In western ethnographic museums, objects are made "ethnographic" by the act of detaching them from their original cultural context and recontextualizing them into western scientific frames of reference. As Kirshenblatt-Gimblett has observed: "Ethnographic artifacts are objects of ethnography ... Objects become ethnographic by virtue of being defined, segmented, detached, and

Figure 2.4 Float created for Indonesian Independence Day parade by Museum Balanga staff. The banner on the side of the truck reads: "The Museum and the Preservation of Regional Cultural Arts. Supporting the Development of the People." The float features structures and objects used in a Ngaju-Dayak *tiwah* ceremony.
Photograph by Christina Kreps, 1991.

carried away by ethnographers. Such objects are ethnographic . . . by virtue of the manner in which they have been detached" (1991:387).

As previously noted, most of the objects in Museum Balanga's collection were classified as ethnographic, and the museum's approach to exhibiting objects was modeled after western-style ethnographic museums. Nevertheless, at the time of my research, none of the museum workers were trained in anthropology or ethnographic methods.[11] They were using a classification system for objects and exhibition styles formulated by the Directorate of Museums. Consequently, the practice of conceptually detaching objects from their larger sociocultural contexts and perceiving them in an abstract manner was incongruous to the way in which many of the staff members viewed the objects. This incongruity became clear to me while observing the preparation of an exhibit on traditional carving of Central Kalimantan.

The title of the exhibition was *The Art of Traditional Carving of Central Kalimantan*, and was held at Museum Balanga from February 29 to March 3, 1992. The exhibition displayed a total of twenty-seven pieces, which were arranged to highlight the objects' aesthetic or formal qualities as well as their functions. The

31

objects included weapons, musical instruments, and carvings originally used in Kaharingan ceremonies and rituals.

A few days before the exhibit was to open, staff members responsible for making object labels and interpretative texts told me they were having trouble preparing the texts. I thought their problem stemmed from difficulties in finding information about the objects. In an effort to help them, I drew their attention to several publications on Dayak woodcarving. However, the workers were reluctant to use these materials because they said the objects illustrated in the books were not the same objects in the museum's collection. Initially, I thought this response reflected the staff's lack of training in formal research methods and an inability to think in the abstract. But later I learned their reluctance had more to do with the nature of the objects and who had the right to interpret them.

The exhibition included various types of *hampatung* and *karuhei*, which are carved wooden figures created by ritual specialists, or *basir*, for use in religious rituals or ceremonies Each object is considered a unique creation, endowed with meanings and powers known only to the *basir* who created it. Knowledge about an object and how to use it is sacred, non-public, and only acquired through lengthy apprenticeship (Schiller 1986, Sellato 1989, Taylor and Aragon 1991). It is also highly personal and based on individual interpretations of Kaharingan. In describing the work of one ritual specialist, Basir Muka, Schiller writes:

> Like other ritual specialists Muka possesses a highly personalistic understanding of his religion based upon his own experience, and the conclusions he has formed about the relationship between man and the supernatural. Basir Muka has produced a permanent record of his religious beliefs in a sculpture that is both sacred artifact and an attempt to preserve Kahayan mythology.
>
> (1986:232)[12]

Therefore, "without the detailed information from the individual who created them, it is impossible to interpret completely the ritual objects . . . or to understand the use of Dayak magical paraphernalia" (Taylor and Aragon 1991:49).

Because objects were made for specific purposes and endowed with singular meanings, museum workers were cautious about usurping the *basir*'s authority and writing generalized statements on exhibit labels about the objects. This attitude stands in contrast to how ethnographic objects are viewed and used in western museum culture where a single artifact is made to represent an abstract totality, such as Dayak woodcarving, art, or culture. As Clifford has pointed out, museum collections and displays "create the illusion of adequate representation of the world by first cutting objects out of specific contexts and making them 'stand for' abstract wholes" (1988:220). Museums deny objects their singularity as "exhibition classifications . . . shift the grounds of singularity from the objects to a category within a particular taxonomy" (Kirshenblatt-Gimblett 1991:392).

The modern museum is typically considered a public entity. Museum collections are theoretically owned by or held in the public trust, and are to be made accessible to the public. Information about collections is, in principle, available for public consumption. "Museums are ... apparatuses for public rather than private consumption ... The public museum was established as a means of sharing what had been private and exposing what had been concealed" (Hooper-Greenhill 1989:68). But in traditional Dayak society, particular kinds of objects, such as *karuhei*, and knowledge about them have not been considered part of the public domain. In fact, knowledge and rights to the ownership and interpretation of some objects, because of their sacred nature, have been the sole preserve of *basir* or other select members of the society.

Out of respect for traditional customs and beliefs associated with certain objects and rights related to the authority of ritual specialists, Museum Balanga workers looked to *basir* for guidance on how to interpret and present objects used in Kaharingan rituals. They also called upon *basir* to assist them in the production of exhibits related to Kaharingan. For instance, on one occasion the museum hired three *basir* to help renovate an exhibit on the *tiwah* ceremony. The *basir* were engaged to advise the staff on how to make the exhibit more authentic or closer to the image of a real *tiwah*. But the *basir* did more than merely advise. They selected objects for display, constructed models of ceremonial structures, and arranged them in their appropriate positions. All the work was carried out in accordance with Kaharingan prescriptions. After the renovation was

Figure 2.5 *Basir*, or ritual specialists, conducting rites at a *tiwah*. The site features *sapundu* (effigy poles), a *sangkaraya* (bamboo structure covered with cloth and festooned with flags), and a *pasah pali* (platform that holds ritual offerings).
Photograph by Christina Kreps, 1991.

33

Figure 2.6 Re-creation of *tiwah* site in Museum Balanga, complete with *sapundu*, *sangkaraya*, and *pasah pali*.
Photograph by Christina Kreps, 1991.

completed, the *basir* performed a cleansing ritual to cast out any lingering bad spirits and to summon good spirits to bestow their blessings on the museum, staff, and visitors.

Collaboration with *basir* is one example of how Museum Balanga was a site of cultural hybridization where local approaches to the interpretation and representation of cultural materials were being mixed with those of a wider, international museum culture. However, to some administrators, these collaborative efforts were unprofessional, too closely tied to religion, and not in keeping with the idea of a museum as a modern, secular institution based on scientific principles and professionalism. As a result, such practices were being discouraged in Museum Balanga.

The politics of culture and the ideology of modernization

Cultural development in Indonesia has officially rested in the hands of the government. The 1945 Constitution made the government responsible for the nation's cultural development and provided the legislative basis for cultural planning and policy making. The People's Consultative Assembly outlines policies and programs for cultural development as part of its 5-year development plans. Cultural development has been inseparable from overall national, socio-economic development and modernization (Sumadio 1985).

The following statement taken from a 1985 government publication outlines the aims of cultural development and the role of the government in the process:

> The government draws up plans for cultural development that imply redis-covering, preserving, developing and telling the people about their cultural heritage, enabling them to avoid the negative effects of certain foreign influences while at the same time being ready to absorb what is good from the outside and can further a necessary modernization.
>
> (Soebadio 1985:10)

Hence, government officials have determined, at least theoretically, what culture is and how it should be developed.

Within the Indonesian government's framework of cultural development, tradi-tional culture has been seen as having both negative and positive attributes. In a positive light, certain elements of traditional culture have been valued for how they reflect primordial values and beliefs thought to give Indonesian national culture its unique character and identity. In a negative light, other aspects of traditional culture, such as traditional religions, subsistence strategies, and forms of social organization have been viewed as obstacles to development and modernization. As such, they have been targeted for change.

Because development and modernization are linked with the new, development programs have opposed and rejected whatever was thought to work against modernization. As Heryanto, an Indonesian social scientist, observed:

> A few things which are "traditional" are tolerated and given the right to exist, but tolerance varies greatly as do the tolerating parties. Those leaders of society who are the most acutely afflicted with the ideology of modern-ization are also the least inclined to tolerate anything which is valued as "traditional" . . . Things which are "traditional" are used as antique or esoteric "spectacles" in the midst of a wave of industrialization.
>
> (1988:22)

In general, traditional culture has tended to be stripped down to what are called the "cultural arts" (*seni budaya*), a category of culture that includes traditional music, dance, drama, costumes, architecture, and handicrafts. Cultural arts have typically received the strongest support from the government (see Acciaioli 1985, Errington 1994 and 1998, Foulcher 1990:303, Pemberton 1994, Yampolsky 1995).

The state's ideology of modernization has informed museum practice in a variety of ways. For example, provincial museums, like Museum Balanga, are supposed to preserve local cultural heritage. But as part of the state apparatus, their ulti-mate allegiance is to the national government and its interests. Material culture is collected and preserved in the museum under the assumption that certain objects will inevitably disappear or become obsolete as Dayak communities become developed and modern. Thus, the preservation of material culture has been favored over the preservation of the traditional values, beliefs, and the ways of life they represent. The ideology of modernization, and the notion that the museum is a modern, scientific institution, have also worked to mask the existence of traditional indigenous curatorial methods, or rather, how local people have had their own methods of collecting, caring for, and preserving objects of cultural significance.

Dragon jars and indigenous curation among the Dayaks[13]

Dayaks, as well as other Indonesian peoples, are well known for their collection, care, and reverence for heirloom property, collectively known as *pusaka*. Examples of *pusaka* include textiles, weapons, gongs, brassware, jewelry, beads, ritual paraphernalia, and ceramics. Museum Balanga's collections include many objects that at one time formed part of a family's *pusaka*. Of special importance is a class of large ceramic jars of Chinese origin known in Ngaju Dayak as *balanga*, from which the museum takes its name. *Balanga* are sometimes referred to as "dragon jars" because of the elaborate dragon designs embossed on their surface (see Harrisson 1990:28–29). Europeans have referred to this jar style as *martavan* (Adhyatman and Rhido 1982:48) while they are also known as *tempayan* or *guci* in the Indonesian language. These jars and other ceramics comprised a large portion of Museum Balanga's collection in 1992, numbering some 400 out of a total of approximately 1,300 objects. Historically, *balanga* have figured prominently in various aspects of Dayak life. Due to their significance, *balanga* have become a symbol of Dayak culture and identity. Today, as a symbol of "Dayakness," *balanga* are displayed on public monuments and buildings throughout the province.

A Dayak penchant for Chinese jars and their high value in local exchange systems is well documented in nineteenth-century European accounts of Borneo as well as in the ethnographic literature (Harrisson 1990, Hose and MacDougall 1966, Scharer 1963, Sellato 1989). Archeological evidence reveals that jars were being imported into Borneo as far back as one thousand years ago (Chin 1988:61). Over the centuries, jars were integrated into Dayak culture and became part of life's most salient occasions. They have been integral elements to healing rituals, marriage ceremonies, ancestor worship, mortuary practices, and ceremonies involving the drinking of rice wine (O'Connor 1983:403). Harrisson describes the importance of jars to Dayaks and how they were treated:

> Among the many peoples of Asia, those of the great island of Borneo developed a most special and lasting regard for large jars. They used them in their daily lives: to keep water cool and sweet, to store rice and other staples securely from pests, or to brew rice wine during festivals. Above all, jars were collector's items. They lined the walls of family rooms and communal galleries [in longhouses]. The farmers who owned them knew many different types. Most precious among them were jars handed down over the generations. Ancestors had paddled them up great rivers, and on their backs, men had borne them across rapids and over mountains. As

Figure 2.7 Monument featuring a *balanga* or "dragon jar" in Palangka Raya, Central Kalimantan. Photograph by Christina Kreps, 2000.

treasured *pusaka*, such jars were surrounded with beliefs and legends. They were treated with ceremony and respect. Privileged families used them as ossuaries for the bones of the dead.

(1990:1)

Even though jars circulated through trade, warfare, inheritance or accidental discovery, in some Dayak cosmologies their genesis is attributed to divine agency. Carl Bock, writing in the late 1800s, reported that Dayaks believed jars were made of the same clay from which Mahatala (the Almighty) fashioned the sun and moon (1988:198). According to Scharer, the Ngaju believed that ancient jars were gifts from divine powers or gods, given as fruits of the Tree of Life (1963:166). Jars were not considered mere inanimate objects, but were centers of vital power capable of action and transformation. Numerous accounts exist relating how jars transformed themselves into animals and people, or had the power to speak or foretell the future (Adhyatman and Rhido 1982, O'Connor 1983:403–404).

In Ngaju cosmology the jar is associated with the underworld, which is presided over by *Jata*, the feminine aspect of the total godhead. *Jata* takes the form of a *naga*, a serpent or dragon, and symbolizes fertility and sources of life such as water. The jar is also associated with death, and has been used as a burial urn for some 3,000 years throughout Borneo. Jars are said to symbolize the female sexual organs in a tomb-and-womb symbolism, whereby the body, buried in a fetal position, awaits rebirth (Sellato 1989:45). The sacred quality given to jars, and their prominent role in religious ceremonies and beliefs have made jars a ubiquitous symbol in Dayak iconography and art. The jar is often represented juxtaposed with the great hornbill bird, the male aspect of the total godhead, known as *Burung Enggang* or *Tingang* (Sellato 1989:45).

To Dayaks, jars are also symbols of wealth and status. Consequently, individuals or families that own many jars have held high status in Dayak society (Adhyatman and Rhido 1982:51). Accordingly, display has been one of the primary reasons for owning jars (Harrisson 1990:28). Traditionally, a family's wealth was measured by the number of jars that lined the walls of its home. As a result, jars have been highly sought after and much attention has been given to their acquisition and care. Many of the customs and beliefs associated with the collection, care, and treatment of these jars are analogous to museum curatorship and connoisseurship.

In former times, jars were acquired through trade, and particular Dayak groups such as the Bajau, Ngaju, Melanau, and Iban are said to have been especially adept at the jar trade (Harrisson 1990:17, O'Connor 1983:403). Dealers, or collectors, traveled on extensive trading expeditions throughout Borneo and the archipelago to obtain and exchange jars. Harrisson writes that "jar festivals" were sometimes held in villages where antique jars were collected (1990:27). Certain Dayak groups favored particular styles and forms, and dealers, or what Harrisson calls "jar experts," were familiar with local tastes and predilections. Jar experts knew the types and values of various jars admired among their own

Figure 2.8 A complex of funerary monuments in Central Kalimantan. On the right is a *sandung*, or mausoleum for remains, surrounded by *sapundu*, or effigy pole, to which the sacrificial water buffalo was tied, and a *sengkaran*, or jar post.
Photograph by Christina Kreps, 2000.

people and other Dayak groups (Harrisson 1990:18–19). Jar experts were concerned with matters of authenticity, provenience, dating, qualities of glazes, form, decoration, and other formal criteria for evaluating a jar's worth (O'Connor 1983:402–405). Harrisson describes the qualifications of a jar expert: "To become an expert, a person needed a keen perception of the touch, sound and look of jars, good memory for their individual characteristics, experience obtained from another expert, and the trust of the community" (1990:21). Jar experts were also known for their skills as "conservators." When jars were broken they were repaired using a mixture of resin, oil, and lime as glue (Harrisson 1990:21).

Antique jars were the most valuable and commanded the highest prices. Harrisson notes that "native connoisseurs" overcame the difficulty of establishing whether or not a jar was genuine by following one simple rule: "Whatever the individual evidence for the local history of any jar might be, only jars with patterns no longer available in the trade qualified as 'genuine' heirlooms" (Harrisson 1990:22). One European traveler, writing in the late nineteenth century, was so impressed with Dayak expertise in identifying authentic jars that he wrote:

High prices paid for jars motivated the Chinese to imitate them. Some have taken the trouble to travel to China with samples in order to have them copied to the smallest detail. I have seen such reproductions and must admit they were perfectly made. I was unable to observe differences between old and new when they were placed side by side. However, not a single Dayak has, so far, been duped.

(Perelaar quoted in Harrisson 1990:21)

Before a family purchased a jar, they might consult community elders and jar experts for an appraisal of a jar's quality and value. This was done also to uphold customary laws surrounding the exchange and use of jars. Because heirloom jars were among a family's most precious possessions, damaging, destroying, and stealing jars, or trying to pass off "fakes" were serious offenses and a threat to the peace of a community. Large fines had to be paid by those who violated laws governing the exchange, use, and possession of jars.

Harrisson wrote in 1990 that little traditional jar expertise still existed in Malaysian Borneo, that antique jars were becoming increasingly rare in villages, and that this was probably true for the whole of Borneo (1990:1). However, during my stay in Central Kalimantan from 1991 to 1992, and in subsequent visits to villages throughout East and Central Kalimantan in 1996, 1997, and 2000, I found this not to be the case. In visits to people's homes in Palangka Raya and elsewhere, I observed large collections of jars. Jars were also essential elements of all Dayak religious ceremonies I attended, such as wedding ceremonies and funerary rituals.[14] Jars still were being offered as bride price and used as payment to settle community grievances according to customary law.[15] I also encountered several individuals who knew a great deal about jars, including their systems of classification, methods of conservation, various customs dictating their uses, as well as legends telling of their divine origin based on Ngaju cosmology. One individual explained that in order to become a "jar expert" one had to *berguru*, or undergo a lengthy apprenticeship, to acquire the requisite specialized knowledge and skills. Specific *syarat-syarat* (rules, requirements, or conditions) have to be observed and payments made for this knowledge. I also heard accounts of families who owned jars with supernatural powers. In sum, jars were still highly valued and revered for both their intrinsic and cultural value, and to a certain extent, curated in line with traditional practices.

Professionalization and the erasure of indigenous curatorial methods

The preceding description of *balanga* and their curation demonstrates that while the museum may be seen as a new and modern institution in Central Kalimantan, curatorial-type behavior has a long history in Borneo. Regardless of this long tradition, and as previously noted, traditional curatorial practices were being discouraged in Museum Balanga in favor of modern, professional museum methods. This tendency was exemplified by the way *balanga* and other ceramics were being curated and displayed in the museum.

Although *balanga* and other ceramics comprised a sizable portion of the museum's collection, at the time of my field research, little information or documentation existed on the collection. Ceramics were displayed as "fine art" with minimum labeling, in keeping with how ceramics were displayed in the National Museum in Jakarta. I was told that not much had been done with the collection because the Directorate of Museums intended to send a ceramics specialist from Jakarta to help the staff identify and document the collection. In June of 1992, a well-known ceramic specialist came to Museum Balanga to assist in the registration and documentation of the collection. He instructed the staff in dating, assigning provenience, and in identifying various types of clays, glazes, and production techniques. He also offered advice on conservation and restoration methods. This project was the first opportunity many Museum Balanga workers had had to receive formal training in curatorial methods.

For the most part, the registration and documentation of the collection conformed to standard professional museum methods. Although some local names for certain jar types were recorded, the collection was not organized around any indigenous classification system. Rather, a classification system was used that had been developed by the Directorate of Museums and presented in the publication *Collection Classification for Provincial Museums* (Suyati 1990). According to this document, an object's place of origin or *lokasi* is one of the criteria used to classify objects. Following the Directorate's guidelines, objects or collections (*koleksi*) can be categorized as *koleksi propinsi* (originating within the province); *koleksi asing* (of foreign origin), or *koleksi nusantara* (originating within the Indonesian archipelago). Because most of the ceramics housed in Museum Balanga were of Chinese origin they were considered "foreign objects," even though *balanga* had been an integral part of Dayak culture for centuries.

During the ceramic specialist's stay in Palangka Raya, I had the opportunity to talk with him about the collection and how it was presented in the museum. He told me that the collection was "not bad" and contained a few "important" pieces. But, for the most part, the ceramics in the museum's collection were not exceptional (in collector's terms) and really could not be considered "fine art" pieces comparable to those in the National Museum or private collections. For this reason, he believed the museum should stress the ethnographic value of the collection and use it as a means of informing the public about the role of ceramics in Dayak culture. He suggested that the ceramics be displayed as ethnographic objects in their cultural context rather than as art.

In November of 1992, Museum Balanga mounted a temporary exhibition titled *Foreign Jars in Central Kalimantan*. In the catalog accompanying the exhibit, jars were pictured with captions that provided the name of the piece, its inventory number, size, provenience, and time period. The catalog explained how tempayan or *balanga* were introduced into Kalimantan as trade goods, and represented contact between the Dayak and Chinese. In addition to this scientific explanation of their origin, the catalog also included a rendition of a Dayak legend that told how *balanga* were originally made from *tanah sorga* (soil from heaven) and brought to earth by two heavenly beings, Sangumang and Raden Tunjung. The legend conveyed the sacred and religious meaning of *balanga* within the context of Dayak culture. Thus, the exhibition acknowledged the historical, ethnographic, and aesthetic dimensions of jars. However, no mention was made of traditional approaches to their care and treatment or the existence of local jar experts.

Museum Balanga's approach to the registration and documentation of jars as well as their display illustrates how the imposition of professional museum methods can work to undermine or mask indigenous curatorial practices. Further training in professional museum methods can help Museum Balanga workers carry out their tasks more effectively and aid in the preservation of valuable cultural materials. But we might also consider what gets displaced in the process, and how increasing professionalization can inadvertently undermine the museum's long-term goal of cultural heritage preservation through the erasure of traditional curatorial methods.

In a discussion with Museum Balanga staff on the role of professional training in the museum, one staff member expressed his concern about preserving traditional knowledge and practices associated with certain objects. He feared that this knowledge and the sacred and cultural value of objects will be lost as Museum Balanga becomes more professional and modern values come to predominate in the museum. Will the museum, in the future, be of interest only to people with a "modern" outlook? In his opinion, the museum should help keep traditional values alive while acknowledging and promoting new ones. This is an important concern because, as Kaeppler has argued, "although all museums can preserve objects and display them, it is up to the local museums to preserve knowledge about them" (Kaeppler 1992:473).

In summary, I discovered that people in Central Kalimantan were museum-minded, but in their own ways. They have their own means of interpreting and appropriating museological concepts to fit into their own cultural patterns. What Indonesian museum leaders see as a lack of museum-mindedness may be a form of resistance to a predetermined idea of the museum's meanings and purposes as well as forms of cultural representation and curation imposed from above and from outside local communities.

Challenging the hegemony of the Eurocentric museum model

Alpha Konare, former President of ICOM and currently the President of the Republic of Mali, has been an outspoken critic of western-style ethnographic museums, especially those established by former colonial governments, and of the problematic nature of applying the model in non-western cultural contexts. For Konare: "The traditional museum is no longer in tune with our concerns; it has ossified our culture, deadened many of our cultural objects, and allowed the essence, imbued with the spirit of the people, to be lost" (1983:146).[16]

In writing on the development of ethnographic museums in Mali, Konare stresses how "each people, each ethnic community will define its own particular conservation structures based on their own traditions" (1983:146). According to Konare, conservation structures take a variety forms, such a shrines and ritual complexes, and are safeguarded through measures embedded in the community's culture.

Konare challenges museologists to explore and create new forms of museums that take local conservation structures and practices into account. He suggests that these new types of museums should be more like family or community museums, based on the community's own cultural traditions, institutions, collective resources, and needs. In the process of creating community museums, Konare stresses that certain guidelines or principles should be followed. For example, in forming collections, local people should decide which objects are to be included. Emphasis should be placed on articles that the people themselves consider to be the most significant, and that they consent to show others. Local values and customs should govern criteria for the selection of objects, and the notion of "quality" must be determined by an object's importance to the local population.

> In all cases, the opinion of the local population should be a determining factor. The conservation of cultural objects should not be carried out against the will of their creators and customary users. An object preserved without the consent of its creators becomes another thing altogether, imbued with a different content, and holding a different meaning . . . Even though its material form disappears, an object exists as long as its spirit remains. It is therefore essential that craftsmen who create cultural objects be particularly involved in the work of compiling inventories and ensuring protection, for these artists are able to recreate objects according to custom and oral traditions.
>
> (1983:149)

In Konare's view, ethnographic museums should be "veritable culture centers" with multiple functions including research and documentation. "Research and the development of community involvement can signify new life and meaning for the object, and the bringing into being a context conducive to renewal and fresh creativity" (1983:148). Furthermore, ethnographic museums should not just concentrate on the past, but also on the present. In general, Konare argues that in order for museums to be relevant to local people and fulfill their goals of protecting their cultural heritage, they should become more democratic and function on the basis of a "self-management approach to culture" (1983:149).

Even though Konare advocates local participation and a "self-management approach to culture," he points out that professional museologists and ethnologists can play a role in the development of local museums by sharing their knowledge and technical training with local people. However, the knowledge and experience of professionals should not take precedence over that of local people because local people or groups constitute "living libraries" whose knowledge and experience are "steeped in popular wisdom" (1983:148).

Konare's examples of local "conservation structures" in Mali stand as further evidence of how museological behavior is not confined to the western world, and how these structures need to be recognized and preserved as part of people's living cultural heritage. Other non-western museologists have made similar assertions, arguing for greater recognition of indigenous models of museums and approaches to cultural heritage preservation.

Hirini Sidney Moko Mead, Professor of Maori at Victoria University, Wellington, New Zealand, also challenges the hegemony of the western-style museum, stressing greater reliance on vernacular systems of cultural heritage management and protection. In the article, "Indigenous Models of Museums in Oceania" (1983), Mead describes museum-like structures in cultures throughout the Pacific and sees them as analogs to the western museum. While Mead points out many similarities between indigenous models of museum and their western counterparts, he also describes some of their differences.

To Mead, the Maori meeting house is an example of an indigenous museum model in which various types of carvings, photographs of deceased relatives, traditional weapons, valued art objects, and heirlooms are kept and displayed. But, according to Mead, the meeting house's primary purpose is not to store or display objects, but rather, to serve as a communal gathering place and center, where the dead are bade farewell and where visitors sleep (1983:98).

Mead also describes "custom houses" found in the Eastern Solomon Islands, asserting that some "look very much like museums." Custom houses are where model canoe ossuaries, skulls in cane containers, decorated bowls, and other valued objects are stored and displayed. Mead explains that custom houses are similar to western museums as places where objects are stored and displayed, and where a wide selection of objects can be observed and studied. He notes that village carvers visit the custom house to study traditional carving styles. Thus, it serves as an educational resource as well as a place for conserving local art traditions (1983:99).

Mead, in illuminating some of the differences between indigenous models of museums in Oceania and western museums, contends that whereas one of the main features of the western museum is the presence of the written or printed word, in indigenous models of museums, communication of cultural knowledge has been primarily transmitted through oral traditions. Mead further points out that, in indigenous structures, there has been no sophisticated technology for prolonging the life of objects. "Eventually, they rotted or were turned into dust by various insects. Replacements were made and the artistic and technological heritage continued for another decade" (1983:100). In this context, "the task of maintaining an art tradition is the primary concern of a community. Display and conservation are of secondary importance" (1983:100).

Mead asserts that indigenous museums are integrated into society in ways that are quite different from their western counterparts. For this reason, he suggests that if the people of the Pacific are encouraged to establish cultural centers or museums they should be advised to model such places on indigenous museums, and the way they have been integrated into people's lives:

> The local museum or cultural centre ought to be a structure that is inte-
> grated into the life of the people and the community. A structure that is

modeled on the western concept is not only too expensive to build in the first place, it is also difficult to maintain.

(1983:101)

Mead argues that the western-style museum is also too specialized and requires trained people to operate it.

> Furthermore, the training favors those who pursue western-type education and leaves outside local people who are quite capable of operating their own familiar structures. In the latter case, training in oral traditions might be far more important than getting a university degree.

(1983:101)

Mead provides examples of indigenous customs and beliefs that serve to protect objects stored in custom and meeting houses, and sees them as a very important aspect of the indigenous museum form. For instance, in most Polynesian and Melanesian custom and meeting houses the articles kept within them as well as the structures themselves are rendered *tapu* (taboo), which functions to restrict access and use. Consequently, there is no need for security guards or systems. But Mead fears that this tradition is being undermined by the increasing influence of western-style museums, which fosters secularization of the knowledge and customs surrounding the meeting houses and the objects within them, making them "common" and devoid of their singular cultural meanings. In general, Mead suggests that "rather than dismantle the belief system of the indigenous people for the sake of setting up a European-style museum, one should work within that belief system as much as possible" (1983:101). The implications of such a suggestion are not without their significance for as Mead argues: "To accept the Western model is to lose control over the culture itself and especially the indigenous philosophy and educational system" (1983:101).

In the next chapter, I provide more examples of non-western models of museums and methods of curation that, in many respects, are analogous to western museum practices. These examples also substantiate the claim that non-western people too have been concerned with the care and preservation of their cultural heritage. The specific characteristics of indigenous museum models and methods of curation vary, but their long-term goal is the same, and that is, the transmission of the culture from one generation to the next.

3

Indigenous models of museums, curation, and concepts of cultural heritage preservation

Many authors have acknowledged that some sort of collecting is probably a universal human activity (Cannon-Brookes 1984, Pearce 1992, Pomian 1994). As Clifford has commented, "accumulating and displaying valued things is, arguably, a widespread human activity not limited to any class or cultural group" (1997:217). Other authors have pointed out how examples of collections and structures with museum-like functions have existed throughout the world since ancient times (Bazin 1967, Simpson 1996). Shrines and temples are said to possess features common to museums, such as the housing and displaying of objects for ritual purposes (Pomian 1994). Neither is the role of curator new. "In their capacity of overseeing ritual objects, healers and priests throughout the ages have acted as the first curators" (Robb 1992:30).

Yet, until relatively recently, collecting and curatorial practices as well as museum-like structures existing outside the western world have largely gone unexplored. In Chapter 1, I suggested that this lack of attention was largely due to the assumption that museological behavior is a uniquely western phenomenon. The predominance of the western museum model has also contributed to this oversight. In the preceding chapter, I demonstrated the extent to which the Dayaks of Borneo exhibit collecting and curatorial practices. In this chapter, I give further examples of non-western museum models and methods of curation that challenge not only Eurocentric museology, but also the assertion that non-western people are not concerned with the collection, care, and preservation of their cultural property. This latter assertion is not merely of academic interest, but has broader implications since it has frequently been used to justify the collection (or some would say plunder) and retention of non-western people's cultural property in museums. The ideological basis of this argument is rooted in narratives of the history of western collecting and museums.

Western collecting practices (at least as they pertain to museums) have been generally distinguished from the collecting practices of others on the grounds that western collecting is systematic and carried out for specific scientific and aesthetic purposes. The history of collecting, as is true with the history of museums, has been associated with the rise of humanist thought, scientific discovery, and the emergence of capitalism in the seventeenth and eighteenth centuries (Ames 1992, Bennett 1995, Clifford 1988, Handler 1988, Pearce 1992, Schulz 1994). As Cannon-Brookes claims in "The Nature of Museum Collections," in the widely used *Manual of Curatorship* (1984):

> The intellectual environment which has provided the essential framework for the assembly of museum collections is Renaissance Humanism, and although the first systematic collections would appear to have been formed in the Greek and Roman world, the fundamental Humanist concept that Man could be understood through his creations and Nature through the systematic study of Her manifestations, positively demanded, for the first time, the formation of collections for study purposes.
>
> (1984:115)

Cannon-Brookes also stresses that "the process of collecting cannot be considered separately from the cultural characteristics of the society undertaking it" (1984:115). Thus, collecting practices must be viewed within their own particular cultural contexts. Nevertheless, Cannon-Brookes sees a fundamental difference between the collecting practices of western and non-western societies. The author bases his claim on perceived differences in the "mentalities" of western and non-western societies in addition to their respective relationships to the material world. This distinction and its explanation warrants quoting Cannon-Brookes at length because his words reveal the commonly held view that non-western societies are not concerned with the collection and preservation of their cultural property, and that such property is not vital to the ongoing transmission of their cultures.

> Seen in a historical context, the vast majority of societies, past and present, are "concept-centred" and for these the individual object is of very limited significance. For these societies the process of collecting/preserving objects is limited to fetishes, totems and so on which perform an ongoing functional role and the transmission of cultural traditions is overwhelmingly oral. However, for the minority – the "object-centred" societies – the accumulation of objects is of crucial importance in the transmission of cultural traditions, and the curiosity manifested by them in artefacts created by the "concept-centred" societies is not reciprocated. Consequently, the relevance today of museum collections to any particular society, and the significance accorded by it to them, varies widely and although museum collections are relevant to most western societies, they are not equally important and may indeed be irrelevant to many societies in the world.
>
> (1984:115)

Cannon-Brookes goes on to say that it is only after such societies have adopted the values of "object-centred" societies (or after they have become sufficiently westernized) that they begin to take on such concerns, and even then, their motivations for doing so are tainted by political interests.

> Mercifully, the impact of collecting on "concept-centred" societies has generally been relatively limited, as might be expected from their characteristics, and much less than is sometimes claimed for them today. But the historical consequence has been for many living societies that the only

artefacts of any age to survive are those which have been collected by the "object-centred" societies. This state of affairs remained acceptable to all the parties concerned until the materialistic values of the "object-centred" societies began to be adopted by all other societies, more as a political manifestation of national cultural identity, cast in an alien mould, than as a newly-developed fundamental need, and the growing demands of previously "concept-centred" societies for the outward trappings represented by museum collections present formidable problems. Indeed, one of the major museum problems of the last decades of the twentieth century is that posed by the ambitions of societies which were "concept-centred" and have subsequently adopted the priorities of an "object-centred" society, and their rights as against those of the long-term "object-centred" societies through whose collecting activities the artefacts of the former have survived.

(1984:116)

The more recent, critical literature on museums and collecting not only illuminates the biases and assumptions of this ideology, but also the historical conditions under which much of this collecting has occurred, that is, under systems of western colonialism and domination (Ames 1996, Barringer and Flynn 1998, Clifford 1988 and 1997, Stocking 1985). Certainly, western practices associated with the collection and preservation of objects can be distinguished from those of other cultures on several grounds. But a more fruitful approach to understanding these practices cross-culturally is to explore, as even Cannon-Brookes suggests, how "the process of collecting cannot be considered separately from the cultural characteristics of the society undertaking it."[1] More succinctly, we might ask: what from the material world do specific groups and individuals choose to collect, care for, and preserve? What are the various methods they have devised for doing so? And what are the purposes of collecting and preserving objects in particular cultural contexts? Of general concern here is the role of culture in the perception, care, and treatment of objects, as well as the function of objects in the transmission of culture.

This chapter focuses on non-western examples of activities that have been at the heart of museum work, i.e. collecting, storage, classification, display, conservation, and education as well as indigenous models of museums. I discuss these practices in terms of how they demonstrate a people's concern for cultural heritage preservation, which, in simplest terms, can be understood as a concern for the transmission of culture through time. In presenting these examples I am not so much concerned with strict or professional definitions of museological terms – for example, of the museum or curation – but more so with the basic functions and aims of museums and curation. As Mead, speaking for Pacific islanders, asserts:

we are not interested in the detail of what a Western museum is, but rather in its basic functions of storing objects of value, of exhibiting them to persons other than their producers and of being a structure that is itself valued because of how it is used and what is in it.

(1983:98)

The goal is to broaden our view of what constitutes museological behavior and its practitioners so we might recognize them in alternative forms.

For instance, the term "curation" derives from the Latin word *curare*, "to take care of," and, as it relates to museums, this means to take care of objects. Those who take care of objects in museums are generally referred to as "curators." Numerous definitions of curator exist in museum manuals and handbooks, and these typically define (in technical terms) what curators do. Edson and Dean define a curator as "a museum staff member or consultant who is a specialist in a particular field of study and who provides information, does research, and oversees the maintenance, use, and enhancement of collections" (1994:290). As useful as this definition may be in defining what a curator does in western museums, it is of limited use when exploring cross-culturally how people care for and protect objects as well as why. It also neglects the social dimensions of curation as well as the role of culture in the care and treatment of objects.

Cash Cash offers a compelling alternative perspective of curation based on the idea that our relationships to objects are ultimately social ones and therefore curatorial work is a form of social practice. Cash Cash defines curation as "a social practice predicated on the principle of a fixed relation between material objects and the human environment" (2001:140). By "the principle of fixed relation" Cash Cash means "those conditions that are socially constructed and reproduced as strategic cultural orientations vis-à-vis material objects" (2001:141).[2] By looking at curation as social practice and as a social construct we can begin to see how curation is situated in particular cultural contexts and is a cultural artifact in itself. This approach also allows us to see the importance of curatorial work in larger social contexts beyond the museum. The point is to liberate the concept of curation from its limited usage in western museology.

Following Cash Cash, this chapter also examines the role of material culture or objects in shaping social relationships, and in the transmission of culture. Every society has its own array of material culture, which embodies, reflects, and reinforces that society's particular social patterns, and, to a certain extent, helps reproduce them. This capacity is not inherent in material culture per se, but is mediated by or realized through human agency. Thus, objects are one means by which humans shape and are shaped by their world (Arnoldi and Hardin 1996:1).

> Material culture is a vital element in the constitution and dynamics of all societies because of two essential factors: it is the product of the interaction of people and their materials worlds; and it is one of the principal means by which culture is stored and transmitted.
>
> (Leibrick 1989:206)

The most distinctive feature of objects is that they are tangible. This means they have the property of being able to exist in time and space independent of people. Since objects endure through time they also have the ability to bridge passing generations, and bring continuity and a sense of cultural connectedness (Leibrick 1989:202). Thus, material culture can play a critical role in the transmission of culture. Objects function in this way as a medium of communication.

"Apart from language, material culture is culture's principal medium of communication, and in the temporary absence of people, it is culture's only means of information storage. For this reason material culture plays a vitally important role for social reproduction" (Leibrick 1989:203). As mnemonic devices, objects can trigger memories and knowledge that may not be used in everyday life and are possibly in danger of being forgotten (Leibrick 1989:202).

But material culture, as a communication medium, can be more complex than language, taking on multiple or new meanings depending on its context. This makes the interpretation of material culture problematic outside its cultural context or apart from the individual or group that produced and used it:

> While the analogy is often made that material culture can function like a crude language, objects can in fact be considerably more evocative, multi-faceted, elegant and ambiguous than language. A single simple object can communicate vastly complex feelings and bundles of information. It can also simultaneously evoke differing, even conflicting types and levels of information, depending on who is viewing it and in what context.
>
> (Leibrick 1989:203)

Ironically, despite this limitation, it is the communicative power of objects that also has been used to justify the collection of non-western people's material culture and its placement in museums. Objects, labeled "ethnographic specimens," have been collected "in the name of science," and for what they can "teach" us about particular groups of people or about human culture in general (see Clavir 2002). Certainly, research on material culture and its interpretation and display in museums have contributed greatly to our understanding of other cultures. But what has been neglected (or in some cases denied) is that objects serve this same purpose in their cultures of origin, and are of great importance for the maintenance and transmission of cultural traditions. The removal of certain objects from their cultures of origin has often led to the demise of certain traditions, especially those related to religious practices and beliefs.

Today, greater sensitivity and awareness of this issue is leading to a reappraisal and reorientation of museum practices as museologists and anthropologists have begun to acknowledge the unequal power relations behind the collection and representation of non-western cultures in museums, as well as the fact that non-western peoples have their own ways of collecting, curating, displaying, interpreting, and preserving their material culture. As I will show in this chapter, the museum and cultural heritage preservation are not new concepts in many non-western societies, and contemporary efforts in museum development are, in many cases, extensions of earlier traditions.

The concept of *pusaka* as cultural heritage in Indonesia

As noted in Chapter 2, Indonesians have a long history of collecting (or keeping) *pusaka*, an Indonesian word that is generally translated into English as "heirloom." However, the word carries a range of meanings in the Indonesian language. In the book *Pusaka: Art of Indonesia* (1992), Soebadio states that the two most established Indonesian dictionaries list three separate meanings for *pusaka*:

> 1) something inherited from a deceased person (analogous to the English noun *inheritance*) 2) something that "comes down" from one's ancestors (analogous to *heirloom*) 3) an inheritance of a special value to a community, that cannot be disposed of without specific common descent (analogous to *heritage* in the sense of "something possessed" as a result of one's natural situation or birth).
>
> (1992:15)

Soebadio claims that the widespread use of the word "*pusaka*" throughout Indonesia (albeit with variations in spelling) indicates that it is an ancient word, and possibly of Malay or Austronesian origin.

Today, *pusaka*, while retaining its more traditional connotations, is also used to refer to symbols of modern nationalism. For example, the first flag hoisted at the Proclamation of Independence on August 17, 1945 in Jakarta is considered national *pusaka*. The nation itself is also said to be *pusaka*. The Indonesian archipelago is known as "Tanah Air" [land and water], and in a popular nationalist song is referred to as "Tanah Air Tanah Pusaka" (Damais 1992:207–208).

The most important aspect of *pusaka*, for the present discussion, is how the concept of *pusaka* has functioned to help protect and preserve valuable cultural property, and transmit cultural knowledge and traditions through the generations. *Pusaka* can take the form of either tangible or intangible cultural property. For example, in addition to objects such as textiles, jewelry, ceramics, weapons, beads, masks, land, and houses, a song, dance drama, or story may be considered *pusaka*. Objects of foreign origin acquired by an individual, family, or group through trade, exchange, warfare, or gift exchange may also be *pusaka*. These include items such as Chinese ceramics, Indian cloth, and European canons and weapons (Hoskins 1998:106, Damais 1992:206). Thus, virtually anything can become *pusaka*, although not everything that is inherited is considered *pusaka* nor are objects necessarily created to play this role. But rather, an object or entity becomes *pusaka* in the course of its social life. As one Indonesian writer put it:

> Whether they are owned by individuals, a family, extended family or clan, collectively by a tribe or ethnic group, or whether they are treasures of a sultan's palace or princely realm, *pusaka* are a creation by a society, which possess them. *It is the meaning a society gives these objects, not anything innate in the objects themselves, which makes them pusaka* [emphasis added]. This is illustrated by the wide range of objects that can become *pusaka*, regardless of who owns them.
>
> (Kartiwa 1992:159)

Consequently, the meanings given to *pusaka* are constructed and interpreted according to context and particular circumstances. For this reason, Martowikrido suggests that it is more appropriate to view *pusaka* as a "social construct" and in terms of social relationships because the quality that makes an object *pusaka* is not inherent in the object itself (1992:132). "*Pusaka* are best understood within the context of an important set of abstract ideas regarding social structure. *Pusaka* emphasize, express or define relationships within society, especially . . . kinship connections" (1992:129).[3]

Pusaka is essential to the maintenance of kinship ties and lineages because it can be one of the most important links to the authority of ancestors, especially founders of families, clans, or ethnic groups. In many Indonesian societies, those in positions of authority claim their positions reside in the authority of their ancestors, who also established rules for its transmission. An heirloom object, which often recalls a founding ancestor in imagery or in stories, symbolizes this authority and thus becomes a "visible symbol of the transmission of traditions" (Taylor and Aragon 1991:43).

In a number of Indonesian societies, ancestors are closely associated with heirloom treasures stored within clan or noble houses. Among the Toraja of Sulawesi, noble houses acquire prestige from myths about the founding ancestors and from the power of the heirlooms stored within them, such as gold and silver ornaments, swords, old Chinese porcelain, textiles, and beadwork (Waterson 1990:165). In some societies, such as the Mambai of Timor, heirlooms have their own names, personalities, and histories. The memorization of the heirlooms' movement from house to house (called the "walk of sacred objects") is frequently used as a substitute for genealogical reckoning (Waterson 1990:34). Genealogical trees, in and of themselves and especially of royal families, can also be considered *pusaka* (Jessup 1981:88).

The transfer of heirloom objects is generally strictly governed by rules of inheritance and customary law (*adat*). Among the Minangkabau of West Sumatra, a matrilineal society, certain kinds of heirloom property customarily descend to nephews and nieces from their maternal uncle. Royal titles, called *sako*, are also inherited in this manner, as are items of property termed *pusako*. "*Pusako* cannot be subdivided, but must be kept intact as received to ensure the integrity of the lineage group. In time, the legacy passes on to the next nephew and niece in line" (Martowikrido 1992:129). In Minangkabau society, the traditional lineage house (*rumah gadang*) itself is a form of *pusako* and is of special significance in the system of inheritance. It is invested with great supernatural powers (*sakti*), and thus cannot be the subject of disputes. Neither can it change hands as other property, such as land, does. In general, the *rumah gadang* is under the control of female kin (Martowikrido 1992:130).

In traditional Indonesian societies, the legitimacy of a ruler, royal house, or kingdom was often bound up with objects, which were considered the "essence" of a palace and vital to its very existence. Royal *pusaka*, such as a crown, staff, or other official heirlooms, were perceived as establishing authority within a court or kingdom (Taylor and Aragon 1991:43). If it fell into the hands of another person that person had the right to be king (Martowikrido 1992:131). Thus, the struggle for power was simultaneously a struggle for the possession of royal *pusaka* (Wagner 1988:145).

It is perhaps in the royal courts of Java that the concept and role of *pusaka* became the most developed. Because of the elaboration of ideas around sacred heirlooms, and the power given to them in Javanese society, the Javanese concept of *pusaka* is distinguished from that of other Indonesian societies through the usage of the Javanese word *pusoko*. Anyone participating in traditional Javanese culture may possess *pusoko*, but *pusoko* belonging to the royal courts are considered the most sacred, and most richly endowed with spiritual power. They are thought to play an important role in protecting Javanese society from harm, and many of the most elaborate ceremonies of the Javanese courts center on *pusoko* objects (Kartiwa 1992:159). Kartiwa describes the nature of royal *pusoko*:

> In the rich ceremonial and spiritual life of the *kraton* [palace], a *pusoko* is much more than merely an object; in fact, it has many human qualities. *Pusoko* have names, feel desires and wishes, and they can communicate through signs with humans. They may possess great power: to foretell events, auspicious and inauspicious, or to protect the people and help them to avoid danger and disaster. To ensure that *pusoko* continue to act in this benevolent way, the people must in turn perform certain services for them, such as periodic provision of offerings, fumigations with incense and ritual bathings. In the courts of Central Java, *pusoko* are cared for and presented with offerings by the Abdi Dalem (courtiers or literally "people of the inner circle" . . .), who pass this responsibility down from generation to generation much as the *pusoko* themselves are passed on.
>
> (1992:159–160)

Of all the objects considered *pusoko*, the *keris*, or Javanese dagger, is the pre-eminent *pusoko* of Central Java. The *keris*, with its sinuously curved blade, is an old and revered weapon. *Keris* are generally beautifully crafted, with handles made of gold, ivory, or rare woods and hilts inlaid with precious gems (see Jessup 1991). But a *keris'* true beauty is said to lie in its blade, and it is often the blade's spiritual power that determines its acceptance as *pusoko* (Kartiwa 1992:160). *Pusoko*, such as *keris*, are said to embody a vital force or power known as *kesaktian*. *Pusoko* are "vehicles for the transmission of *kesaktian*. As such, they are considered sacred" (Damais 1994:206). A *pusoko keris* is always treated with special reverence, and even sacrifices are offered to it, which are thought to enhance its spiritual and magical power (Wagner 1988:162).

It is customary for *pusoko* to be regularly "washed" and sanctified according to traditionally specified rituals. Each *pusoko* is washed in a different way, using substances such as opium, flowers, incense, cigarette smoke, and coffee (Kartiwa 1992:164). The blades of *keris* are sometimes polished and treated with citrus juice and arsenic (Richter 1994:26). These practices are carried out not only to protect an object's spiritual integrity, but also to preserve its physical integrity.

In general, and throughout Indonesia, because of its high value, much attention has been given to the care and protection of *pusaka*. *Pusaka* are usually carefully stored in specially designated areas within houses, such as attics, rafters, lofts, or platforms. As repositories of a family's or group's treasured sacred heirlooms, these spaces are often considered sacred in and of themselves. In Rindi, East Sumba, the spirit of the clan's founding ancestor is said to be present in the roof peak of the clan's origin house, where the house treasures are stored. Therefore, a number of prohibitions and restrictions limit access to this space because the objects stored within it are heavily charged with sacred power (Waterson 1990:227). Only older men of the lineal group that owns the house, or ritual functionaries are allowed to enter (Waterson 1990:179). The most sacred spot in the traditional Achenese house of North Sumatra is a platform high up in the roof, beneath the gable, on which the *peusaka* is stored (Waterson 1990:183). In some cases, entire houses are sacred owing to the presence of sacred heirloom property. Waterson writes that among the Nualulu of Seram, traditional houses are called *numa morie*, or "sacred houses," whose sacredness does not lie so much in the building itself as in its contents, the heirlooms stored in it. "The house is properly viewed as a 'depository for sacred objects,' rather than as a sacred structure in its own right, and even less a habitation for human beings, *which is virtually incidental*" (1990:45, italics in the original).

As discussed in Chapter 2, the Dayaks of Borneo are renowned for the collection and veneration of Chinese jars as *pusaka*. But Dayak *pusaka* can also include beads, weapons, brassware, gongs, textiles, and old porcelain. Traditionally, the Dayaks stored these prized possessions in trunks or containers in the rafters and lofts of their longhouses. A longhouse is a dwelling composed of individual family apartments under one long, continuous roof. Longhouses can still be found in some parts of Borneo, although most Dayaks today live in individual houses.

Pusaka, such as jars, may be stored out in the open as a display of a family's wealth or kept from public view and only brought out on special occasions. Schiller noted, when observing the funeral rites of one Ngaju family in Central Kalimantan, that, "death is the only occasion when the family displays . . . treasured heirlooms" (1997:44). Metcalf describes a similar practice among the Berawan of Sabah, Malaysia, where heirlooms are also brought out at the time of death and displayed with the corpse. Until this time, valuables are kept in safe storage. "Every family has a substantial wooden chest tucked away somewhere, in a sleeping cubicle or high up under the rafters, which contains all the fine things that are rarely brought out" (1982:39). Metcalf indicates how both practical means and social mores serve to protect heirloom property:

> The box is not for security against theft. Anyone so deranged as to try to steal heirloom property from his own people could easily carry off the whole box. Rather it is to keep them away from the prying fingers of little boys, against whom nothing else is proof, and to preserve modesty about these possessions.
>
> (1982:39)

Rights to the ownership of heirloom property vary according to the customs of each Dayak ethnic group. For instance, Alexander writes that in the longhouses of the Lahanan of Sarawak (a state of Malaysian Borneo) the longhouse and its

Figure 3.1 Kenyah Dayak woman of East Kalimantan displaying her heirlooms or *pusaka*. Photograph by Christina Kreps, 1996.

contents as well as land and heirlooms (*laven pusaka*) are owned by the founding family of the longhouse (*tilung pu'un*). The author explains that heirlooms, including beads, gongs, brassware, and jars, "provide a symbolic focus for the *tilung pu'un*" (Alexander 1993:40). Rights to the heirlooms are held by all members of the *tilung pu'un*, regardless of where they live. But custody of heirlooms is entrusted to the senior member of the *tilung pu'un* (Alexander 1993:40). In contrast, among the Berawan, heirloom property is not owned by the residential group, but rather, by individuals:

> When an old person dies, his or her heirloom property is divided among all the children. The deceased may have indicated how this was to be done before death. If not, the sharing is approximately equal, save that the person who looked after the old person deserves a larger share.
>
> (Metcalf 1982:18)

In Borneo, and throughout the Indonesian archipelago, *pusaka* is also stored in family granaries or rice barns (*lumbung*) (Waterson 1990).[4] In many parts of Indonesia, the rice barn is characterized as having a sacred aspect, and is thus treated with great reverence. The rice barn is sometimes attached to the house, but can also be a separate building. The importance of the granary is reflected in the fact that it is often more elaborately decorated than the house itself. The number and size of a family's granaries and the quality of their workmanship serve as a visible sign of the owner's wealth and prestige (Waterson 1990:59).

Like all aspects of culture, traditional practices associated with *pusaka* continually undergo change in response to other cultural changes, especially those related to religious practices and beliefs and systems of social structure and organization. The concept of *pusaka* has proven to be adaptive to changing social conditions and circumstances. As such, it is an enduring concept in Indonesia that can tell us much about what from the material world people choose to value and thus preserve, as well as how they conceptualize and protect their heritage. In the words of Adji Damais, an Indonesian scholar and museum professional:

> Whether we are talking about sacred and powerful protective objects worn by ancestral heroes or the symbols of modern nationalism . . . it is clear that the concept of *pusaka* is a pervasive one, close to the heart of Indonesian ideas about objects, and therefore about the world . . . We need to understand the idea of *pusaka* in order that we may relate to – and constitute – our heritage.
>
> (1992:208)

Heritage is intimately linked to identity, and *pusaka*, either individually or collectively owned, is central to Indonesian people's identity. "*Pusaka* are objects and property left to us by our ancestors, and like any other heirlooms of long standing, are central to the sense of identity of their owners" (Martowikrido 1992:129).

Museums and pusaka

In Chapter 2, I pointed out how many of the objects in Museum Balanga's collection were once part of a family's, individual's, or group's *pusaka*. This is also true of other provincial museums throughout Indonesia. Thus, provincial museums, in certain respects, have taken over some of the roles of the traditional caretakers of *pusaka*, that is, families, titled individuals, ritual specialists, and so on. Yet, in some cases, despite their placement in museums, *pusaka* objects are still revered as *pusaka* and treated accordingly by community members. This is especially true in museums that were formerly the residences of noble families and the home of royal *pusaka*. Thus, in these museums one can see how traditional beliefs and behaviors associated with *pusaka* are still at work in addition to deeply embedded systems of social hierarchy and status.

Bambang Sumadio, a former director of the Directorate of Museums, suggested in an interview that in my study of Indonesian museum development it was important to consider how museums, in spite of being "modern" institutions, are superimposed on communities where "feudalistic" social structures and relationships are still played out. He emphasized that such factors affected museum operations, and at times, created professional dilemmas for museum staff.

Several provincial museums in Indonesia were previously the palaces of regional sultanates. For example, the Provincial Museum of East Kalimantan, Mulawarman, occupies the former palace of the sultanate of Kutai. Although the museum is officially owned by the state and thus intended to function as a public museum with all the accompanying democratic attributes, the royal family still uses the palace and some of the collection for royal functions and ceremonies. According to one of the museum's staff members, the sultan's family also has considerable say in museum matters.

Museum Mulawarman's collection consists of ethnographic objects from the various Dayak groups that inhabit the province, antiquities from the Hindu period in East Kalimantan, and contemporary sculptures. However, a large percentage of the collection is made up of objects related to the history of the sultanate in addition to the family's heirlooms. These include royal regalia, such as the *Lembu Suana*, or coat of arms of the Sultan of Kutai, Kartanagara XIX, staffs, and articles of clothing. These items are not only of great symbolic importance, but are also still used by members of the royal family. One museum staff member told me that periodically they had to take the clothing off display so it could be worn in ceremonies and official gatherings. In her view, this was not "good museum practice," but, she conceded, working in a museum that is also a palace requires compromise.

Taylor provides an example of a similar situation in his description of the Sultan's Palace Museum of Ternate, in the Province of Moluku. According to Taylor, the Sultan's Palace Museum was founded in 1916, but continued to be a functioning palace long afterwards. In 1976, it was integrated into the national provincial museum system of the Directorate of Museums and renovated. However, soon after the renovation took place, the descendents of the former sultanate began moving into the museum and occupying it as their home. Taylor wrote in 1994 that the Ternatese still treated the son of the last sultan, who lived in Jakarta and was a member of the Indonesian parliament, as the sultan for purposes of carrying out some traditional ceremonies.

Taylor explains that "although the sultan's palace is officially a museum it remains one of the most powerful symbols of the sultan's power along with the regalia" (1994:73–74). The museum houses the "foremost object of local veneration and pre-eminent example of regalia," the crown of the sultan of Ternate. For a few years after the museum was renovated, the crown was on public display. But later, it was placed in a private room where it was shielded from public view. Regardless of this move, Taylor observed:

> The museum-going-public brings bottles of water each day to place at a prayer-rug altar set up outside the room containing the crown. There prayers are carried out three times a day, after which the museum-goers return to take the blessed water home to cure fevers and illnesses.
>
> (1994:74)

The practice, on the part of community members, of coming to museums and making offerings to particular objects is not uncommon in Indonesian provincial museums. A Directorate staff member told me that on such occasions museum workers generally "look the other way," meaning the practice is tolerated but not encouraged. While the practice of making offerings to objects in the museum may not be condoned by museum staff, it tells us something about how local people find ways of fitting the museum into their cultural patterns and traditions regarding *pusaka*.

Pusaka and other objects have been preserved through the generations because they have fulfilled material and spiritual needs. As prestige objects they have been used to reinforce social position and status and signify wealth. As ceremonial objects they have been integral to religious beliefs and practices. Although many Indonesians still hold onto the traditional values and beliefs surrounding *pusaka*, today most Indonesians are either Muslims or Christians. Thus, for these people, *pusaka* objects have lost much of their traditional meanings and have become "antiques."[5] Yet there is still concern for their care and preservation as part of people's "cultural heritage." This sentiment is expressed most clearly in Indonesia's developing "museum culture," as well as in the wider society as it becomes increasingly "museum-minded." Such concern can be seen in the incentives behind and negotiations surrounding the collecting strategies of museums, such as those of the Provincial Museum of Central Kalimantan, Museum Balanga.

The principle means by which Museum Balanga acquired objects for its collection was through donations, purchases, and field collecting. Donations took a variety of forms, but were mostly objects that had been in a family's possession for generations, such as jars, brassware, and historical items. For example, one elderly man gave the museum a flag commemorating a battle between the Dayaks and the Dutch that took place in 1902. He gave the flag to the museum because he believed it was more secure in the museum than in his home.

Additionally, some community members, aware of the rapid rate at which Central Kalimantan's cultural heritage was being lost to traders and collectors, chose to give objects to the museum so future generations would know something of their heritage.

The loss of cultural property to the domestic and foreign art and antiquities market[6] was a major concern for the museum, since one of its main purposes was to care and preserve the province's cultural heritage. The museum staff was aware of the fact that the high prices paid for Dayak "art" and antiques enticed people to sell their heirlooms.[7] In an effort to address this problem, Museum Balanga staff conducted field surveys in villages to make inventories of people's collections and to purchase objects for the museum's collection. Field surveys also gave museum workers the opportunity to inform villagers about the museum and its role in preserving the province's cultural heritage.

In July 1991, I accompanied one staff member on a survey trip to villages upriver from Palangka Raya. In one village, we visited the home of an older man who had formerly been the *kepala desa* (village head). This man was eager to talk about his *pusaka*, and especially his collection of *balanga*, which lined one wall of his house. He proudly described the qualities and uses of each *balanga*, stating that one was used to brew rice in while another was reserved for ceremonies. He recounted how he had given one valuable jar to his son-in-law when he married his daughter. "One jar for one woman. That is *jalan adat* [customary way]."

The man told us that he thought the work of the museum was important, and that it was good that the government was concerned about "old things." He said many objects were disappearing from his village, and, in fact, during the previous year, several *sapundu* (mortuary effigy poles) had been stolen. He approved of the government sending people to villages to inform them about their *budaya* (culture) and the value of "old things." Perhaps this would help prevent the further loss of things like *sapundu* and *balanga*.

Although villagers welcomed us on this trip, museum workers informed me that such a warm reception was not always the case. In fact, they said they often had to gain the trust of villagers before they could proceed with their work. They told me several stories about how they routinely had to explain who they were, why they had come, and the purpose of the museum. One worker said that once when she and four other staff members arrived in a village, the people refused to talk to them. After consultation with one villager, the staff discovered that the villagers were wary because they suspected the museum workers were there to take their *pusaka*. The villagers had heard stories about strangers coming to villages and coercing the people to sell their heirlooms.[8] Eventually, the workers were invited into homes and allowed to photograph collections. However, the villagers refused to sell any of their heirlooms to the staff. Yet in another village when the museum staff inquired about purchasing a *sapundu*, the villagers refused to sell it. Instead, they offered to give it to the museum. Apparently, the villagers felt it was an honor to be able to make a gift to the museum. But before the staff could remove the *sapundu* from the village, a purification ritual had to be performed to release its spirit. This ceremony made it safe for the staff to transfer the *sapundu* to the museum, and absolved the villagers of any further ritual obligations. According to one staff member, each village has its own *adat-istiadat* (laws and customs) that regulate the proper use and treatment of certain objects.

The above anecdotes show that while attitudes and values regarding *pusaka* objects are changing, people are still concerned about their care and preservation. Indonesian museums are increasingly becoming the custodians of *pusaka*, which is seen as not only a critical element of people's local and regional heritage and identity, but also that of the nation. Taylor sums up the situation neatly.

> Indonesians are beginning to fill museums with collections, and will continue to do so as museums expand and as traditional methods of keeping such treasures change. The museums maintain materials . . . for which traditional methods of care have been abandoned as the population has converted to Islam or Christianity . . . Indonesians are creating new concepts of the museum's place in society, particularly as a mediator between local traditions and national identity. In other words, in their approach to the museum . . . Indonesians have taken a European model and are starting to create something distinctly theirs.
>
> (1994:86)

Indigenous models of museums and curation in the Pacific

Since the 1970s, museums and cultural centers have been growing at a rapid rate throughout the Pacific. But as previously noted, the museum concept and curatorial-type work are not new phenomena in the Pacific, rather, they are extensions of long-standing traditions. A number of other authors have made similar observations, suggesting that contemporary museums and cultural centers in the region are based on or inspired by indigenous museum models and curatorial methods. In many cases, present-day museums and cultural centers are fusing elements of local traditional forms with the western idea of the museum to serve individual communities' contemporary needs and purposes.

Simpson, writing on indigenous models of museums in the Pacific, is among those who counter the claim that the museum is a foreign concept to non-western peoples and thus, presumably, inappropriate for that audience. Echoing Mead, she observes that "in some non-western cultures there have been traditions of having buildings or sites in which were stored collections of objects of religious or ceremonial significance, which are in some respects analogous to the western concept of a museum" (1996:108). Simpson further argues that when western museum curators suggest that indigenous museums and cultural centers are not really museums, they are not seeing how these facilities "do indeed function as museums and, in some instances, lead the way in developing methodologies which are relevant to the communities they serve, yet conform to the basic philosophies of the museum" (1996:107).

Simpson makes the important point that while certain characteristics of indigenous museums, such as their exclusive or non-public nature, may run counter to the democratic ideals and public orientation of western museums, this should not disqualify their status as museums. But rather, such facilities offer "evidence of the concepts of collection, storage and preservation being applied within a particular cultural framework as an extension of earlier traditions, but with the adoption, in some instances, of modern museological environmental, security and recording methods" (1996:107). What is of critical importance is how museological methods are "being adapted to suit the demands of current social needs within a particular cultural context" (1996:107). To say that museums are irrelevant or inappropriate for any society is to overlook not only how people have their own museological models and concepts, but also how these are malleable cultural expressions that can be transformed over time to meet changing circumstances and interests. Clifford makes a similar observation in responding to the question: "Why have museum practices proved so mobile, so productive in different locations?" (1997:217). He writes that

> several interlocking factors are at work. The ability to articulate identity, power, and tradition is critical, linking the institution's aristocratic origins with its modern nationalist and "culturalist" disseminations. Museums also resonate with a broad range of vernacular activities of collecting, display, and entertainment.
>
> (1997:217)

The traditional meeting or men's house, described in the previous chapter, is common to a number of societies throughout the Pacific and often cited as an example of an indigenous structure with functions similar to those of the museum. "Centers of community ritual, political, and artistic activities were almost universal in the traditional cultures of Oceania, and have often been labeled 'men's houses' – such as *tambarans* in the Sepik areas, long houses in Asmat, and *marae* in Polynesia" (Nero and Graburn 1978:147). Several authors have described the nature and function of these structures and the forms they are taking in contemporary society.

The peoples of the Abelam and Sepik River regions of Papua New Guinea are well known for their richly decorated men's houses called *haus tambaran* (*korombo* in Abelam and *haus tambaran* in Melanesian Pidgin) (Smidt and Guigan 1993:121). Their styles and uses vary according to the traditions of specific ethnic groups, but in general, they have been used as a meeting place and for ceremonies and rituals, especially those related to male initiation rites. *Haus tambaran* have also served as workspaces for the production of ritual objects and other arts as well as places to display and preserve them. Lewis describes traditional *haus tambaran* as "sacred repositories where objects were ritually preserved" (1990:159). As places used for preserving valuable objects and for teaching younger generations about tribal history, beliefs, and cultural practices, *haus tambaran* have been important centers for the preservation and transmission of local culture. Simpson writes that "objects were stored and preserved in the *haus tambaran*, in so far as the climate would allow, for future generations"

61

(1996:112). Cultural storehouses, such as the *haus tambaran*, "played a particularly important role in non-literate societies in which people relied upon oral traditions and the communicative power of objects to educate the young and the uninitiated and to provide historical records" (Simpson 1996:113).

Today, *haus tambaran* serve similar purposes as they did in the past, but may also provide storage and display areas for objects specifically made for sale to tourists (Lewis 1990:159). Traditionally, women and uninitiated males were typically prohibited access to the *haus tambaran* (Kaeppler 1994:21). However, this practice is being modified to accommodate changing traditions as well as the influx of tourists. In some cases, outsiders as well as women may be given honorary male status so they can enter the *haus tambaran*. According to Simpson, the *haus tambaran* can be seen as a form of an indigenous museum where "villagers guide visitors and explain the functions and stories of artefacts, an appropriate means of interpretation in a society which has relied upon oral history for the recording and dissemination of its history and lore" (1996:113).

The example of the huas tambaran shows that the museum is not a new concept in Papua New Guinea, but rather, part of continuing traditional practices. Stressing this point, G. Mosuwadoga, a former director of the Papua New Guinea National Museum in Port Moresby, explains:

> The necessity for building a communal type of house to secure and to house these objects is not a new or uncommon practice. Papua New Guinea was doing this long before the museum reached our country. The name and function of a museum can be looked upon in our society today as fitting into our basic ideals, which were with us long before any influence actually reached us.
>
> (quoted in Edwards and Stewart 1980:157)

The men's houses of Papua New Guinea not only represent an indigenous model of a museum, but also provide examples of indigenous forms of curation. In some men's houses – for example, those of the Mountain-Ok people of Central New Guinea – objects are systematically classified and arranged in carefully ordered displays in men's "cult houses." Craig describes these displays as "relic and trophy arrays," which include the sacred relics of ancestors, animal trophies, and ritual objects. According to Craig, the arrays reflect the people's relationships to ancestors, animals, and their environment, and are "a symbolic arrangement acting as an ecological model of animal resources in relation to human settlement and environment" (1990:201). Craig explains that all relic and trophy arrays are associated with the cult of ancestors, whose rituals are performed to ensure fertility of crops and domesticated animals, success in hunting and warfare, and good health for all members of the community (1990:207). Reflecting the central role of ancestors in people's lives and the ecosystem, ancestor relics are placed centrally at eye level within arrays. "These relics are intimately related to the quality of life of the inhabitants of the settlement, in particular to the activities essential for survival: gardening, hunting, and pig husbandry" (1990:201). Craig makes clear that there is a great deal of variation, even within certain groups, in exactly how the relic and trophy arrays are arranged in various houses as well as in their symbolic connotations. Cult leaders, which Craig describes as "cult house curators" are responsible for setting up and maintaining the arrays (1990: 207–208). It is not a stretch to say that, in their systematic and taxonomic character, the relic and trophy arrays lining the walls of cult houses recall images of the studiously constructed typographical displays of early western natural history and ethnographic collections.

Another interesting curatorial aspect of men's houses is how certain conservation measures were taken to protect and preserve objects. Davenport writes that in the men's houses of Santa Cruz Island, "racks were constructed over the central, communal hearth on which were kept all valued items that had to be protected against rats, mold and mildew" (1990:103). Along these lines, Craig also noted how the smoke from hearth fires acted to preserve the animal bones displayed in relic and trophy arrays (1990:205).

Viane Tutai, Assistant Director of the National Museum of the Cook Islands, provides another example of indigenous museological concepts and structures that can be seen as analogous to museums. In a workshop held at the Papua New Guinea National Museum and Art Gallery in 1989 on museums and cultural centers in the Pacific, Tutai stated: "Our societies had museums prior to the coming of the Whiteman. It was not called a museum then because it had various traditional names. But the functions or activities of such institutions were similar to modern day museums" (1991:201).

Tutai describes how, during "precontact times," the museum was known as *Are-Vananga*, *Are-Kariei*, *Are-Korero*, and *Pia-Atua*.

> These vernacular terms captured the activities involved and the function of such museums. *Are-Vananga* referred to a house of esoteric knowledge where astronomy was taught and also the history of the people. *Are-Kariei* was the entertainment house where the art of warfare was taught. *Are-Korero* was where history was taught and *Pia-Atua* highlighted religion. The staff who manned these institutions was called *Taunga* or experts in their own right. They displayed our objects of *mana* and dressed and fed them on the *marae* or sacred grounds. The house where these things were kept was *tapu* [taboo] to the public just as our storerooms are today. But the open ground of the *marae* was public and served as a kind of open-air display room.
>
> (1991:201)

Tutai explains that the work of indigenous curators was interrupted by colonial rule, subverted by missionary zeal and the "new order" of the colonial government.

> With the death of the special houses and the deportation of some of the artifacts, the museum as a special place of respect died on the lips of our curator-artisans who suddenly found themselves unemployed or redundant under the new order.
>
> (Tutai 1991:202)

63

But the museum institution resurfaced, albeit in a modified form, with the establishment of the Cook Islands Museum in 1964.

> As a place or institution, the museum disappeared from our midst during our early colonial period. Like the prodigal son, it returned to a feast of welcome and celebrations, after independence and home rule. In 1821 it disappeared from the Cook Islands scene for 143 years until 1964. The year 1821 represents the date of meaningful missionary contact to our shores. And the year 1964 represents the date of the new museum's physical establishment.
>
> (1991:201)

Since its inception, the Cook Islands Museum has been dedicated to the representation of the culture of Cook Islanders as well as other Pacific Islanders in an effort to revive, preserve, and promote the cultural heritage of the region.

Since the 1970s, indigenous museums and cultural centers have been at the center of cultural revitalization and heritage preservation movements throughout the Pacific. In many cases, they have been enlisted to aid in the struggle for indigenous rights and to promote self-determination. Self-determination has brought with it a strong desire to re-identify with traditional culture and history. Museums and cultural centers, established either by local communities or with the help of outsiders, have provided a venue for restoring and strengthening indigenous cultures and promoting a renewed sense of cultural identity (see Edwards 1980, Eoe and Swadling 1991, Hanson and Hanson 1990, Kaeppler 1994, Newton 1994). As Dark suggests:

> There seems to be a general concern among Pacific Islanders for the restoration of their heritage. "Restore" means to give back, to make restitution of things taken away. In various ways some things have been returned, whether an object or an illustration of it, skills that had been abandoned have been revived, and knowledge that might slip away has been sought and recorded.
>
> (1990:244)

Today, community-based museums and cultural centers are often the focus of community activities, offering a venue for cultural activism and involvement where public education and social issues are brought to the forefront. As Simpson observes,

> they provide a showcase for cultural representation in a context, which is neither insensitive to the host community nor alien to Europeans. They provide evidence of the community's ability to care for artefacts and therefore strengthen claims for the retention or return of cultural patrimony; and they present artefacts and information using formal interpretative methods and the written word, upon which so much emphasis is placed in western culture. The museum, then, is a useful and powerful tool for politicisation and promotion of culture.
>
> (1996:114)

Indeed, it is their attention to promoting and sustaining living culture that places them in the forefront of contemporary, alternative museum movements. "Pacific cultural centers may be in the forefront of the museum movement – not only forging national or cultural identity but leading the way for cultural rather than object, preservation" (Kaeppler 1994:32).

In the book *Being Ourselves for You: The Global Display of Cultures* (1998), Stanley discusses how the creation of indigenous museums and cultural centers in the Pacific exemplifies a form of "indigenous curation." Indigenous curation reflects how indigenous communities are attempting to integrate aspects of traditional and modern life on their own terms. For Stanley, those involved in indigenous curation are "seeking to embrace tradition in the name of modernity" (1998:87). Indigenous museums

> act as the locus for the reintegration of material objects from the past into contemporary instruction. There have been a number of attempts in widely varying locations in the South Pacific to develop the concept of an indigenous museum . . . Each has its reference to museological procedures and objectives.
>
> (1998:88)

Citing the work of Michael O'Hanlon, Stanley describes the creation of the Onga Cultural Centre in the New Guinea Highlands. The Centre was established in the late 1980s by a local Romonga man who wanted to create a museum in his own community after seeing museums in Port Moresby and elsewhere. The man's main motivation for creating the museum was "so that in [the] future people should know how their forefathers had lived" (O'Hanlon quoted in Stanley 1998:89). The museum comprised a traditional Hagen men's house and a woman's house from the pre-contact period, recreated with "exceptional fidelity and stocked with a truly remarkable array of material culture." The museum was also created with tourism in mind, serving as an arena for cultural performance. Stanley contends that the Onga Cultural Centre is a site where "the past and tradition are integrated into a forward-looking organisation, which accommodates new as well as old" (1998:89).[9]

The Gogodala Cultural Centre at Balimo in the Fly River area of Papua New Guinea can also be seen as an indigenous museum in the sense that it was modeled after a traditional men's house and functions to promote and preserve local cultural heritage. Unlike the Onga Cultural Centre, which was a local initiative, the Gogodala Centre was established in 1973 through the initiative of the National Cultural Council of Papua New Guinea and with the assistance of Australian anthropologist Tony Crawford (Meister 1999:113). It was built entirely of "bush materials" and consists of a *komo* (sleeping place for men) and a *sikil* (sleeping place for women). The *komo* is an open area where artifacts and other objects are displayed. According to B. Mula, manager of the Centre in 1989, the mission of the Centre is "to revive the cultural traditions, arts and customs of the Gogodala people" (1991:72). The Centre is a multifunctional facility where children are taught traditional songs, legends, and dances, and traditional arts are displayed and sold. The Centre also sponsors patrols to

villages and schools to stimulate cultural awareness. Another important function of the Centre is to conduct research on local cultural traditions and to
publish results of this research. Mula states that elders of the community act as
"cultural teachers" who instruct children in the traditional arts of carving, canoe
making, singing and dancing, and weaving. For Mula, cultural revival is at the
core of the Centre's activities:

> To revive cultural activities, we have to teach our young children about the
> culture and traditions of the Gogodala tribe. Our aim is to teach the old
> culture and traditions to our new generation so that these are not
> forgotten. Culture and traditional activities are very important and are a
> key element in our tribe. The Cultural Centre is where local people and
> tourists come to see the culture and traditions of the Gogodala of the
> Western province.
>
> (1991:73)

Similarly, Nero and Graburn, in their observations of the Gogodala Cultural
Centre's activities in the late 1970s, observed how the Centre provided a psychological stimulus for the revival of many traditional ceremonies that had not been
performed for more than a generation. It was also playing a significant role in
the revival of traditional arts (1978:152).

Among the many museological developments in the Pacific has been the revival
and recreation of the concept of the *bai* of Palau, western Micronesia. The *bai*
is a form of a traditional meeting house, which "served both as the major expression of the material arts in most villages and as primary locations for other
artistic activities – dancing, narratives, and the making of crafts – as well as
serving as secular centers for both men and women" (Nero and Graburn
1978:148). Traditional *bai* were erected, maintained, and used by men's associations or "clubs" of a "social-political character," but were also used by women
on certain occasions. The houses were built on raised stone platforms and were
covered with a pitched thatched roof. They were highly decorated, and thus
works of art in themselves. "The most spectacular artistic expressions were the
painted relief carvings on the huge gables on either side of the *bai*, the corners
of the exterior, and along roof beams" (Nero and Graburn 1978:148). *Bai* took
a tremendous amount of labor and materials to erect and lasted many years.

Under colonial domination, beginning with that of the Germans, the men's clubs
were repressed and their functions transferred to other newly introduced institutions. Consequently, old traditional-style *bai* were destroyed or eventually
deteriorated by the elements. Nero and Graburn wrote that by 1978 only one
nineteenth-century *bai* remained that served its traditional purpose as a community meeting house. But during the 1970s, the people of Palau, as part of a
cultural revitalization movement, began recreating *bai* to meet both traditional
and contemporary needs. For instance, in 1976, a new "club *bai*" was built in
Koror, Palau by a Koror young men's club. Nero and Graburn state that initially
the new club *bai* was the most functionally traditional of a group of new
community centers in Koror, serving as a gathering place and a facility for both
modern and traditional chanting and dancing. A few years later, however, it had

also become "one of the most popular nightclubs for modern music and dancing" (1978:149). Another community center in Koror operated as a pan-Palaun cultural center until it was destroyed by a typhoon. This *bai* also contained a museum within a partially enclosed interior (Nero and Graburn 1978:152).

In Australia, museums and cultural centers are also being created that are inspired by ancient traditions but modified to serve contemporary purposes. Simpson writes that traditionally Australian Aboriginal communities "kept sacred and some everyday objects stored away in caches in caves or rock shelters" (1996:108). This practice is of particular note in light of the fact that traditional Australian Aboriginal people often have been characterized as some of the least materialistic people in the world, and thus unconcerned with the care and preservation of their cultural materials. In fact, Cannon-Brookes, in the previously cited text, used Australian Aboriginals as an example of a "concept-centred" society uninterested in the collection and preservation of objects. "Australian aboriginals and Bushmen, are fundamentally opposed to the collecting of objects because of the danger of interfering with the spiritual dimensions of all objects, and thus the concept of the museum collection is totally unacceptable to them" (1984:116). Simpson soundly refutes this claim in her discussion of the concept of the Aboriginal "Keeping Place" in both traditional and contemporary contexts.

Building on their tradition of safeguarding objects in caves and caches, Simpson describes how today Aboriginal communities maintain "Keeping Places" where secret and sacred materials can be securely stored. This practice evolved out of a concern that such caches were vulnerable to discovery and theft by non-Aboriginal people. Similar to the traditional *haus tambaran* and *bai*, Keeping Places are restricted to initiated individuals. According to Simpson, "although the Keeping Places serve to preserve secret/sacred material, their role is to maintain the secrecy of the objects and so restrict access rather than widen it" (1996:108–109). However, Simpson notes that the European model of the publicly accessible museum and cultural center is also being adopted. These places function as educational facilities in which Aboriginal communities can interpret their history and culture to non-Aboriginal communities. They also serve as a facility to display and sell Aboriginal arts. Thus, individual communities have adopted those aspects of museums that best suit their particular purposes and needs, and in so doing, have developed two distinct entities: the Keeping Place, serving a traditional role, and the museum or cultural center addressing contemporary educational and economic needs (1996:119).

Simpson points out that indigenous museums in general are typically devoted to the collection and display of objects from their own communities or indigenous products,[10] in contrast to western museums whose collections may be encyclopedic in nature representing cultural artifacts and natural history specimens from throughout the world. In this regard, it is important to consider how indigenous museum models may differ in purpose from their western counterparts. "The traditional indigenous museum-like model differs most significantly in purpose; most of the objects continue to fulfill their original function, and indeed are frequently still in regular usage" (1996:113). In reference to contemporary Keeping Places, or "museums," Simpson relates how they provide accessible storage and enable

> the context, function and symbolism of artefacts to be communicated to others within the community through oral traditions such as storytelling, song, dialogue, and through events such as dances, ritual and ceremonies, but only within traditional cultural parameters and subject to restrictions of ownership, initiation, and so on.
>
> (1996:113)

And perhaps most importantly, the extension of these activities to cultural centers allows the Aboriginal community to "take control over its own representation" and create cultural awareness among a wider audience, including outsiders.[11]

It is important to point out that the creation of indigenous museums throughout the Pacific, as well as elsewhere, is not without its dilemmas and contestations. Certainly, as Stanley remarks, "indigenous curation does not offer neat or easy solutions in locally sponsored venues" (1998:114). For instance, some museum activities, such as the removal of objects from their living cultural context, has met resistance in some communities. While some communities have found ways around this dilemma, as in the case of Australian Aboriginals and their Keeping Places or museums, others have found this practice problematic and resisted such efforts. In Micronesia during the 1970s, Nero and Graburn found that

> an increasing number of Micronesians are actively supporting museums and the reconstruction of traditional meeting centers in an effort to retain those arts and crafts which still exist . . . However, at times the filling of the museums is another problem, as this entails removing the objects from their social context and meaning, something which Micronesians and other Pacific Islanders resist to this day.
>
> (1978:153)

Similarly, in Tonga, the authors observed that huge *tapa* (bark cloth) sheets were still being made for ceremonial exchange, marriage gifts, markers of rank, etc., alongside the more commercial *tapa* arts. However, "it is the traditional objects of similar significance which are still in use that the present Micronesians will not give up to museums" (Nero and Graburn 1978:156). Nero and Graburn suggested that the placement of such objects in museums was problematic for "the relationship between the objects and the audience is thereby depersonalized even if the objects are better physically preserved. Hence the relationship between the maker and the appreciator/audience is also depersonalized, independent of ongoing social ties" (1978:156).

Joseph describes how the Cook Islands Museum has faced a similar dilemma in its effort to collect and preserve examples of traditional Cook Island material culture:

Each individual tribe has its own [collection of sacred objects] and it is its responsibility to ensure its preservation or conservation. There are "taboos" on these objects and members not belonging to the tribe are afraid that if they trespass they will die. This fear prevails today. And because of it, most of these objects are shut away from general view. Nevertheless, we are able to preserve and conserve some of the portable artefacts we are able to get hold of. But there are many more with individual families, who are reluctant to part with them.

(1980:142)

Certainly, as communities throughout the Pacific continue to explore ways to protect and preserve their cultural heritage they must find means of doing so within culturally accepted parameters. And like small, community-based museums nearly everywhere, Pacific island museums and cultural centers must struggle to find ways to become sustainable in the long run, overcoming shortages in funding, staff, and other resources. As a case in point, Meister wrote in 1999 that the previously discussed Gogodala Cultural Centre "has nearly collapsed" due to a lack of funding and outside support (1999:101). Clearly, any museum or cultural center anywhere cannot fulfill its mission if it can not remain in operation.

The integration of indigenous curation into mainstream museums

Indigenous communities throughout the Pacific also have been working with mainstream museums to bring about changes in practices and policies surrounding the care and treatment of their material culture in these museums. For example, Awhina Tamarapa, Collections Manager of Maori Collections at the Museum of New Zealand Te Papa Tongarewa in Wellington, describes developments that have been taking place in the museum since its restructuring in 1991. Tamarapa describes these developments as steps toward the institutionalization of the concept of biculturalism in the museum.[12]

In relation to Te Papa Tongarewa, advocating the concept of biculturalism is the most important institutional change ever made in the history of this museum. There are a number of ways this has manifested itself through management and policy, exhibitions, collection management, public programs, curatorial research and protocols.

(1996:164)

Arapata Hakiwai, a Maori curator at the museum, claims that the Bicultural Policy affirms "the right of Maori to manage their *taonga* [cultural treasures] in the most appropriate ways" (1999:10).

According to Tamarapa, a critical element in the institutionalization of biculturalism has been training Maori people in the museum profession and recruiting them for employment in museums. "For us as Maori, increasing the number of trainees in this profession was a tremendous leap. Only a lonely

69

handful of Maori were previously working in museums . . . but now there are more than fifty" (1996:161). With the restructuring of the Te Papa Tongarewa, the museum increased its Maori staff by adding a Maori protocols officer and hiring a Kaihauti (Maori leader) in a position equivalent to that of the CEO of the museum. The Kaihuati is responsible for the overall management of Maori *taonga* held in the museum and is directly responsible to *iwi* (tribes) (Hakiwai 1999:11). Through the efforts of the Maori curators and *kaitiaki* (guardians) and the protocols officer, non-Maori staff members were educated in "appropriate Maori protocol in relation to their work and the Maori collection" (Tamarapa 1996:165).

Tamarapa relates that one of the first changes to take place in the museum was the institution of a policy that restricted food from being carried through or placed near *taonga*, either on display or in storage. This policy was instituted because the *mauri*, or life-force of particularly sacred items, is made *noa*, or neutralized, by the presence of cooked food (1996:165). Additionally,

> water bowls placed at exit ways from *taonga* in storage permit people to sprinkle themselves with water, spiritually cleansing themselves of the *tapu*, or sacred forces, of the *taonga*. This enables a person to walk freely in the world of light – this world – without any unforeseen forces upon him or her. *Karakia*, or prayers, are usually spoken when a new *taonga* comes into the museum or is moved to or from display, or to and from the museum.
>
> (1996:165)

Tamarapa explains that "our goals are collections-based, and that the primary responsibility we have as museum workers is the physical and spiritual well-being of the collection for education and benefit of future generations" (1996:165).

Rose Evans, Object Conservator at the museum, writes that "all conservation treatment of Maori *taonga* is carried out under the premise of *tikanga* [protocol], which is very much rooted in a commonsense and respectful approach. With a few exceptions this parallels good conservation practice" (1999:15). During treatment, restrictions are placed on the consumption of food and drink, standing or walking over carvings, use of saliva for treatments, and blowing on carvings. Women must not work on carvings during menstruation.

> Reasons for all these are based in the maintenance of a spiritual and physical worldview. The same considerations also impact upon the support and location of *taonga* in storage, movement and handling. If deemed necessary, prayers are said to remove a *tapu* (bringing the artifact into the realm of the ordinary) from the carvings prior to treatment and replace it afterwards.
>
> (1999:15)

Conservators at the museum are now obliged to consult with *iwi*, or tribes, on the proper care and treatment of objects (see Clavir 2002:217–244).

A new classification system for storage was also implemented. Collections are now classified not only by typology, but also by tribal (*iwi*) affiliation. Furthermore, "objects related to food and everyday function (*noa*) objects, are stored apart from sacred (*tapu*) or ceremonial objects" (Tamarapa 1996:166). The most sacred objects in the collection are kept in a special *wahi tapu* (sacred place usually referring to a burial ground) (Tamarapa 1996:166). The public is allowed access to the storage area through organized tours. Prior to the tours, however, groups are briefed on Maori protocol and advised that no cameras or videos are allowed because of tribal copyright restrictions.

Sharing power in decision making is critical to the institutionalization of biculturalism in the museum. This means that the two mainstream cultures of Aotearoa New Zealand, i.e. Maori and Pakeha (people of European descent), engage in genuine partnership. In Tamarapa's words: "*Iwi* liaison is the most fundamental aspect of one's responsibility as a *kaitiaki* [guardian or custodian] Maori. If this museum is to make credible commitment as a bicultural institution, then tribal consultation must certainly be the foundation for cultural partnership" (1996:167). As part of this effort, the museum established a Maori consultants group to advise on policy decisions and provide *iwi* liaison.

> *Iwi* liaison is our key to the future. It is hoped with expertise, knowledge and care and with the guidance of our *iwi*, the *taonga* of our collections will be able to be seen by those interested, in the manner appropriate to their origin and history.
>
> (Tamarapa 1996:168)

In the preparation of new exhibits in the museum, staff members consulted with *iwi* on how they would like to see their *taonga* represented and interpreted in the museum. For the Maori curators, the goal was not only to give Maori people the opportunity to tell their own stories, their own histories, but also to reconnect the *taonga* with their people, "make them live," and acknowledge their *mauri* or "living life force" (Hakiwai 1999:11). "Our mission was literally to break down the walls of the museum, reconnecting the umbilical cord between *taonga* and people, building two-way highways so that life could be given back to *taonga* that had been sleeping for years" (Hakiwai 199:12).

For the Maori, like for many indigenous people, their cultural treasures are not mere objects, but living entities with names, personalities, lineages, and spirits. They are living things and are treated like people (Clavir 2002:223). They are mediators between the past and present and links between the living and dead (Hooper-Greenhill 2000:52–53). Thus, they are bound up in personalized relationships whereby the Maori take care of their *taonga* and the *taonga* take care of them. "The histories of the *taonga* stay alive when they take part in gatherings and ceremonies and are talked over, touched, and wept over" (Hooper-Greenhill 2000:52). The primary value of *taonga* then derives from its history and association with particular ancestors, which embody spiritual links that bind Maori identity. It is this spiritual dimension of objects that is of the utmost concern to the Maori (Kaeppler 1994:28).

71

Figure 3.2 Maori *Pataka* (storehouse) displayed in the Margaret Mead Hall of the American Museum of Natural History, New York. According to the object's label, the *pataka* was used by a chief and contained valuable greenstone ornaments, weapons, special tools, and feathers worn as a symbol of rank. The *pataka* has its own name and history related to the carved ancestral figure at the gable peak. The owner's personal *mana*, or power, is invested in the *pataka* and ensures its security.

Photograph by Dave Berliner. Courtesy of Department of Library Services American Museum of Natural History Library, 2002. Neg. No. 63925.

The Te Papa Museum has also institutionalized tribal involvement and a team-based approach to major conservation treatments. For example, when the museum decided to deinstall and relocate a Maori storehouse or *Pataka* Te Takinga, which had been constructed by the Ngati Pikiao (a North Island tribe) in 1820, it employed Ngati Pikiao representatives to work on the project. Evans states that "the relationship between the Ngati Pikiao and Te Takinga was basic to this project. In acknowledging this relationship we needed to plan and manage a process to ensure credible *iwi* involvement" (1999:14).

A *pataka* is an ornately carved, elevated storehouse on carved piles. It is a symbol of wealth and status among the Maori, and traditionally was used as a place to store implements, precious garments, and preserved foods.[13] The Ngati Pikiao considered the Te Takinga *Pataka* to be a physical embodiment of a major ancestor from whom the tribe's descendants trace their ancestors. The museum acquired the *Pataka* in 1906. Because early attempts to reconstruct the *Pataka* in the museum were considered inappropriate, the museum elected to deinstall, restore, and move the *Pataka* to a new building. Through collaboration with Ngati Pikiao tribal members, the *Pataka* was restored and relocated in keeping with both professional conservation and tribal protocols. The goal was to preserve not only the *Pataka's* physical integrity but also its cultural integrity. According to Evans, the project represented a positive museum initiative by providing museum staff with the opportunity to engage in direct dialogue with tribal representatives and thus learn more about the cultural significance of the *Pataka*, while giving Ngati Pikiano tribal members educational and employment opportunities (1999:14). As Evans remarks:

> The Te Takinga project represented the first major conservation treatment at Te Papa incorporating *iwi* involvement to such an extent. Through this project, a new process was developed that enabled both *iwi* and museum concerns to be addressed, and which respected both cultural and physical aspects of the storehouse's ongoing well being.
>
> (1999:15)

The museum also has begun repatriating Maori cultural property, which, according to Tamarapa, was "unheard of" prior to the museum's restructuring. In Tamarapa's opinion, repatriation can work to the advantage of both the museum and the Maori people, and help forge mutually beneficial relationships in the long run. For example, when the Rongowhakaata people negotiated to have six painted church panels repatriated they requested that the museum, in exchange, act as the custodian of their carved meeting house.

> Contrary to the fear of many museum professionals, *iwi* [tribes] are not looking to pull out all their *taonga* from their institutions. Many Maori are aware of the benefits that museums have as places of professional care and responsibility. *Iwi* are currently discussing their ownership of *taonga* – land, fisheries, material culture and language, and the future. Perhaps one day we will have our own tribal museums, with professional Maori staff to organize them. I would certainly see this as an exciting prospect, but right now, we are at the cutting edge of breaking down the barriers between museums and Maori people for the benefit of future generations.
>
> (Tamarapa 1996:167)

Indigenous models of museums and curation in Africa

Similar to cultures in the Pacific, African peoples historically have created special places such as altars, shrines, and temples to honor their ancestors, carry out rituals and ceremonies, and to display and store valued objects. These too have been likened to museums in their basic functions and purposes, and have served as a means of protecting and passing on cultural heritage.

Okita, in an article titled "Museums as Agents for Cultural Transmission" (1982), points out that although museums are one of the new and probably most explicit forms of transmitting cultural heritage in contemporary Nigerian societies, a number of agents existed in traditional communities for cultural transmission previous to the introduction of the modern museum.

> The different ethnic groups or communities that came to be known as Nigeria had various ways of transmitting the cumulative creation of man known as culture or cultural heritage from one generation to another . . . Before the coming of Islam, Christianity and Western education, cultural heritage was transmitted through folklore, music and dance, festivals and shrines, and elders in their different roles.
>
> (1983:4)

Of particular interest here are shrines, which Okita states, "are a traditional agent that transmit cultural heritage" (1982:8), which have performed functions similar to museums (1982:16).

According to Okita, religion is the *raison d'être* of communal or family shrines. As the focus of religious beliefs and practices, they have been used for the performance of rituals, ceremonies, and festivals (particularly related to ancestor worship), and to house ritual objects related to these practices. However, Okita emphasizes that the importance of shrines extends beyond religion, and is ultimately linked to nearly all aspects of life:

> The importance of shrines as a vehicle, transmitting a people's cultural heritage, does not only emanate from the fact that shrines are the embodiment of socio-religious ideas that give meaning and sustain life in a traditional society. The objects kept in the shrines, the worship or festival that takes place there are all symbolic acts that sometimes deal with the tradition of origin of a people, the rather inexplicable natural forces or phenomena that must be personified or certain norms or laws considered necessary for the sustenance of society all of which are invariably connected with the life cycle.
>
> (1982:9)

And furthermore, "the ideas behind or the significance of festivals, shrines and the objects connected with them, are what every traditional society wants to pass on from one generation to another" (1982:10).

Okita writes, "shrines are so widely spread that it is almost impossible to think of a traditional community or society without one" (1982:7). Among the Igede, for example, each clan has a god known as Eke-Eji with a shrine that represents and symbolizes his presence, typically located at the village center. Shrines had their own "curators" charged with their care and protection." The custodianship of the shrine is the responsibility of the village or clan elder known as

Ogabwo, and it is he who is also in charge of all communal worship at the shrine" (1983:7).

Okita contends that the acceptance of Islam, Christianity, and western education (resulting from British colonial control) has led to a decline but not a complete abandonment of the traditional ways of transmitting and communicating cultural heritage. The perpetuation of these traditions stands as a testimony to their importance in people's lives as well as a concern for cultural heritage preservation, a concern that has often been denied for African people.

In a fascinating article titled "Traditional Preservation Methods: Some African Practices Observed," Nicklin writes, "it is frequently assumed or asserted that Africans living in rural communities are not usually concerned with controlling or preventing the physical deterioration of their cultural property" (1983:123). Nicklin asserts that this assumption is not only false, but has also been used by collectors and curators to collect African materials. "The supposed nonmaterialistic attitude of Africans to their art is seen to justify its removal from them, for accumulation in private collections and museums in Europe and North America" (1983:123).

Nicklin states that there are certain categories of art, which once used are discarded or freely exposed to the elements. But this is by no means always the case. For instance,

> in the Cross River region of southeast Nigeria and West Cameroon there are many examples of successful attempts made by villagers to preserve their artefacts. There is no reason to assume that the Cross River area is unique in this respect. Whether or not efforts are made to preserve such objects is largely determined by their significance to the owners.
>
> (1983:123)

Nicklin provides several examples of traditional preservation methods found in the Cross River region of eastern Nigeria and West Cameroon.

Among the Oron of eastern Nigeria, carved wooden figures known as *Ekpu* are housed in the *obio*, a building with an open front and a roof supported by large posts. The *obio* and its contents form a shrine to the ancestors, who are believed to participate in the affairs of the living and can be approached through the *Ekpu* shrine to bring fertility to women and farms, and to banish epidemics. Ritual sacrifices are made at the shrine at the time of planting and harvesting to solicit the help and goodwill of the ancestors. The word "*Ekpu*" literally means "dead ancestors." Nicklin states that even after the *Ekpu* cult began to decline in the late nineteenth and early twentieth centuries with the advance of Christian missionization, the *Ekpu* figures continued to be venerated, and "Oron people were reluctant to allow them to be removed by outsiders" (1983:124).

According to Nicklin, many of the carvings that were in existence up until the outbreak of the Nigerian civil war of 1967–1970 were thought to have been at least two hundred years old. This made them some of the oldest wooden sculptures extant in sub-Saharan Africa (1983:123). The collection of figures in the

Oron Museum numbered 661 in 1966.[14] Nicklin claims that the figures have survived for so long "because of the durability of the wood, which is relatively resistant to termite attack, and the care taken in their preservation" (1983:124).

An example of this care is seen in the way in which the figures were positioned within the *obio*. "The sculpture stood upright with their bases on or in the ground, but if the bases decayed they were leant against the wall or supported from behind by a cross bar" (1983:124). Thus, the *obio* itself provided shelter and ventilation for the figures. "Except for the obvious problem of the base of the carving being set in the ground, it would be difficult to imagine a more effective method of storage for such objects at a simple level of technology" (1983:124).

Ekpu figures endured not only due to these basic conservation measures, but also because of the effectiveness of the "institutional arrangements" adopted by the people to protect their ancestor figures. *Ekpu* figures were under the care of the most senior branch of the lineage segment, and if this branch died out the nearest surviving one took over the care of the founding ancestor figure. Nsugbe, cited in Nicklin, also suggests that *Ekpu* survived because they "served as an aid to social memory."

> It can be assumed that the passion which still exists over *Ekpu* figures is largely explained by the fact that they indeed served to conserve and protect in wood collective lineage rights and claims, lineage history, and lineage identity and welfare.
>
> (1983:124)

In this respect, *Ekpu* have also functioned as "agents of cultural transmission."

Nicklin also describes techniques used to preserve skin-covered masks, commonly found in the Cross River region. Such masks were made of lightweight woods and were covered with animal, or in the past, human skin. Although the choice of the wood is practical since lighter-weight woods are easier to carve and the resulting mask is light to wear and carry, soft woods were particularly prone to fungal and bacterial attack in the hot humid climate of the region. These woods were also susceptible to insect and pest infestation. The skins covering the mask were easily damaged by humidity as well as by rats and mice attracted to the skin. Despite the problems posed by these environmental hazards and choice of raw materials, Nicklin observed that the masks were carefully preserved and survived for considerable periods of time. Their survival was due to the "highly effective methods of skin-covered mask preservation" (1983:125).

Preservation methods included the use of various traditional preparations of oil, which were rubbed into the masks to preserve the skin. Nowadays, commercially produced petroleum jelly is sometimes used to preserve the skin on the masks. Nicklin explains that after the oil is applied, the mask is then placed in the sun so the oil can be absorbed into the skin. Afterwards, it is wrapped in a material, such as a particular kind of bark cloth, which is resistant to termite attack. The wrapped mask is then suspended from house rafters, generally near the cooking area or kitchen, which Nicklin says is a particularly suitable space for storage since it is constantly filled with smoke and has a relatively uniform warm and dry atmosphere.

> Here the mask is safe as it can be in a tropical village environment from the attacks of insects and fungi, and bacterial decay. The effect of the oil and percolation of smoke probably cause a certain degree of tannage to the skin. Over a period of time a patina builds up, shiny in texture and rich in colour, which is appreciated not only by the foreign connoisseur but also by the original owners.
>
> (1983:127)

In addition to these technical means of preserving masks, Nicklin notes that certain members of the mask association were responsible for their care and protection, who, in essence, acted as the curators of the masks.

> It was a widespread practice for each mask association to appoint one of its members as a custodian for its ceremonial paraphernalia. He was often the leader of the association, another respected elder or chief, or a carver. He was liable to be held responsible for damage or loss.
>
> (1983:126)

Other authors have noted measures taken to protect not only individual objects but also entire ritual complexes. For example, among the Bobo Fing of the Upper Volta, subterranean houses or temples were created for the family cult, which were thought to represent the founding ancestor of the family (Denyer 1978:68). The practice of constructing temples or shrines underground had a protective effect for "apart from the more obvious advantage of concealment, they were more secure against fire" (Denyer 1978:67).

Konare describes similar "conservation structures" in Mali. He writes that in some family compounds, there are specific rooms set aside for storing family relics. Certain family or community members are prohibited from entering the rooms. Particular areas in the family compound may also be protected because they house the tombs of ancestors or the guardian fetish of the family. In some villages, sites used for initiation ceremonies and sacrifices are protected as well as the objects contained in this area. In some cases, entire villages are regarded sacred and thus preserved (1983:146–147).

According to Konare, "certain guilds, traditional associations of young people and women and initiation societies are responsible for the conservation of these sites and objects" (1983:147). While some of these sites and the objects within them may be open to all, at others, "often only a select audience enjoys this privilege, access being granted only to initiates and members of associations, each bound by strict rules governing his role and position" (1983:147).

Granaries can also be seen as conservation structures in terms of being places where valuable goods are stored and where certain restrictions to access are applied. Barley writes that among the Dowayo of Cameroon "a woman's granary . . . is an intensely personal object. It is where precious and secret things are kept, identity papers, medicines, money. To look in another's granary without asking permission is a grave offence" (1994:116). Granaries are also a medium for artistic expression, which in turn, becomes an expression of individual identity. "Each woman has a mud granary that is built by a man but that she decorates entirely according to her own tastes . . . The granary is the core of individual identity. It is the only large and valuable thing that is individually owned" (Barley 1994:116). Here one can see parallels among the Dowayo granaries, Indonesian rice barns, and the Maori *pataka* or storehouses. They are all indigenous conservation structures, which symbolize each culture's sense of aesthetics, ways of constructing identity, and values regarding the ownership of property.

The above examples demonstrate that while the museum may be a new and more explicit form of cultural transmission and preservation in Africa, indigenous Africans have a long tradition of preserving their cultural heritage, in both tangible and intangible forms, through various means. The many other examples of indigenous models of museums and curation presented in this chapter show that museological behavior and a concern for cultural heritage preservation is by no means limited to western cultures.

4

Reclaiming the spirit of culture: Native Americans and cultural restitution

The numerous examples of indigenous models of museums, methods of cura-tion, and concepts of cultural heritage preservation presented in the previous chapter clearly demonstrate that non-western people have long been concerned with the care and preservation of highly valued objects. They also show that such objects have been crucial for the transmission of culture from one genera-tion to the next. Greater recognition of these phenomena and the rights of indigenous peoples to their cultural property is leading to a reassessment of the basic philosophies and motivations behind the collection and preservation of indigenous people's cultural property in museums.

The motivations for collecting other people's material culture and preserving it in museums have been varied, including the belief that it needed to be "rescued" from an inevitable extinction (Watson 1997:24). But perhaps one of the most persistent rationales, at least for anthropology, is that such material holds scien-tific value, and is necessary for the advancement of knowledge of non-western cultures and humankind in general (see Clavir 2002, Pearce 1991). And although much can be said regarding the politics of cultural representation in museums,[1] it remains true that anthropologists and museologists have been motivated by the conviction that the presentation of people's material culture in museums contributes to cross-cultural awareness and understanding (see Haas 1996). Notwithstanding this idealism and its humanistic motivations, museums, in the post-colonial era, are now challenged with re-evaluating their justifica-tions for collecting and retaining indigenous people's cultural property (see Messenger 1989, Simpson 1996). The collection of indigenous objects for the sake of preservation, exhibition, and education for the public's benefit is no longer considered sacrosanct, and the cultural prerogative of museums. "It is not a revelation that many objects – often those considered most significant – should never have been removed from their original contexts, 'collected,' as they were, to be held in museums" (Harth 1999:279).

In the United States, changes in museum sensibilities have come about very much as a result of the passage of the Native American Graves Protection and Repatri-ation Act (NAGPRA) in 1990 by the United States Congress. The Act, in addi-tion to creating measures to protect Native American burial sites, required all museums receiving federal funds to make inventories of Native American, Eskimo, Aleut, and Hawaiian human remains and associated funerary objects. These inventories were to be completed by November 1995. Museums were also to prepare written summaries of unassociated funerary objects, sacred objects, and objects of cultural patrimony by November 1993. This process was to be carried out in consultation with federal agencies and Native American tribes or Hawaiian organizations. Museums were also required to make the inventories and summaries available to Native American tribes or Hawaiian organizations, and provide access to any pertinent information for determining tribal affiliation to NAGPRA covered materials. Once cultural affiliation and appropriate ownership rights are proven, tribes may request the repatriation of human remains and artifacts (covered by the definitions of the Act) to lineal descendants or affiliated tribes (Simpson 1996:205).

As a result of NAGPRA, museums have been made increasingly aware of the value of their holdings to their cultures of origin. NAGPRA has also led to greater appreciation of the necessity of certain objects for the perpetuation of cultural traditions, and the importance of a community's cultural heritage to its sense of identity, self-respect, empowerment, and overall well-being. Viewed from the perspective of human dignity, requests for the return of cultural property are increasingly being seen as part of larger moral, ethical, and legal discussions on the cultural and human rights of indigenous peoples (Berman 1997, Bray 2001, Harth 1999, Mihesuah 2000, Tsosie 1997). As museums continue to negotiate their changing relationships with indigenous peoples they are being increasingly drawn into the human rights arena.

Galla, in "Indigenous Peoples, Museums and Ethics" (1997) draws attention to the need for museologists to become aware of the significance of indigenous people's issues to museums as well as the significance of museum collections to indigenous peoples. Galla states that the immediate challenge for museums is to explore the historical background of the relationship between museums and indigenous peoples, a relationship that has been tainted by colonial structures of power and dominance. "The evolution of museums in the past two centuries has inevitably been intertwined with colonial factors, often disenfranchising and reducing indigenous people as prisoners of collections and archives" (Galla 1997:143). Museums must come to terms with their pasts and their special relationship to indigenous communities as these communities continue to fight for greater self-determination and control over their own culture.

> The focus of museums, which has been largely collection-centred, will come under greater scrutiny from indigenous peoples who have been striving for wider objectives of community-based cultural conservation and self-determination within the context of social justice strategies. The argument is that there is a direct and primary link between cultural control, heritage, health, and social well-being.
>
> (Galla 1997:142–143)

Galla acknowledges that in several parts of the world, museums and indigenous peoples are beginning to negotiate more constructive partnerships and work toward redressing the imbalances in current practices of cultural heritage management. Introspection on the part of museum professionals and collaborations with indigenous communities are leading to a reassessment of museum practices within the larger framework of indigenous people's human and cultural rights.

Various national and international museum bodies, such as the International Council of Museums (ICOM), have established codes of professional ethics intended to guide and guarantee ethical behavior in all areas of museum activity. While these codes of ethics have gone far in promoting ethical principles and actions in museum matters, Galla suggests that other international protocols, such as the United Nations Draft Declaration on the Rights of Indigenous Peoples, have important implications for museological practice and associated codes of conduct (1997:143).

The Draft Declaration on the Rights of Indigenous Peoples is "law in the making" (Quesenberry 1999:106). In its final form, it will be part of a set of international legal instruments dealing with human rights, such as the United Nations Declaration of Human Rights. The Draft reflects both existing and evolving standards of international human rights law related to indigenous peoples. As in the case of other United Nations conventions, it will provide the legal basis and political momentum for the eventual adoption of a United Nations convention on indigenous people (Quesenberry 1999:106). The Draft was drawn up by the Working Group on Indigenous Populations (WGIP), which is a United Nations human rights body created by the Sub-Commission on the Prevention of Discrimination and the Protection of Minorities of the Economic and Social Council of the United Nations. The WGIP has been the main forum for participation at the international level by indigenous peoples, and is one of the largest United Nations forums in the field of human rights. The Draft Declaration, prepared by the WGIP, was adopted by the Sub-Commission in 1994, and forwarded to the United Nations Commission on Human Rights for ratification (Quesenberry 1999:107). To date, the Declaration has not been ratified by any State and is still under debate.[2] Despite its unsettled legal status, the Draft Declaration has drawn greater attention to and generated increased international dialogue on indigenous peoples' issues.

Galla provides extracts from the Draft Declaration in his article and makes note of specific parts and articles of relevance to museums. He states that his purpose for doing so is "to challenge museologists to reflect on ways in which their practice could be modified within the framework of international protocol and obligations and their own ethical and professional conduct" (1997:144). At the time of this writing, the Draft Declaration contains nine parts and forty-five articles. Part III and Articles 12, 13, and 14 are of particular relevance since they relate to the cultural, religious, spiritual, and linguistic identity of indigenous peoples, and according to Galla, have direct significance to museums and other agencies managing cultural heritage.

> Article 12: Indigenous peoples have the right to practice and revitalize their cultural traditions and customs. This includes the right to maintain,

protect, and develop the past, present and future manifestations of their cultures, such as archaeological and historical sites, artifacts, designs, ceremonies, technologies, and visual and performing arts and literature, as well as the right to the restitution of cultural, intellectual, religious, and spiritual property taken without their free and informed consent or in violation to their laws, traditions, and customs.

Article 13: Indigenous peoples have the right to manifest, practice, develop and teach their spiritual and religious traditions, customs, and ceremonies; the right to maintain, protect, and have access in privacy to their religious and cultural sites; the right to the use and control of ceremonial objects; and the right to the repatriation of human remains. States shall take effective measures, in conjunction with the indigenous people concerned, to ensure that indigenous sacred places, including burial sites, be preserved, respected and protected.

Article 14: Indigenous peoples have the right to revitalize, use, develop, and transmit to future generations their histories, languages, oral traditions, philosophies, writing systems, and literature, and to designate and retain their own names for communities, places and persons. States shall take effective measures, whenever any right of indigenous peoples may be threatened, to ensure this right is protected and also to ensure that they can understand and be understood in political, legal, and administrative proceedings, where necessary through the provision of interpretation or by appropriate means.

(Draft Declaration on the Rights of Indigenous Peoples
quoted in Galla 1997:144–146)

Although the Draft Declaration on the Rights of Indigenous Peoples is still under revision and not yet "law," it serves as an additional guideline and code of ethics for the professional museum community vis-à-vis their relationships to indigenous peoples. In its current form, it is the "spirit" of the Declaration that holds the most power since it draws attention to the need to honor and respect indigenous peoples' rights and for States and other bodies to take measures to protect these rights. As Galla suggests, it provides another framework for ethical and professional conduct.

Such guidelines are necessary, Galla contends, because cultural heritage institutions like museums have been at the tail-end of social justice agendas. But the time has come for these institutions to stand at the forefront of such agendas.

Institutions managing cultural heritage have to become important focal points for the critical discourse of the borders and subaltern histories in emerging post-colonial societies. They should put into practice the rhetoric of community centeredness and liberate themselves from the colonial bondage to the romanticism of decontextualized objects. The focus should be on cross-cultural heritage consciousness and the crossing of cultural borderlands in the center of power and authority in the cultural industry.

(Galla 1997:154–155)

This chapter discusses developments that have been taking place in the United States since the passage of NAGPRA as an example of the changing nature of relationships between museums and indigenous peoples, and how this reflects greater respect for indigenous people's human and cultural rights. NAGPRA is seen as human rights legislation since it embodies the basic principles and concerns expressed in human rights instruments such as the United Nations Draft Declaration on the Rights of Indigenous Peoples. NAGPRA, as a federal law, is an example of how a State, in this case the United States of America, has taken measures to help ensure that indigenous peoples' (i.e. Native Americans, Hawaiians, and Alaskan Natives) rights are protected, at least as they pertain to certain categories of cultural property and human remains as well as some religious beliefs and practices. While legislation such as NAGPRA may be seen as a progressive move on the part of the United States government and museums, it is also important to acknowledge that NAGPRA came about largely as a result of the perception that the American professional museum community had not gone far enough in recognizing and respecting the rights of Native peoples. "The principal justification for the law was the conviction that, unless forced to do so, museums would not be responsive to American Indian requests for the return of . . . objects to them" (Merrill *et al.* 1993:524). In this respect, NAGPRA highlights how a professional body's code of ethics and standards of behavior are not always adequate in addressing certain issues. "The law is sometimes the last resort for those confronted by unethical acts" (Edson 1997:27).

NAGPRA is fundamentally concerned with the issue of cultural restitution as legislation designed to redress wrongs of the past. The term "restitution" means: "1) the act of restoring to the rightful owner something that has been taken away, lost, or surrendered. 2) The act of making good or compensating for loss, damage, or injury; indemnification or reparation. 3) A return to or restoration of a previous state or position" (The American Heritage Dictionary of the English Language, 1981). As it relates to the repatriation of cultural property, the term "restitution" captures much of the sentiment behind the changing relationships between museums and Native Americans in the United States.

The chapter describes changes in mainstream museum policies and practices as a result of NAGPRA, and how these changes exemplify efforts to go beyond the "letter of the law" and enact the "spirit of the law." Spirit of the law means honoring the traditions, values, and beliefs of Native Americans regarding their cultural property and adjusting museum practices to accommodate them. Signs of change include the growing presence of Native American representatives, religious leaders, curators, and scholars in museums, and the co-curation of collections. One of the many outcomes of these collaborations has been an increase in our knowledge of indigenous curatorial methods, or what is commonly referred to as "traditional care." The chapter also covers developments taking place within the Native American museum community such as the creation of the National Museum of the American Indian as well as tribal museums and cultural centers. These developments demonstrate how Native people are taking greater control over the management and preservation of their own cultural heritage.

The Native American Graves Protection and Repatriation Act

The Native American Graves Protection and Repatriation Act provides nation-wide standards and procedures for the repatriation of Native American human remains and certain protected objects from museums and institutions receiving federal funds, including federal agencies such as national and state parks, monuments, and historical societies. The United States Department of the Interior and National Park Service are charged with overseeing the implementation of NAGPRA and compliance with its mandated procedures.

Under NAGPRA, museums were required to create an inventory of their Native American collections, in consultation with tribal representatives and federal agencies, and determine the "cultural affiliation" of human remains, "associated and unassociated funerary objects," "sacred objects," and "objects of cultural patrimony." Because of the difficulty in defining exactly what constitutes a "sacred object" or "cultural patrimony" (see Simpson 1996, Haas 2001), NAGPRA provided specific definitions of these and other categories of objects to guide museum workers in making their inventories. These definitions are reproduced here for the reader because the "language of the law" very much captures the spirit of the law, in the way it acknowledges the religious significance of these objects to Native Americans and their ongoing cultural importance. These definitions are also significant because, as a result of NAGPRA, terms such as "sacred" or "ceremonial object" have become common in American museological discourse, taking on more power and meaning, at least for those working with indigenous collections.

According to Section 2 of NAGPRA titled "Definitions," "associated funerary objects" are

> objects [that], as part of the death rite or ceremony of a culture, are reasonably believed to have been placed with individual human remains either at the time of death or later, and both the remains and associated funerary objects are presently in the possession or control of a federal agency or museum, except that other items exclusively made for burial purposes or to contain human remains shall be considered as associated funerary objects.

"Unassociated funerary objects" refers to objects that

> as a part of the death rite or ceremony of a culture, are reasonably believed to have been placed with individual human remains either at the time of death or later, where the remains are not in the possession or control of the federal agency or museum.

Sacred objects are defined as "specific ceremonial objects which are needed by traditional Native American religious leaders for the practice of traditional Native American religions by their present-day adherents."

Cultural patrimony refers to

> an object having ongoing historical, traditional, or cultural importance
> central to the Native American group or culture itself, rather than prop-
> erty owned by an individual Native American, and which, therefore,
> cannot be alienated, appropriated, or conveyed by any individual regard-
> less of whether or not the individual is a member of the Indian tribe or
> Native Hawaiian organization and such objects shall have been considered
> inalienable by such Native American group at the time the object was sepa-
> rated from such group.
>
> (Native American Graves Protection and Repatration
> Act reproduced in Bray 2001:233–234)

The passage of NAGPRA was the culmination of decades of struggle for Native
American tribal governments and people to protect graves against desecration,
to repatriate thousands of human remains, and to return stolen or improperly
acquired religious and cultural property to Native Americans. NAGPRA is part
of a series of laws passed since the 1960s designed to address the United States
government's and other institutions' long history of suppressing Native American religious practices.[3] For example, in the early 1800s, Congress authorized
and appropriated monies for the "Civilization Fund," which provided Christian
denominations with federal funds and franchises on particular Native groups for
converting Indians to Christianity and European ways. This practice continued
on into the twentieth century. It was also common military practice to stop
Native peoples from carrying out religious ceremonies throughout the 1800s.
In 1904, the Secretary of the Interior published *Regulations of the Indian Office*,
which banned all traditional religious activities, ceremonies, and dancing,
mandating the Christian only/English only education of Indian children (Harjo
1996:5).

According to Trope and Echo-Hawk, individuals who were both involved in
deliberations leading up to the passage of the law, NAGPRA is landmark legislation because it represents fundamental changes in basic social attitudes toward
Native peoples by the museum and scientific communities as well as the public
at large. "NAGPRA is, first and foremost, human rights legislation. It is designed
to redress the flagrant violation of the 'civil rights of America's first citizens'"
(2000:22). Congress viewed NAGPRA as part of its trust responsibility to Indian
tribes and people, and stated that it "reflects the unique relationship between the
Federal Government and Indian tribes and Native Hawaiian organizations"
(Trope and Echo-Hawk 2000:23). The Act constituted a compromise forged by
representatives of the museum, scientific, and Indian communities. It was
designed to create a process that would reflect both the needs of museums as
repositories of the nation's cultural heritage and the rights of Indian people.
"Most importantly, NAGPRA was intended to 'establish a process that provides
the dignity and respect that our Nation's first citizens deserve'" (Trope and
Echo-Hawk 2000:23). Congress also hoped that NAGPRA would encourage a
continuing dialogue between these groups and promote greater understanding
among them.

Trope and Echo-Hawk assert that one pattern that has defined Indian and non-Indian relations in the United States is the one-way transfer of Indian property to non-Indian ownership. This property has included both land and material culture.

> By the 1870s, after most tribes were placed on small reservations, the Government's acquisition of Indian lands had in large part been accomplished. Thereafter, the pattern shifted from real estate to personality and continued until most of the material culture of Native people had been transferred to White hands.
>
> (2000:13)

Although some of that property transfer was through legitimate trade and intercourse, a significant amount of Native cultural property was acquired through illegitimate means. NAGPRA establishes a national standard and procedure for the return of this property.

NAGPRA has not only provided a legal framework through which Native people can request the return of their cultural property, it has also brought Native American and museum and scientific communities into greater dialogue and interaction. Because of NAGPRA, museums have had to "engage with and respond to concerns, values and desires of Native American constituencies" (King 1998:110). Such interactions have led to changing views on Native American material culture and its treatment. As Cash Cash, a Native American scholar with an extensive background in repatriation, points out:

> In recent years, Native communities and museums have reached an unprecedented level of interaction. The nature and import of this interaction is beginning to transform the way anthropologists and museum professionals view and treat Native American material culture, particularly as it relates to the enduring cultural status of the objects in their care. Clearly, the present situation is quite different from what it was around the turn of the century when the intellectual interests of anthropological sciences and museums merged in a concerted effort to "salvage" remnant Native cultures.
>
> (2001:139)

In this passage Cash Cash is referring to "salvage ethnography," which was the dominant paradigm of American anthropology during the late nineteenth and early twentieth centuries among anthropologists studying Native American cultures (see Hinsley 1981). During this period, Native American cultures were experiencing rapid change as a consequence of the disintegrative impact of Euroamerican expansion and domination. Anthropologists, many under the sponsorship of the United States government's Bureau of American Ethnology, fanned out across America to document the seemingly "vanishing" ways of life of Native Americans and to collect their material culture. The work of salvage ethnographers fed American museum collections and archives where Native American cultural materials could be preserved for the sake of science (Stocking 1985:114).

Salvage ethnography was grounded in an ideology of inevitability and ethnological collecting of this era rested on the belief that "it was necessary to use the
time to collect before it was too late" (Cole 1986:50). Preservation efforts
focused on the collection and preservation of material culture rather than the
living culture of Native Americans as the loss of the latter was seen as inevitable
in the wake of progress and an assumed assimilation. "American anthropology
developed in large part to preserve Native American culture for posterity – not
to help them fit into the new society" (Garza and Powell 2001:44).

The ideological impulses of salvage ethnography also had political implications.
John Wesley Powell, an anthropologist and head of the Bureau of American
Ethnology, convinced the United States Congress that "anthropology would
be useful in getting Indians peacefully allocated to reservations" (Stocking
1985:113). The salvage work of American anthropologists of the era exemplifies
what James Clifford has called the "salvage paradigm," or rather, "a geo-
political, historical paradigm that . . . denotes a pervasive ideological complex"
(Clifford 1987:121). As Cash Cash writes, "the vast inventory of Native material culture now housed in Western repositories is eloquent testimony to the
larger historical realities and colonial processes through which Native lifeways
were suppressed and cultures disenfranchised" (2001:139).

Today, anthropologists have largely denounced salvage ethnography for being
authoritarian and paternalistic (Sharma 1999:54). Nevertheless, its lasting
effects continue to mark relationships between museums and Native Americans.
But, as Cash Cash attests, Native Americans have transcended this history and
today are taking control over the management of their own cultural heritage and
its preservation.

> While these early efforts helped to establish and foster a distinctly
> American social science based on fieldwork and the acquisition of ethno-
> graphic information, human remains, and artifacts, the one-way transfer
> of intellectual and cultural property that ensued has had a lasting and
> profound effect on Native communities. No matter how benign or socially
> responsive the anthropological project has since become its cumulative
> impact across time and space has been significant. Even so, Native com-
> munities today, through their collective efforts, are beginning to transcend
> this history and are now attempting to reconcile the past with the future
> through self-determined strategies of cultural renewal and preserva-
> tion.
>
> (2001:139)

Anthropologists and museum professionals are now challenged with a new
accountability. Today, they must be accountable not only to their scientific and
professional communities and the public, but also to the cultures whose collections they previously held in "perpetuity." The "sacred trust" of museums to
hold objects in perpetuity for the benefit of the general public (or humanity as
a whole) has now been called into question. "The notion of permanence – that
museums hold their collections in perpetuity – can no longer be taken for
granted" (Harth 1999:279).

87

Although the implementation of NAGPRA has given rise to numerous problems and concerns on the part of both Native Americans and the museum and scientific communities, it marks a dramatic shift in attitudes and law, favoring Native Americans (see Bray 2001, Mihesuah 2000). And even though the wording of the Act is not wholly satisfactory to the various interested parties, it has been at least considered "workable." As Jonathan Haas, a curator at the Field Museum of Natural History in Chicago and participant in discussions on the final wording of NAGPRA, contends

> while the language of NAGPRA may be murky, patronizing, clumsy and unrealistic, the law in many ways is working. All parties concerned with collections and repatriation, e.g., curators, lawyers, tribal officials, traditional leaders and many others, are finding ways to deal with both the letter of the law and the spirit of the law. With a decade of experience since the passage of the Act, it appears that many of the dire predictions of vast collections flowing out of museums have simply not come to pass. Increasingly, we see that the idea of repatriation in most museums, with notable exceptions, is viewed less and less as a threat and more commonly embraced as an opportunity to build new kinds of relationships with the Native communities whose objects are represented in their collections and exhibition halls.
>
> (2001:120)

Many museums in the United States, in an effort to create goodwill between their institutions and Native communities, are going beyond the "letter of the law" and working more in the "spirit of the law" by returning objects not covered by NAGPRA. As a case in point, Curator David Bailey of the Museum of Western Colorado returned a beaded vest and a buckskin dress decorated with elk teeth to the Northern Ute families they once belonged to. In discussing the need to return family heirlooms, Bailey said:

> We never put ourselves in their place and that's a mistake. Everybody benefits when we return items and receive valuable information back. Other curators seem to believe their job is to fill their museum's storerooms and lock the door, but I would rather have a dialogue and exchange with living Indians to gain their respect and insight into our collections.
>
> (quoted in Gulliford 2000:53)

In return for repatriating the vest and dress, the Museum of Western Colorado received new beaded items as a gift from the tribal chairman, as well as stories and information about them.

Thomas Livesay, Director of the Museum of New Mexico, also relates how his institution's repatriation policy has brought it much closer to tribes in New Mexico, a state with a sizable Native American population. According to Livesay, tribal members have gone through the museum's storerooms and provided staff with additional information about many of the objects. As a result of such interactions, these museums have not been confronted with the formal, adversarial relationship that is sometimes brought about by the implementation of NAGPRA (Gulliford 2000:53).

Reciprocal exchanges such as these are now common and exemplify how the transfer of objects and knowledge has begun to work both ways. Although NAGPRA and the repatriation of objects often has been portrayed in terms of conflict, as Davis pointed out back in 1989 before the passage of NAGPRA, it is important to remember how both sides can benefit from repatriation. "In presenting the issue as a political conflict, the chroniclers of repatriation are missing what is shared in common by the combatants: both sides value the material culturally, and there are times when both enjoy sharing that knowledge" (1989:4).

It is also important to note that many museums throughout the United States had already begun to establish collaborative relationships with Native communities before the passage of NAGPRA in 1990. For example, the Denver Museum of Nature and Science (formerly the Denver Museum of Natural History), created a Native American Advisory Committee in 1968 when the Crane American Indian Collection was donated to the museum. The Advisory Committee, a multi-tribal, Denver-area group, provided museum staff with advice on how to curate the collection in a culturally sensitive manner and

Figure 4.1 Transfer of Keet S'aaxw (Killer Whale Clan Hat) of the Tlingit Dakl'aweidi Clan of Angoon, Alaska during a repatriation ceremony at the Denver Museum of Nature and Science. The clan delegation receiving the hat included Mark Jacobs Jr, Harold Jacobs, Lydia George, Edwell John Jr, and Michelle Metz.

Photograph by Annette Slade. All Rights Reserved, Photo Archives, Denver Museum of Nature and Science, 1997.

assisted with planning exhibitions in the Crane American Indian Hall that opened in 1978. The Committee also "guided the staff in setting aside a sacred storage room for about 700 objects and invited traditional spiritual leaders for blessing ceremonies. Thus, the experience of interacting with the Indian community in a meaningful manner was established early at the Museum" (Herold 2001:6).

Many museums had also begun to repatriate objects before the passage of NAGPRA.[4] One notable case was the return of Zuni "War Gods" or *Ahayu:da* to the Zuni people. Among the many museums to repatriate *Ahayu:da* was the Smithsonian Institution Museum of Natural History, which returned two in 1987, and the Denver Art Museum, which returned three in 1980 (Merrill *et al.* 1993:527). The museums' actions were in response to the Zuni's request for the return of the War Gods, which the Zuni claimed, were inalienable, communal property. According to Zuni tradition, no person could ever have had the right to remove or sell an *Ahayu:da* and thus they must have been stolen. The Zuni also based their claim on the belief that "the harmony of the universe and the future of Zuni in particular is endangered as long as a single War God is out of its shrine" (Childs 1980:5).

The repatriation of the *Ahayu:da* was the result of a Zuni effort that began in 1978 to recover the *Ahayu:da* from museums and private collections. A "Statement of the Religious Leaders of the Pueblo of Zuni Concerning Sacred Zuni Religious Items/Artifacts" was drafted, which emphasized that the theft of religious artifacts from sacred shrines was the most distressing problem facing the modern Zuni people. In conclusion, the Statement read:

> because of the many adverse effects and conditions that have been experienced by the Zuni people, we have made a decision to respectfully request the return of all our communal religious items/artifacts currently on display or in storage in the world's museums and to try to stop the theft and sale of sacred Zuni religious items . . . This decision is based on our desires to perpetuate our Zuni culture in its totality.

> (quoted in Childs 1980:6)

According to Edmund Ladd, a member of the Coyote clan of the Zuni Pueblo and anthropologist, in Zuni culture the War Gods are the patron of sports. The Sunfather created them at the beginning of time. Images of the War Gods are recreated annually by the Deer and Bear clans and are placed at various shrines around Zuni land for the protection of the Zuni people and the world at large.

> This is why the *Ahayu:da* are considered "War Gods." Beyond the fact that they are attended by the bow priests, they have nothing to do with war. Rather, they are considered the protectors of the Zuni people and the world in general, guarding against both human-produced and natural disasters.

> (Ladd 2001:107)

When a new image of the *Ahayu:da* is installed in a shrine, the "old" one is removed and transferred to a place where all the previous gods have been lain.

Ladd emphasizes, however, that this does not mean the images have been discarded or thrown away:

> Like a chain, each god that is replaced adds to the continuum that augments and reinforces the protective powers of the *Ahayu:da*. It is through the process of disintegration that these gods realize their protective powers. It is therefore imperative that they not be removed, collected, or preserved; such acts are both dangerous and insensitive.
>
> (2001:107)

Thus, the makers of the gods never intended them to be preserved. Their power is realized through their disintegration (Ladd 2001:108).

When the Denver Art Museum repatriated the *Ahayu:da* to the Zuni, it issued a statement saying that it was presenting the War Gods to the Zuni people because "in Zuni religion . . . the War God is a deity and a present animate object of worship, rather than a symbol or art object" (Childs 1980:6). The Museum Trustees concluded that while the museum was responsible for preserving its collection in public trust, it was also concerned with "strengthening its relations with the Zuni people and other creative cultures as an institution which displays and preserves art objects from all cultures with sensitivity and appreciation" (quoted in Childs 1980:6). In response, the Zuni commended the museum for "taking an enlightened step in recognizing the importance of Native American religious practices" (quoted in Childs 1980:6).[5] The museum also assisted the Zuni in planning a high-security facility to be constructed around the shrine where the *Ahayu:da* were to be placed. "This facility was designed to protect the *Ahayu:da* from theft while meeting the religious requirement that the shrine be exposed to the elements" (Merrill *et al.* 1993:539).[6]

Native American traditional care in mainstream museums

Another important outcome of NAGPRA and the increasing presence of Native American representatives in museums is the growing awareness of Native American views on the care and treatment of cultural materials, as well as the differences between professional museum curatorship and that of Native peoples. In response to Native people's concerns, museums are beginning to change their practices to accommodate tribal wishes, especially regarding the treatment of "culturally sensitive objects." Charles Smythe, formerly of the Department of Anthropology Repatriation Office of the Smithsonian National Museum of Natural History, describes culturally sensitive objects as

> those that may be considered to be of special significance in a particular culture. In many cases these objects are believed to be, or have been in the past, spiritually active or possessing spiritual power. Objects used by shamans, for example, may retain some of the power they were endowed with at the time of use. Other examples of culturally sensitive objects are those that are used exclusively by men and for which handling by women would be culturally inappropriate.
>
> (quoted in Williamson 1997:2)[7]

Developments such as these demonstrate how, "across the United States, Native Americans are asserting hegemony over their own cultural values insisting on curatorial change in the nation's museums" (Gulliford 2000:42).

As true for other indigenous peoples discussed in the previous chapter, many Native Americans are concerned about the "public" nature of museum collections, and rights governing access to and use of collections.

> The very concept of a collection of tribal objects, seen, studied, and cared for by outsiders can be viewed as being inconsistent with tribal tradition. Some tribal objects were never intended for all tribal members to see, handle, or use. Some could only be seen and touched by men, others only by women. Some objects were only seen and touched by members of particular tribal societies, organizations, or families. The fact that public collections exist is a source of social problems in Indian communities.
>
> (Parker 1990:37)

And as Peter Jemison, from the Seneca tribe proclaims:

> The concept in the white world is that "everyone's culture is everyone else's." That's not really our concept. Our concept is there were certain things given to us that we have to take care of and that you are either part of it or you are not a part of it. If you are not a part of it, then you don't have to worry about it. But if you are a part of it, then you have got to be actively taking care of it on a yearly basis, or on whatever basis it is taken care of. We think that it's the ones out there that are uncared for by us [that] are causing problems with our own communities internally.
>
> (quoted in Parker 1990:37)

Jemison's views on curatorial authority are consistent with those of many other tribes.

> Some tribal members think that tribal objects, sacred or not, can only be appropriately cared for by those responsible for such duties within the tribe. Sacred objects should not be in collections where they are handled by people other than the appropriate spiritual authority.
>
> (Parker 1990:37)

In light of these concerns, some museums try to familiarize themselves with each tribe's cultural protocol and work with "qualified caretakers." Smythe describes qualified caretakers as

> an individual who knows the culturally prescribed rules for handling and maintaining culturally sensitive objects. In some cultures, the caretaker has the responsibility for keeping the artifacts safe on behalf of a larger group until they are passed on to subsequent generations, i.e. another caretaker.
>
> (quoted in Williamson 1997:3)

For many Native peoples, such as the Zuni, objects are imbued with a spiritual or life-force or energy, which endows them with certain powers (Clavir 2002, Davis 1989, Rosoff 1998, Simpson 1996). This belief stands in sharp contrast to the perception of objects in western science and museology where objects are considered inanimate, and emphasis is placed largely on their physical integrity and attributes as evidence of cultural, historical, or scientific phenomena. But because objects are alive and embody their own powers, many Native peoples find certain museum practices offensive because they debase the spiritual integrity of the objects. For example, because objects are alive, they need to breathe. Thus, many Native people are disturbed by the standard practice in museums of storing objects in sealed containers or in plastic. In the following statement, Conrad House, a Navajo, expresses his dismay in finding masks stored in plastic when visiting a museum:

> At the museum, I saw a number of sacred masks covered up with plastic. In our way, this is wrong. The masks have to breathe because there's energy in them – in the Navajo way, they're alive. You can't suffocate them or they'll be angry in time to come.
>
> (1994:95)

Furthermore, because objects are alive they have a life cycle. Consequently, some Native Americans find the conventional museum practice of conserving objects to prolong their life disturbing since it arrests the life cycle of the object. "Curation is not only a problem of outsiders caring for objects that they have no right to touch; curation also changes the character of an object by artificially prolonging its life" (Parker 1990:37).

While this may be the case for some objects, Jemison points out that, in their traditional context, certain objects were made to last and measures were taken to prolong their life.

> There are some things that deteriorate through use, and that is the way they were made. Nobody ever thought that these things would last forever because of the nature of the materials they were made from. If you are using it actively, it will wear out. Some of the parts you can replace, take care of it and put it back together again. There are some things, like wampum belts though, that are made of material that we consider to be very permanent. Wampum Quahog clamshell is really very permanent; if you step on it and break it, then you can restring it. That does require some care. It does require that you replace the leather that holds it together. It does require that you store it in a place that is safe, that nobody is going to go and steal it if they have the opportunity and someone is unscrupulous.
>
> (Jemison quoted in Parker 1990:38)

As museums have been made increasingly aware of such concerns and the fact that Native Americans have their own methods of caring for and preserving objects, they have begun to integrate Native philosophies and methods of traditional care into the curation of their collections. This is true for both NAGPRA-related and non-NAGPRA objects. Museums are attempting to respond to Native wishes and alter their practices accordingly, especially in terms of how objects are stored and whether or not they should be displayed. It is now standard practice for museums to remove NAGPRA-covered objects from displays. In some cases, objects are replaced with a sign telling visitors that the object has been removed out of respect for Native wishes and in compliance with NAGPRA. Since every tribe has its own traditions regarding the use and treatment of objects, museums must consult with individual tribes to obtain information on how best to accommodate their particular wishes.

In a session on NAGPRA and curation at the annual meeting of the American Association for State and Local History in Denver, Colorado in 1997, Gordon Yellowman of the Cheyenne-Arapaho Tribes described some of the sensitive curation issues surrounding Great Plains objects. He pointed out, for example, that male and female objects should not be stored together. Care must also be taken when objects are moved because some should be positioned upright, while all objects need sunlight. Yellowman also expressed concern about the handling of sacred objects, which can have an impact on anyone who handles them. Thus, sacred objects must be appropriately curated and stored (Gulliford 2000:51).

In a consultation sponsored by the National Museum of the American Indian on traditional care and handling issues, Greig Arnold, of the Makah tribe of Washington state, described how Makah headdresses are displayed only on certain occasions:

> Once we have a headdress out on the floor and it is being danced, the person with that headdress is supposed to put it on right away and come out – he is that thing, whatever it is that he is doing. If he is wearing a thunderbird or if he is wearing a wolf, he is that on the floor. As soon as that song is over and that energy is gone, he comes off and then transforms. Then he is back to who he is as a person or she is as a person. All that gear is then put away and stored after that, not to be seen until it is danced again.

> (quoted in Rosoff 1998:39)

As part of the same consultations, Bob Smith, of the Oneida, related how Iroquois Medicine and False Face masks should be stored.

> At one time . . . the masks were actually buried with the individual. But the way I understand it and the way these masks are up here now [in the storage area of the National Museum of the American Indian] . . . that isn't the way that they would be stored; you wouldn't hang the mask face out. If the mask was to be hung, it would be facing towards the wall and it would be covered. The proper way of storing the mask would be to store it face down, because if you store the mask face up, it connotes something that is dead or dying.

> (quoted in Rosoff 1998:39)

Today, most museums containing NAGPRA-covered materials, or sacred objects and human remains, have created procedures for handling and storing these materials. At the University of Denver Museum of Anthropology, human remains and unassociated and associated funerary objects have been isolated from the general collections and are stored in a separate NAGPRA vault. Items of cultural patrimony and sacred objects are also stored in a specially designated NAGPRA vault. Access to these rooms is restricted to museum staff and tribal representatives, and entry is only permitted for tribal visits or for maintenance such as cleaning and pest monitoring. Women are not allowed to enter the storage room or to handle NAGPRA-related items during menstruation or, in some cases, pregnancy. Efforts also have been made to store material according to the wishes of tribal representatives who have voiced their particular concerns through the course of NAGPRA consultations. For example, human remains and associated funerary objects are not stored in plastic or lidded boxes. Instead, muslin and acid-free tissue paper are used in storage containers so the remains and objects can breathe. Tribal representatives are also permitted to feed or make offerings to objects at the time of their visits. Although some organic matter, such as corn meal, is not allowed to remain in the storage area due to its potential to attract pests, others, such as sage, cedar, and tobacco, can remain with the collections. Smudging may also take place, which is a process that requires the burning of an offering; usually tobacco, sage, or sweet grass to create smoke that "washes" over the object. If smudging is requested, advance notice is given to facility management staff so fire alarms can be disarmed ahead of time. In addition, the museum does not allow any research to be conducted on NAGPRA collections, and their associated documentation is kept confidential. NAGPRA procedures are updated regularly in the course of ongoing consultations with tribal representatives.

As a further example of the efforts that have been made to honor and accommodate tribal wishes a survey was sent to all tribes represented in the collection in preparation for the museum's move to a new facility. The "Packing, Transporting, and Rehousing NAGPRA-Related Collections Survey," prepared by the museum's NAGPRA Coordinator and Specialist, was sent to 209 tribes, Alaska Native corporations, and Native Hawaiian organizations. The survey was funded through the National Park Service NAGPRA Grants Program. The purpose of the survey was to obtain information on any concerns or suggestions tribes might have regarding how NAGPRA collections should be moved. Survey questions addressed packing, transporting, handling, and rehousing. Twenty-nine responses were received.

The majority of respondents did not object to the museum staff determining the methods of and materials used for packing humans remains, associated funerary objects, and sacred items as long as packing was done in a respectful and careful manner. The use of plastic bubble wrap was permissible for a brief period in order to offer the greatest protection against breakage. The majority of respondents emphasized that they did not want human remains and associated funerary objects separated during transport. Several respondents stressed that human remains and funerary items (or items of the deceased) should never be located near sacred material or cultural patrimony (items of the living). A third of the tribes responded that they thought a tribal representative or religious leader should be present during transport. Invitations were extended to those tribes. However, due to the timing of the move, no tribal representatives or religious leaders were able to be present. In general, the respondents wrote that they trusted the museum staff "to do the right thing," and appreciated being consulted before the move. As one respondent wrote: "We trust you will make every effort to pack, transport, and rehouse in accordance with desires of the appropriate tribal authorities; wish you every success and appreciate your continued sensitivity to the concerns of Native peoples."

In the article "Merging Traditional Indigenous Curation Methods with Modern Museum Standards of Care" (2001), Flynn and Hull-Walski discuss policies and procedures that have been instituted for the care of culturally sensitive materials in the Department of Anthropology at the National Museum of Natural History, Smithsonian Institution. Commenting on the arguments for and against integrating aspects of traditional care into modern museum standards they state:

> Some museum professionals would argue that museums as scientific entities should not be vehicles for religious expression and should manage collections in a strictly objective manner. [But] incorporating the religious and ritual meaning of an object as presented by the indigenous culture into its care and preservation enhances its information value and adds an additional story to the object's life history.
>
> (2001:31)

The authors encourage other museums to develop a standard policy and set of procedures for the care of culturally sensitive materials because a standard methodology allows museums to identify emerging care issues in a consistent and reasonable manner.

Flynn and Hull-Walski state that the Department of Anthropology, over the past twenty years, has responded to many requests to alter its methods of caring for collections. In an effort to accommodate these requests, the Department's staff has developed a set of guidelines for identifying and managing culturally sensitive materials and instituted a number of changes in its practices. These changes include rehousing objects, creating special mounts and containers for them, moving materials to new locations, and creating new identification labels to reflect changes.

According to Flynn and Hull-Walski, the Department has received a number of requests to reorient objects in their storage units. These requests, on occasion, have required the construction of special mounts to hold objects in an appropriate position. For example, a Cheyenne religious leader from the Cheyenne and Arapaho Tribes of Oklahoma requested that a Sun Dance buffalo skull be oriented to face east when in storage. It was also to be stored upside down. This position signifies that the skull is not an "active" sacred object. However, while the request for the east-facing position was implemented immediately, the upside down position required that a special mount be built so the skull would not be resting on its fragile horns (2001:34).

Flynn and Hull-Walski explain that the issue of access presents a particularly difficult dilemma for their museum because it is a public institution receiving federal funding, precluding it from discriminating or supporting any particular religious view. As a means of circumventing this problem, the Department devised a method to accommodate the wishes of groups who request restricted access while avoiding violation of the law. Storage units containing objects with cultural restrictions are labeled with the relevant information so those who wish to obey the restrictions may do so.

One of the most challenging care issues for the Department of Anthropology is how to handle the leaving of offerings or the ceremonial feeding of sacred objects. As previously discussed, because offerings are typically of plant material, such as tobacco, sweet grass, sage, cedar, and corn pollen, they pose the risk of harboring or attracting pests. The Department has established several options to eliminate this potential risk. Offerings may be enclosed in sealed polyethylene bags or placed in a box next to the object. Pest strips are placed nearby, which are then monitored regularly. The Department is also currently developing a space at its storage facility that can be used for the private viewing of objects during consultations and for carrying out ceremonies requiring smudging.

The Department's policies and procedures for caring for culturally sensitive materials do not just apply to its Native American collections. It also honors requests from other culture groups whose collections are housed in the museum. The Department of Anthropology at the National Museum of Natural History cares for one of the largest and most diverse ethnographic collections in the world. While it is particularly strong in collections from North America, it also contains collections from Central and South America, Asia, Africa, and the Pacific. The size and diversity of the collections and the cultures and spiritual beliefs they represent make the development of a standard policy challenging. In this regard, Flynn and Hull-Walski remind us that "while all objects should be treated with care and respect, it is also necessary to remember that not all cultures view their sacred, ceremonial, or culturally sensitive material in the same way" (2001:31).[8]

Conservators have become especially sensitive to issues surrounding the care and treatment of sacred or ceremonial objects, because of the potential of their work to change an object's physical, and possibly, spiritual integrity. Wolfe and Mibach, in a paper on ethical considerations in the conservation of Native American sacred objects, advise:

> we should consider the circumstances under which sacred objects undergo modern, scientific conservation treatment, since the very process of handling, documentation and treatment could constitute interference with the integrity of the object and destruction of its functional and spiritual value.
>
> (1983:1)[9]

According to Wolfe and Mibach, the American Institute for Conservation Code of Ethics and Standards of Practice provides conservators with directions in how to approach sacred objects. According to the Code, conservators are to be "governed by unswerving respect for the aesthetic, historic and physical integrity of the object." Wolfe and Mibach suggest, however, that this integrity should imply "more than the physical evidence of use or signs of modifications constituting the historical record of the object. Sacred objects are considered by some to be living sources of power; as such we must be as careful of their spiritual integrity as we are of their physical integrity" (1983:3).

Wolfe and Mibach write that because conservators are not in a position to know what constitutes an object's spiritual integrity, they should consult with tribal religious leaders to learn how to appropriately care for sacred and ceremonial objects. They point out that a distinction is made between "care for" and "conserve" because "a great many sacred objects require periodic ceremonial maintenance. This ceremonial maintenance ranges from prayer ceremonies involving the use of a religious bundle, to the feeding of False Face Masks" (1983:4). The authors further relate how some of the traditional practices associated with ceremonial maintenance are akin to those of their own profession.

> Some of these ceremonies include procedures, such as the annual inspection by trained people and regular "fumigation" with smoke smudge of sweetgrass or other aromatic substances. Many aspects of traditional maintenance are thus very similar to preventive conservation techniques; they have, after all, preserved the objects, often for a century of more in unfavorable environments, until they arrived in our collections.
>
> (1983:4)

Wolfe and Mibach suggest that answers to conservation problems related to the care and treatment of sacred materials and other ethnographic objects may lie in traditional techniques, and encourage conservators to seek out this knowledge.

The authors point out that some of the approaches conservators have developed for the maintenance of collections have long been in use among Native groups. For example, Mibach found through her work with the Northern Cree of Canada, that the Cree have historically used rendered skunk oil for dressing rawhide containers containing sacred objects. Skunk oil is used instead of fish oil, goose, or bear grease because it does not yellow over time and remains fluid even at cold temperatures. Mibach asserts that "these reasons for choice closely parallel those used by conservators," and further "it appears that the ethical systems and maintenance procedures used by conservators are closely paralleled and preceded by those used by Native people" (n.d.:99).

Museums are also finding ways to accommodate Native people's concerns regarding the private nature of many sacred objects and rights to their care and handling. Mibach and Wolf Green recount how the Provincial Museum of Alberta, Canada has approached the issue.

> In the Provincial Museum of Alberta . . . all sacred material was acquired through traditional transfer ceremonies from previous owners who expressed the wish that the material should remain in permanent safekeeping in the museum. The new ceremonial owner, a museum staff member, is the only person allowed to handle or examine the sacred material. He also performs the necessary ceremonial caretaking functions associated with these materials.
>
> (1989:61)

Many other museums throughout Canada and the United States follow similar protocol or have appropriate elders visit the museum for ceremonial purposes.

Museum professionals and the scientific community have come to realize that the removal of sacred materials from Native communities has constituted a tremendous loss for Native peoples. It has also limited the ability of traditional religious practitioners to maintain the necessary ritual control, maintenance, and appropriate care of sacred objects for the benefit of Native communities. Their removal and retention in museums have also forced Native communities to divulge sacred or esoteric forms of knowledge to substantiate their claims to these items or to ensure their appropriate disposition, often without the guarantee this knowledge will be protected (Cash Cash 2001:144). However, as the above examples show, the situation has begun to change.

> Traditional religious practitioners are now beginning to experience greater freedom to introduce and apply indigenous forms of curation within the museum. As indigenous curators, they bring to the museum a newly added dimension of human potential and experience that is testimony to the immediacy, vitality and power of objects to mediate the lived, everyday world we have now come to share.
>
> (Cash Cash 2001:144)

In general, the above examples demonstrate how NAGPRA and other developments have called into question the hegemonic and Eurocentric nature of the museum's previous claims to indigenous peoples' cultural property. As Cash Cash contends:

> At sites where cultures intersect, such as museums, the mobilization of meaning and ritual expression often loom larger than life when originating cultures assert claims of authenticity and authority over objects. More often than not, these indigenous claims are counter-hegemonic since they often arise out of lived cultural realities that exist outside the boundaries of the museum. As a result, the exclusive domains of property, representation, and control that constitute the common, everyday functions of the museum are directly challenged, thus calling into question traditional museum policies and practice.
>
> (2001:141)

The dialogues between Native Americans and museums that have been taking place over the past ten years or more clearly show how Native communities maintain a distinctive non-western view of their material culture. They also reveal how this material has enduring symbolic qualities and attributes that are of great importance to present-day communities. This new understanding

> also includes the notion that certain objects are imbued with power or possess sacredness and have the capacity to mobilize community histories, ritual, and cultural institutions. Within the Native community, objects are often perceived as locales of transcendent meaning and purpose apart from the normative importance of their physicality and form.
>
> (Cash Cash 2001:142)

99

Cash Cash, in his discussion of Native people's rights to sacred cultural property and the potential role of indigenous curation in museums, has sought to "liberate the concept of curation from its supposed neutrality in the institution and situate it within a specific cultural and historical context" (2001:140–141). He argues that curation should be viewed as social practice and within the context of social relations. In this respect, curation is as much a political act as a cultural one.

> So long as curation is maintained as the privileged enterprise of the museum institution it is reasonable to conclude that its categories and contradictions will inspire opposition. By restoring curation to a larger conceptual framework, we begin to account for direct experiences of individuals and cultures whose ontology is deeply embedded in the things we call "museum specimens."
>
> (2001:144)

Traditional care in the National Museum of the American Indian

President Bush signed the National Museum of the American Indian (NMAI) Act into law on November 28, 1989. The Act, among other things, provided for the creation of the National Museum of the American Indian. The museum is tentatively scheduled to open in 2003, and once completed, will be the fifteenth museum of the Smithsonian museum complex on the Mall in Washington, DC. It will be the first national museum in the United States dedicated exclusively to the history and culture of the indigenous peoples of the Americas. The NMAI Act authorized the purchase of the collections of the former Museum of the American Indian, Heye Foundation located in New York City, and the development of a new museum in New York City founded on these collections. The Museum of the American Indian contained one of the largest collections of Native American materials in the world with over 1 million objects and a library of 40,000 volumes relating to the archeology, ethnology, and history of Native American peoples. This new museum opened in November 1994 after collections of the Museum of the American Indian were transferred to the newly renovated historic Alexander Hamilton United States Customs House in Lower Manhattan. In addition to this facility the Act also provided for the building of a Cultural Resources Center in Suitland, Maryland. The Center, which opened in 1998, functions as the museum's research and collections storage facility. In 1999, the NMAI began moving its collections from New York to the Cultural Resources Center in Maryland. The undertaking is expected to take approximately five years.

The creation of the NMAI, and all its components, has had a critical impact on Native American efforts to repatriate their cultural property, and exercise greater control over how such property is curated and presented in museums. The NMAI is required to oversee the return of certain materials to tribes long considered government "property." "Its very founding charter is, thus, at odds with the traditional mandate to acquire and hold collections in trust, in perpetuity, for the 'whole' public" (Harth 1999:277).

The NMAI Act required the Smithsonian Institution, in consultation with Indian tribes and traditional Indian religious leaders, to inventory human remains and funerary objects in their collections.[10] The Act mandated that a special committee be formed to monitor and review the "inventory, identification, and return of Indian human remains and Indian funerary objects and to assist in the resolution of disputes concerning repatriation" (Trope and Echo-Hawk 2000:21). The NMAI Act preceded NAGPRA and set an important precedent later cited by supporters of NAGPRA while it was being debated before Congress (Trope and Echo-Hawk 2000:20). The repatriation provisions in the NMAI Act were designed to redress wrongs of the past and were created in a spirit of restitution. "The NMAI Act's repatriation provisions were aimed at rectifying 'some of the injustices done to Indian people over the years'" (Trope and Echo-Hawk 2000:21).

The NMAI Act and NAGPRA were intended to further policy articulated in the American Indian Religious Freedom Act of 1978, which acknowledged, in part, that "laws and policies often deny American Indians access to sites required in their religions, including cemeteries and at times prohibit the use and possession of sacred objects necessary to the exercise of religious rites and ceremonies" (quoted in Harjo 1996:3). The American Indian Religious Freedom Act, the NMAI Act and NAGPRA are laws that "provide some small measure of justice for Native Peoples in the modern era for the generational suffering and hardship imposed by policies and practices that outlawed Native religions and violated fundamental rules of human decency" (Harjo 1996:3).

The NMAI Act acknowledges Native people's claims that the retention of sacred objects in museum collections is a violation of their customs, and infringes on their rights to freedom of religious practice, theoretically protected by the American Indian Religious Freedom Act (Trope and Echo-Hawk 2000:13). It also acknowledges that the retention of religious materials in museums is, more generally, a violation of Native people's human rights. This was made clear in the hearings that preceded the passage of the Act, in which the United States Select Committee on Indian Affairs heard testimony from many individuals and organizations representing museums and tribal interests. Oren R. Lyons, Faithkeeper of the Onondaga Nation, Fire Keepers of the Haudenosaunee (Six Nations Iroquois Confederacy), in reference to collections held at the former Museum of the American Indian, claimed that the "possession and display of the [Haudenosaunee] Medicine Masks violates the Human Rights of our people, and the group rights of those Medicine Societies and the people that they serve" (quoted in Simpson 1996:207). Lyons also argued that the retention of wampum belts was a "violation of the human rights of the Council of Chief of the Haudenosaunee" (quoted in Simpson 1996:207), and should be returned because they were required for religious purposes.

The National Museum of the American Indian has been a leader in establishing standards for the sensitive and appropriate representation and curation of

Native American cultural materials. One of the distinguishing features of the museum is the overriding importance of the "Native voice" in all museum activities. Richard West, Director of the NMAI and member of the Cheyenne and Arapaho Tribes of Oklahoma states: "From the start, our new museum has been dedicated to a fresh, and some would say radically different approach . . . We insist that the authentic Native voice and perspective guide all our policies, including, of course, our exhibition philosophy" (2000:7). West also asserts that research and scholarship on Native peoples must now include multiple perspectives, especially the voices of Native peoples themselves (West 1993). In the context of the NMAI, "the incorporation of the Native voice restores real meaning and spiritual resonance to the artifacts we are privileged to care for and put on display" (West 2000:8).

The fact that the United States' national museum system now includes a primarily Native-run museum exemplifies the kind of profound changes that have been taking place not only in the American museum community, but also in American society as a whole regarding its views of Native American cultures. Despite such changes, Native Americans are still constantly confronted with popular culture stereotypes of their cultures, and the myth of the "vanishing Indian" (see Clark 1997, Nason 2000). To many Americans, Indians and their traditional ways of life are a "thing of the past." This view of Native American cultures as "dead" or "dying" was confirmed by surveys conducted by the NMAI from 1991 to 1995 as part of the planning process for the creation of the museum, its facilities, and exhibitions. As James Nason, Comanche and Professor of Anthropology and Director of the American Indian Studies Center at the University of Washington, relates: "Time and again we heard that, among other things, there are no more Indians – they all died . . ." (2000:39). In light of these perceptions, one of the NMAI's main purposes is to make the general public better aware of contemporary Native cultures and their continuing vitality. The museum's Mission Statement underscores this objective.

> The National Museum of the American Indian shall recognize and affirm to Native communities and the non-Native public the historical and contemporary culture and cultural achievements of the Natives of the Western Hemisphere by advancing – in consultation, collaboration, and cooperation with Natives – knowledge and understanding of Native cultures, including art, history and language, and by recognizing the museum's special responsibility, through innovative public programming, research and collections, to protect, support, and enhance the development, maintenance and perpetuation of Native culture and community.
>
> (quoted in Harjo 1996:30)

Since the NMAI was established, the museum staff has been consulting with Native people about the nature and function of the museum. As a result of these consultations, the museum has begun to integrate Native world-views and standards into all aspects of the museum's activities. This integration is mandated in the museum's Mission Statement and Collections Policy, which encourages the "direct and meaningful participation of Indian People" in all aspects of the museum's activities. Rosoff, a former staff member of the NMAI, states that in addition to providing detailed procedures for documentation, acquisition, repatriation, exhibition, care and handling, and other museum functions, the Collections Policy "respects and endeavors to incorporate the cultural protocols of Indian people that define: cultural and religious sensitivities, needs, and norms; the utilization of cultural knowledge and information; and restrictions outlined by specific tribal groups" (NMAI Collections Policy quoted in Rosoff 1998:33).

One of the museum's highest priorities has been the repatriation of all human remains in its collection. Because human remains in the museum's collection had never been adequately identified and inventoried, museum staff had initially to conduct a shelf-by-shelf search for remains. At the end of the survey, a total of 524 remains were identified. All of the remains found in the search were then consolidated into one room designated "Human Remains Vault." The remains were removed from old crates and other containers and all artificial materials such as plastic coverings and mothballs were discarded. According to Rosoff, as each part of the remains was wrapped in muslin it was sprinkled with a mixture of sage, sweet grass, tobacco, and cedar. All four plants were used because it was unknown which plants were sacred to the individual in question. All human remains were also reunited with their associated funerary items. The remains and objects were rehoused in acid-free boxes with cedarwood chips as packing materials to "cushion them for the journey home" (Rosoff 1998:34).

Sacred objects are another important category of objects the NMAI is concerned with repatriating. Each Native group is to determine which objects are sacred to it, if the objects should be repatriated, and if not, how the museum should care for and exhibit them. Since its inception, the NMAI has been consulting with tribal representatives to obtain information on how to integrate methods of traditional care into the curation of human remains and sacred materials. In response to Native people's concerns, Rosoff writes that the NMAI has begun to implement the following traditional care practices into its storage facilities in New York.

> The Human Remains Vault is smudged with a mixture of tobacco, sage, and sweetgrass, and cedar every week; drawers containing sacred materials such as bundles [medicine] have been flagged so that people know where this material is and can show it proper respect; during the full moon, the sacred Crow objects in the Plains vault are smudged with sage.
>
> (Rosoff 1998:37)

Rosoff stresses that the museum staff is not performing ceremonies, but only trying "to take care of these things the best way that we can" (1998:37). She explains that this statement characterizes the situation quite well because there are no pan-Indian ways of dealing with all the Native cultures represented in the museum's collection. "Until we receive specific instructions from a tribe, we leave the care of the collection to the discretion of Native staff members to treat the objects in the most respectful way possible according to their own cultural knowledge and customs" (1998:37).

In keeping with the heightened concern of conservators to approach the treatment of sacred objects in an ethically and sensitive manner, the collections and conservation staff of the NMAI also has been exploring new methods for taking care of culturally sensitive objects. Rosoff observes that current standard conservation treatments for deterring or eliminating insect infestation such as the use of plastic bags, freezing, and low-oxygen atmospheres may be inappropriate for certain objects because they might "suffocate" a living entity. Consequently, the staff has been investigating traditional Native American fumigation techniques such as regular smudging and the use of certain botanical substances in sachets. However, before any procedures are undertaken, museum staff consults with the appropriate tribal representative. Also, culturally sensitive and sacred objects are not repaired or stabilized unless the conservation department first gets permission from the Native group concerned. In general, the "department is experimenting with procedures that satisfy both Native communities and professional conservation standards" (Rosoff 1998:38).[11]

Because the museum is focused on a cultural present as much as it is on a cultural past, its policies and activities are directed toward helping sustain the living culture of Native American communities. As Richard West has said:

> The National Museum of the American Indian is not only about the preservation of physical objects, or things. It is also about the preservation of cultures, of ways of being. Native Communities throughout the Hemisphere have persisted, against almost overwhelming odds, to this very day. And their cultural viability, including, as it always has, response, adaptation, and innovation grounded in timeless tradition, not only continues to exist but is experiencing a profound renaissance.
>
> (quoted in Gulliford 2000:41)

In keeping with this philosophy, the museum's Collection Policy also contains a provision that allows tribes to borrow sacred objects and regalia for use in ceremonies and to manifest their spiritual beliefs. In borrowing these materials, "some tribes feel that they are fulfilling a responsibility to utilize cultural materials as they were intended" (Rosoff 1998:38). Such requests are considered on a case by case basis.

As a result of consultations with various tribes and in an attempt to respect the traditional values and practices associated with certain materials, the NMAI has also removed certain objects from exhibit. For example, the Sacred Pipe of the Sioux, *ptechincala hu cannupa*, was removed from display, and in its place a label explains: "When a pipe bowl and stem are joined a consecration occurs and the pipe becomes an instrument of divine communication" (Gulliford 2000:48). Pipe bowls and stems are traditionally stored separately when not in use. Plans have been made at the NMAI to ensure that "pipes which have long been exhibited with their bowls and stems joined will be separated and purified and removed from display" (Gulliford 2000:48).[12] Removal of sensitive objects from display at the National Museum of the American Indian represents a significant shift in curatorial practice and increasing respect for Native cultures. As one Native American staff member explained, "when exhibits become redefined and artifact collections are returned, the larger American society will continue to learn of Native American traditions – but on our terms, in our time, by our people" (quoted in Gulliford 2000:54).

Rosoff admits that, despite such attempts to be culturally sensitive, it is not always feasible for the museum to implement traditional care practices, in light of the fact that tribal preferences are not uniform. Implementation also poses challenges because the museum's collection of over 1 million objects is hemispheric, has a temporal range of tens of thousands of years, and represents some 600 tribes. But the goal and the hope for the institution's many different facilities is that "they will be welcoming places that incorporate the special spiritual requirements of all Native people" (Rosoff 1998:40).

Native American museums and cultural centers

The United States National Park Service reported in 1990 that there were more tribal objects held in collections owned or managed by non-Indians than held by Indians (Parker 1990:34). While this situation may never be adequately brought into balance, it has begun to change as objects are being repatriated to Native American tribes and as more and more Native communities are establishing their own museums and cultural centers. Today, there are over 200 tribal museums or cultural centers in the United States (Simpson 1996:137). They range from small community-based museums staffed by just a few dedicated individuals to large complexes with multi-million dollar budgets. The growth of tribal museums and cultural centers represents how Native American communities are increasingly exercising greater control over their cultural property and management of their cultural heritage. "The critical issue from a tribal perspective . . . is the control and management by native peoples of their cultural patrimony" (Parker 1990:41).

While some tribal museums and cultural centers are similar to western-style museums in their basic functions, how they carry out these functions and for what purposes often differ dramatically from mainstream museum practices. In the words of Richard West: "The most radical departure from traditional museum practice is perhaps best represented by the growth of Indian-run institutions, which have a considerably different perspective from that of traditional museums" (2000:8–9). As is true for other indigenous models of museums and curation, Native American tribal museums differ from western museums most notably in their goals and purposes as well as the political and historical conditions under which they are being created. Each museum or center expresses the unique cultural identity of its community and its own ways of curating, interpreting, representing, and preserving its culture. Through their activities they help reaffirm a sense of cultural identity and provide a venue for the perpetuation of cultural traditions.[13] "The advent of tribal museums, which are both repositories and community centers, provide Native Americans with a positive sense of historical identity and an opportunity to look toward the future by sharing the past with the next generation" (Gulliford 2000:53).

Even though many Native communities have embraced the museum idea, some find the term "museum" itself offensive because of negative perceptions of museums and museum practices. Gloria Cranmer-Webster, Director of the U'Mista Cultural Centre in British Columbia, expressed this sentiment in saying: "We don't want museums. The word museum has a negative connotation signifying the place where dead things lie and where native people don't go" (quoted in Clavir 2002:85). For this reason, many communities prefer the term "cultural center," to reflect the dynamic nature of their institutions, which are as much concerned with the present as the past.

On the differences between mainstream or majority museums and those of Native peoples, Clifford writes, "speaking schematically, majority museums articulate cosmopolitan culture, science, art, and humanism – often with a national slant. Tribal museums express local culture, oppositional politics, kinship, ethnicity and tradition" (1991:225). Clifford asserts that the tribal museum also has different agendas:

> (1) its stance is to some degree oppositional, reflecting excluded experiences, colonial pasts, and current struggles; (2) the art/culture distinction is often irrelevant, or positively subverted; (3) the notion of a unified or linear History (whether of the nation, of humanity, or of art) is challenged by local, community histories; and (4) the collections do not aspire to be included in the patrimony (of the nation, of great art, etc.) but to be inscribed within different traditions and practices, free of national, cosmopolitan patrimonies.
>
> (1991:225–226)

However, Clifford also adds, the tribal museum's vision is not just inward or locally directed. Rather, "the tribal or minority museum and artist, while locally based, may also aspire to wider recognition, to a certain national or global participation" (1991:226). Even though tribal museums may exploit familiar "museum effects," they do so largely on their own terms and in their own ways.

The activities of tribal museums and cultural centers are far ranging, extending beyond the conventional parameters of historical or cultural preservation. What tribes seek to preserve through their various cultural heritage preservation programs is the integrity of their living culture and community in general. Thus, many are taking an integrated or holistic approach to cultural heritage preservation or "cultural resource management" (Anyon et al. 2000). In addition to the establishment of museums and cultural centers, many tribes are setting up their own heritage management programs, which encompass a wide variety of activities. Such activities may include efforts to preserve and transmit languages and oral traditions, arts and crafts skills, knowledge of traditional uses of plants and land, and traditional religious practices. The protection of sacred sites may also be a crucial element of preservation programs. Preservation in this context means "cultural preservation: the active maintenance of continuity with indigenous values and beliefs that are part of a community's identity" (Clavir 2002:73).

Through their heritage programs, many tribes are also exercising greater control over archeological and ethnographic research conducted on their lands and in their communities. In many cases, researchers must now obtain permission from tribes before embarking on any research project that affects them. "Maintaining the privileged nature of esoteric religious knowledge and traditional cultural information, and protecting the legal rights of research subjects, are the driving concerns in instituting control of ethnographic research" (Anyon *et al.* 2000:137).

Although tribes may receive support from outside sources for developing their programs, for example from government agencies and museum professionals, they are concerned with maintaining and creating their own approaches to cultural heritage preservation. In the words of Alan Downer (Navajo): "What a tribal program is about is a tribe establishing standards and policies in controlling its own cultural resources rather than letting someone else do that" (quoted in Parker 1990:13). Each tribal program approaches heritage management in a different way to fit its own needs, goals, and culture.

As individual tribes institutionalize their own cultural preservation programs, they are striving to establish criteria and processes consistent with tradition. And similar to their counterparts in the Pacific and elsewhere, Native American museums and cultural centers often exhibit approaches to cultural heritage preservation that are extensions of older traditions. Carla Roberts, director of ATLATL, a Phoenix-based Native American Arts organization, stresses how "there have always been mechanisms in native communities for transmitting cultural values from one generation to another" (Roberts 1994:27). In some cases, traditional mechanisms and institutions are now serving as models for contemporary facilities. As a case in point, Roberts, in the essay "Object, Subject, Practitioner: Native Americans and Cultural Institutions" (1994), describes how the Yup'ik in south-western Alaska were developing a cultural center in conjunction with a Council of Elders. The new cultural center is modeled on the traditional community house or *gasgig* with adaptations to its contemporary context.

> The elders liken the organization's function to the gasgig, or community house, which was the place in other times where young people acquired the skills they needed in the lifeways of the Yup'ik. The operational structures and models that are being examined for the new cultural association are a hybrid of traditional social structures and contemporary business structure. The organization will meet legal criteria for arts funding, but will be uniquely Yup'ik.
>
> (1994:28)

Roberts further explains that "native peoples believe the old ones know how to care for objects made from natural materials, but these techniques do not always conform to 'museum standards'" (1994:29).[14]

One of the distinguishing characteristics of tribal museums and cultural centers is their approach to the "ownership" of the objects in their collections as well

107

as to their access, use, and curation. At the Hoopa Tribal Museum in California, two-thirds of the museum's collection was acquired through donations from families living on the Hoopa Valley Indian Reservation. However, objects are not "owned" by the museum, in the conventional sense of the term, but are loaned to the museum on a long-term basis. According to Lee Davis, an anthropologist who has worked with the Hoopa for several decades, family members donated objects to the museum

> because the museum is better protected than their homes against theft and fire, because their materials can be properly handled and repaired by the museum staff, because family members are able to take the materials out of the museum to use in cultural activities, and because people are proud to display their family heritage at the tribal cultural center.
>
> (1989:6)

Davis states that the museum's relationship with its donors is modeled after the traditional Hoopa way in which regalia and heirlooms are kept together under the care of a family "curator." This curator is responsible for keeping the materials in good repair, attends to the spiritual needs of the items and brings the objects out to dance during ceremonies. Family collections are also displayed together in the museum exhibits.[15]

Davis also points out how the materials in the museum constitute "Indian wealth." Ownership or curatorship of such wealth is a responsibility replete with supernatural power and danger. For this reason, the director of the Hoopa Museum must be a man, just as the traditional keepers of family regalia are men (Davis 1989:7).[16]

Important to the work of tribal museums and cultural centers is the documentation of traditional knowledge, especially that of elders. However, tribes want to design their cultural preservation programs in ways that permit the continuance of traditional methods of managing information, which again, may not adhere to professional museum or scholarly standards. Certainly, as Roberts writes:

> The American obsession with the right of access to information does not always translate into native culture, in which information access is based on the individual's right to know. Some information is available only after initiation into specific cultural or religious societies.
>
> (1994:29)

The Makah Cultural and Research Center (MCRC) in Neah Bay, Washington state provides an example of how some tribes are creating information management systems that reflect traditional hierarchical social structures. The Center contains tribal archives, which hold recordings of Makah oral traditions. However, unlike most non-Indian archives, the recordings are not available to the general public, researchers, or even certain tribal members unless the contributing tribal elder expressly gives permission.

> This is because in the traditional information management system of the Makah Nation, different kinds of knowledge are the property of particular

age, sex, and kin groups. The Center reasons that if they are truly to preserve Makah oral tradition, they must also preserve the cultural traditions by which it is transmitted.

(Parker 1990:53)

Ann Renker, Executive Director of the MCRC, explains that although this policy runs against the grain of professional societies like the Society of American Archivists and American Association of Museums, it has been instituted "to protect the ancestral information management system" of the Makah (quoted in Simpson 1996:77).

The MCRC has also established a "tribal-appropriate collections management system" that merges tribal values and concerns with the management of collections. The MCRC was established in 1979 on the basis of over 55,000 well-preserved artifacts recovered from the Ozette archeological site. The site contained four houses that had been buried by a mudslide over 300 years earlier. The Ozette collection was originally organized for archeological research purposes according to functional and technological categories. However, in preparation for the installation of the Ozette collection in a newly constructed curatorial facility, the collections staff instituted a new management system that better reflected traditional property rights and sanctions concerning the handling of certain items. For example, each of the Ozette houses represented a family or household unit whose property belonged to its occupants. Consequently, the staff began separating and storing the Ozette artifacts not only by type, but also by the household from which they were recovered. The staff also imposed gender restrictions in collections management.

> In traditional Makah society, certain restrictions based on gender were applied to the handling of some tools; whaling gear, for example, could not be touched or handled by women. Because such values were traditionally associated with the Ozette artifacts and are still held to some degree in the Makah community, the shelves containing such artifacts are flagged with a symbol indicating a gender restriction. These restrictions apply to staff, researchers, and visitors alike.

(Mauger and Bowechop n.d.: 4)[17]

One of the primary missions of the Center is to support and preserve the use of the Makah language. Consequently, the staff began labeling artifacts in both English and Makah, and classifying them according to their Makah roots and/or suffixes. In Makah, for example, containers are indicated by the suffix /sac/. Bentwood boxes, however, lack this suffix despite the fact that they functioned as containers. Their Makah name, rather, refers to the unique woodworking technique of kerfing and bent corners. Because the boxes lacked the container suffix /sac/, they were classified according to their technology rather than function and are stored separate from containers.

> Physically storing and labeling the Ozette collection according to Makah language encourages analysis of the cultural meanings and affinities between artifacts in the collection and provides insights into both Makah

language and thought. The MCRC collections management system, then, is not only an organizing device for accessing information and artifacts, but a tool for reflecting, understanding, and preserving the cognitive system within which the artifacts were produced and used.

(Mauger and Bowechop n.d.:5)

At the Ned Hatathli Cultural Center Museum on the Navajo reservation, Navajo and non-Navajo methods of historical interpretation and communication are used in the museum's exhibitions. Although the museum is open to the general public, it serves a predominantly Navajo audience (80–90 percent) and caters primarily to its needs. For example, one of the museum's exhibits is devoted to Navajo history, and both Navajo and non-Navajo interpretations of the origins of the Navajo people are used in the exhibit. Murals depict scenes of the Navajo creation story, but are displayed without written labels or interpretative text. This technique reflects the Navajo tradition of oral history and the primary function of the museum, i.e. the education of the younger generations in Navajo history and culture. Written words are not necessary because the Creation story is a familiar and relevant part of Navajo life (Simpson 1996:162). Without previous knowledge of Navajo concepts of creation, the museum's exhibits are not fully understandable. "Their meaning is imbedded in cultural coded imagery inaccessible, on all but the most superficial level, to the uninformed outsider" (Simpson 1996:163).

The Ned Hatathli Cultural Center Museum also loans objects from its collection, such as medicine bundles, for use in religious and healing ceremonies. The museum has accumulated a large collection of Navajo medicine bundles as a result of a successful campaign to repatriate Navajo religious paraphernalia. Because the bundles are still used as part of current healthcare practices the museum has developed a lending system whereby medicine men can borrow bundles for use in ceremonies. Medicine bundles, in Navajo tradition, are powerful, religious objects, which, when used by qualified men and women, are effective instruments for healing. However, due to their sacred and powerful nature, access to and use of medicine bundles is restricted. They are also not exhibited in the museum. According to Harry Walters, a curator at the museum:

> The medicine bundles . . . are living things, which should not be kept locked up as they need to breathe. In early spring when the vegetation starts growing, they are opened, then a blessing is performed in the autumn at the harvest. When they are used in ceremonies, the medicine bundles are restored and regenerated; their continued use is, therefore, a part of their necessary conservation as well as facilitating the continuation of Navajo traditional practices.

(quoted in Simpson 1996:163)

Although tribal museums and cultural centers are concerned with developing approaches to cultural heritage preservation that are consistent with tribal traditions, many also recognize the value of gaining professional museum training. At the same time, tribal curators may also be obliged to receive training from tribal experts in order to learn the appropriate traditional methods used to care for and handle various kinds of objects (Parker 1990:39). Consequently, tribal museums are selecting those aspects of professional museum practice that best suit their needs and purposes. Today, throughout the United States there are a number of museum studies programs that offer special courses and training programs specifically designed for Native American curators and staff, such as the Smithsonian Institution's American Indian Museum Studies Program (AIMS). According to the program's website, AIMS "responds to the training needs of Native Americans working in tribal museums and American Indian cultural centers. Through workshops, publications, and consultations, the AIMS program assists Native Americans in the continuation and interpretation of tribal cultures as they define them." Workshops and seminars held throughout the United States and Canada create forums for dialogue and the exchange of information among Native museum professionals, the Smithsonian and larger museum community. The American Indian Museum Studies Program was initially funded through the NMAI Act.[18]

Tribal museums and cultural centers can also seek advice and assistance from the National Museum of the American Indian. An essential element behind the concept of the NMAI is to extend its activities and "community" beyond its facilities in Washington, New York, and Maryland and link them to tribal museums and other Native organizations throughout the Americas. This decentralization effort has been called the "Fourth Museum," and is designed to help ensure that distant or isolated Native communities have access to resources, programs, collections, and exhibitions at the NMAI (see Barreiro 1994, Simpson 1996). Internships are also available through the NMAI's Internship Program. The program is designed to create educational opportunities for Native students in museum practice. One of the primary goals of the program is to expand the pool of Native museum professionals. Since its inception in 1994, more than one hundred students have participated in the program. The Visiting Professional Program of the NMAI offers Native non-students working in museums access to the NMAI collections and resources. In addition to receiving further training in museum practice, program participants continue to serve as vital links between the NMAI and their communities.

The NMAI Act also provides funding for museum training through the Indian Museum Management Fellowship Program, which awards stipends for training in museum development and management. The NMAI Act also established the Tribal Museum Endowment Fund, which

> makes grants to Indian organizations, including Indian tribes, museums, cultural centers, educational institutions, libraries and archives, for renovation and repair of museum facilities and exhibition facilities to enable such organizations to exhibit objects and artifacts on loan from the collections of the Smithsonian Institution or from other sources.
>
> (NMAI Act reproduced in Bray 2001:229)

In 1989, prior to the passage of NAGPRA, Davis criticized the professional museum and scholarly community for not paying more attention to tribal museums. She wrote that tribal museums have valued non-Indian museums, but non-Indian museums have not valued tribal museums. "From a cultural perspective, this is morally wrong, but from the perspective of good scholarship this one-way flow of information is simply unproductive" (Davis 1989:9). Davis further argued that "by keeping Indian people out of the museum system, museums are keeping themselves away from the kinds of knowledge they already value" (1989:9).[19] Today the situation looks quite different, as mainstream and tribal museums continue to engage in greater dialogue and exchange. NAGPRA and other developments such as the creation of the National Museum of the American Indian have been a primary impetus for change, leading the museum and scholarly community in new directions.

Tribal museum curators, staff, and scholars are also increasingly joining the ranks of professional museum and academic associations, and are becoming regular participants in national conferences and forums, such as the American Association of Museums and American Anthropological Association. The increasing prominence of the Native voice in such forums is one of the most distinctive signs of changing times, and marks the emergence of what Richard West has called the "new inclusiveness" in research and scholarship on Native peoples.

In an article based on an address to the American Anthropological Association, West, the Director of the National Museum of the American Indian, outlined the museum's approach to research and scholarship. He emphasized how research and scholarship on Native peoples must be guided by principles of inclusiveness, or more specifically, multiple perspectives that include the voices of Native peoples. In the following statement West explains that non-Native scholars and researchers will not be excluded from the NMAI, but must keep in mind that "the rules of the road" have changed:

> I have no intention of imposing a new, reverse exclusivity to replace the old exclusivity that typified the museum community's frequently defensive attitude toward the participation of Indian America in its work. Quite the contrary, our purpose is to expand the circle of research rather than contract it . . . But I also want to be candid in stating that *the rules of the road have changed* [emphasis added]. So yes, our research agenda will reflect directly the stake of Native communities in what we do and their active participation in the establishment of that agenda. And yes, Native peoples will be entitled to call upon the research resources and programs of the National Museum of the American Indian in the direct support of their efforts to preserve culture.
>
> (1993:7)

Indeed, "the rules of the road" have changed dramatically. NAGPRA and other developments have shifted the grounds on which mainstream museums and the discipline of anthropology have solidly stood. They have called into question the fundamental purposes behind the museum and its practices, challenging some of its most entrenched assumptions about collections, curation, and preservation. Museologists and anthropologists have had to rethink the basic premises on which their work is founded and the interests it serves. An ideology that justified the collection, study, and preservation of collections for the sake of an abstract *humanity*, is giving way to more thoughtful consideration of how the museological and anthropological enterprise affects actual *humans* and their lives.

While museums and anthropology cannot be held wholly responsible for the historical repression of Native peoples, they can be, nevertheless, accused of a certain complicity as institutions that reflect and reinforce the dominant values of a society. As many have pointed out, museums and anthropology did benefit from earlier state policies designed to eradicate Native cultures or assimilate Native peoples into the wider society. In this respect, museums and anthropology have been part of larger forces that have worked to dehumanize Native peoples. Subsequently, the debates over repatriation and indigenous peoples' human and cultural rights have brought to light one of anthropology's greatest ironies: that a science dedicated to the study of humans also, at times throughout its history, has had its dehumanizing elements. As Suzan Shown Harjo (Cheyenne and Hodulgee Muscogee) succinctly puts it:

> The major policy achievement and the hardest-fought battle in the development of repatriation laws has been the humanization of Native Peoples – the legal recognition that we, too, have the human right to get buried and stay buried, to recover our people and property from those who want to own them, to worship in the manner and with the objects of our choosing.
>
> (Harjo 1996:3)

Indeed, in their struggles for cultural restitution, Native Americans and other indigenous peoples are reclaiming the spirit of culture, not only for themselves but for us all, by helping move a seemingly dispassionate science and society toward a renewed sense of humanity.

5

Museums, culture, and development

In the previous two chapters, I demonstrated how indigenous communities are using museums and cultural centers to help reclaim and preserve their cultural heritage. Often times, these museums build upon earlier traditions concerned with the protection and transmission of culture. Another important distinguishing feature of these museums is how they are expanding conventional museum functions to encompass overall community development. In many cases, the goal is to maintain the integrity of the community as a whole and improve social and economic conditions through a culture-based approach to community development.

This integrated, holistic approach is in keeping with movements in the field of international development, which have become increasingly concerned with the "cultural dimension of development." Several decades of development work have shown that cultural factors can be a critical determinant in whether or not a project succeeds or fails. Since culture, in all its varied forms, contributes to the construction of what people value, it also determines, to a certain degree, how and toward what goals they will direct their energy. Consequently, development workers are beginning to pay more attention to the relationship between culture and development, and how cultural resources, such as museums, can be used to promote community development. Today, it is not unusual to find that plans for the creation of a museum or cultural center are the centerpiece of a community development project.

In this chapter, I discuss the growing importance of culture-based approaches to community development and specifically, the role museums and cultural work can play in the process. I draw on insights gained from my experience as a consultant to the World Wide Fund for Nature (or World Wildlife Fund [WWF]) Indonesia Programme on the development of a community-based museum program in East Kalimantan. The program, known as the Kayan Mentarang People's Museum Development Program, was directed toward both environmental and cultural conservation. I show how this type of cultural work can strengthen conservation and development efforts by creating what Charles Kleymeyer calls "cultural energy" in a community. According to Kleymeyer, cultural energy is a force that is generated through cultural activities, which in turn, can be harnessed to bolster a community's sense of pride, self-respect, and identity, giving people renewed energy and motivation to take on the challenges faced in their lives (Kleymeyer 1994b). "Cultural energy is a powerful force in the creation and reinforcement of group solidarity, organizational efficacy, participation, and volunteer spirit – all of which are basic ingredients of successful grassroots development initiatives" (Kleymeyer quoted in Healy 1994:17).

In describing the program, I concentrate on methodological concerns and make suggestions about how projects of this nature may be approached and carried out. Of critical concern is the role of "outside" consultants, project designers, and sponsors in conceptualizing and planning projects, in addition to the importance of "participatory approaches." This "people-centered" approach emerged in the 1970s via non-governmental and grass-roots organizations in response to "top-down" development patterns, which were largely controlled by the elite. In contrast, participation is a "bottom-up" approach that ideally involves the intended beneficiaries in all phases of a project, especially decision making. Field observations as well as analyses of specific projects have demonstrated that when people influence or control decisions that affect them, they have a greater stake in the outcome and will work harder to ensure a project's success. The approach is a means of empowering people to take control over their own course of development. Participation provides both a conceptual framework and body of techniques not only for facilitating the participatory process, but also for making seemingly alien institutions and practices more compatible to local contexts. Based on democratic principles, participatory approaches aim to bridge the gaps between outside professionals and local community members, suggesting that the knowledge and skills of local people hold as much value as those of "experts" (see Burkey 1993, Rahman 1993, World Bank 1996).

Although participatory approaches have been created for use predominantly in rural development projects such as healthcare provisioning, agriculture, and natural resource management, they are also applicable to museum development initiatives. As they apply to museum projects, participatory approaches encourage the active involvement of local people in all aspects of their planning, implementation, and management, building on people's own knowledge, experience, and resources (Kreps 1997).

My interest in participation and community-based museum development evolved out of my research on government-sponsored museum development in Indonesia (discussed in Chapter 2) and the disadvantages I saw in "top-down," centralized museum planning and development. Needless to say, this approach allowed little room for community participation. I also learned that when predetermined museum models are imposed on local communities, they are often seen as alien institutions, existing for outside interests and purposes. And furthermore, when museum development projects are directed by outside "experts" there is a tendency to reproduce western-style, professionally oriented museum models. In this chapter, I suggest that just as international development work has shown the need to use culturally and environmentally "appropriate technologies" in diverse settings, museum development projects should also be shaped to fit each community's needs and interests. In short, they should build on people's own concepts and systems of cultural heritage management.

In order to understand the broader implications of the role of museums in development, I begin the chapter with a discussion of the relationships between culture and development. This discussion provides a background for better understanding the significance of projects like the Kayan Mentarang People's Museum Development Program.

Culture and development

The term "development" carries different meanings for different people, but in the field of international development it is broadly defined as a means of improving the material and social conditions of a society through planned social change. Since the 1950s when development became a formal field of study and target of official state policy, particularly in post-colonial "developing nations," it has been defined primarily in material or economic terms. Dominated by macroeconomic approaches, development has been measured mostly through economic indicators such as gross national product, per capita income, and growth rates, to name a few. Cultural variables and the human dimensions of development were largely left out of development equations. In fact, culture, especially "traditional" culture, was generally seen as an obstacle to development, something to be overcome so the process of development and modernization could proceed unencumbered (see Dove 1988, Schech and Haggis 2000).

However, today theorists and practitioners alike recognize that development cannot simply be measured by or reduced to economic variables; that economic growth alone does not necessarily lead to the improvement of people's living conditions and their overall well-being. More and more, those working in international development are seeing that development is a profoundly cultural matter, in the sense that it is intertwined with and affects a people's whole way of life. "It is in this sense that all forms of development, including human development, ultimately are determined by cultural factors" (UNESCO 1995:24). In addition, because ignorance of cultural factors has often led to the failure of development projects, today, culture is more aptly seen as an asset or driving force behind development. For development to be socially and environmentally sustainable it must take into account and draw upon the values, traditions, and cultural resources of the people it is theoretically designed to serve (see UNESCO 1995 and 1996).

But merely taking the cultural dimension into account can relegate culture to a secondary role. Instead, culture should be seen as foundational to development and an essential point of reference by which all other factors are measured. This means that development cannot really be successful or sustainable without the recognition of culture's vitalizing force, since culture represents the totality of people's framework for living. A development strategy that incorporates the cultural dimension constitutes an integrated approach to development, which not only comprises concrete development actions in key areas such as education, communication, technology and science, healthcare, etc., but also seeks to utilize the creative energies of people.

One of the dominant features of conventional development paradigms has been the "transfer" of western models of development to developing areas. This approach has involved not only the transfer of technology, scientific know-how, and western-style institutions, but also the transfer of western cultural values. In effect, this style of development has worked to undermine other cultures' own technologies, knowledge systems, and institutions as well as their values and sense of identity. A culture-based approach to development counters the profoundly ethnocentric nature of earlier development models. It acknowledges that an external experience, technique, or model cannot be successfully integrated by mere adoption or reproduction, but needs to be reinterpreted or reinvented through the filter of a society's cultural identity and value system.

Healy refers to culture-based approaches to development as "ethnodevelopment," which "strategically places culture at the center of development planning" (1994:14). Local development projects that take this approach demonstrate how indigenous culture, in the form of technologies, knowledge, organizational skills, and talent, can be engaged for effective and sustainable development. It is a strategy for self-reliance and local empowerment. Ethnodevelopment shifts the focus of development thinking from the "macro" level, which assumed that western models of development were universally or generally applicable, to the "micro" level where development efforts are adapted to a particular community's own culture, needs, and circumstances. This type of development is generally pursued by alternative institutions, which are usually independent from top-down, politically driven government agencies. These include non-governmental organizations (NGOs), research institutions, and indigenous alliances. These alternative institutions have developed ways to restructure market relations, refocus educational programs, and increase indigenous self-management capacities and opportunities. They also draw on "cultural recovery and identity revalidation for socioeconomic development" (Healy 1994:15).

Culture-based approaches to development frequently promote the use of "appropriate technology," which has been defined as technology that is appropriate to a given situation and need. Appropriate technology uses mostly local or easily obtainable and inexpensive materials and skills to meet community needs (Ryan and Vivekananda 1993:20). It also has been described as a process that combines people's indigenous skills with modern knowledge to upgrade indigenous skills (Rahman 1993:129). Central to the concept of appropriate technology is that the technology must match both the user and the need in complexity and scale (Hazeltine and Bull 1999:3). Advocates of appropriate technology argue that if a new technology is introduced it should be related to existing technology because this is less disruptive to the local social structure and can be adapted to it more readily. "If a new technology is similar to the existing one, the user can adapt it most effectively to the local situation" (Hazeltine and Bull 1999:6). Appropriate technology by definition is small-scale,

117

and can foster self-reliance and responsibility because the people directly involved control it.

The appropriate technology movement is attributed to E.F. Schumacher, a British economist, who was highly critical of orthodox, western economic development thinking, which placed too much emphasis on "macro-level, rational decision-making with insufficient attention given to the human impact of change" (Schumacher quoted in Ryan and Vivekananda 1993:24). As an alternative, Schumacher proposed a fundamentally "humanistic change strategy" that entails a systematic study of more cost-effective ways of achieving acceptable societal goals with minimal means. In Schumacher's words, "Appropriate Technology is technology that is non-violent and would not undo the natural, cultural, economic, and ecological cohesion of rural societies" (quoted in Ryan and Vivekananda 1993:20).[1]

Appreciation of how important cultural factors are to development goes hand in hand with the realization that people's material well-being is also contingent on their emotional, psychological, and spiritual well-being. For several decades, social scientists have been assessing the "social costs" of development and now know that people's culture and a strong sense of cultural identity are vital to their well-being (Appell 1988). It has become evident that weakened identities and negative group image are obstacles to development. When people lack a sense of dignity, self-esteem, and respect, they can feel culturally and socially impoverished. As a result they can experience reduced motivation and energy, which can perpetuate their being disadvantaged in a material sense. As explained by David Mayberry-Lewis, Founder and President of Cultural Survival:

> People . . . cling to their cultures . . . because it is through them that they make sense of themselves. We know that when people are forced to give up their culture, or when they give it up too rapidly, the consequences are normally social breakdown accompanied by personal disorientation and despair. The attachment of people to their culture corresponds then, to a fundamental human need.

(1994:xiv)

In this respect, the right of people to determine their own course of development within the context of their own culture and on their own terms is a basic human right.

Because of the importance of culture to people's lives, cultural heritage should be seen as an essential element of development work. However, this does not mean that people's cultural traditions should be maintained in some static or pristine state, even if that were possible. Cultural traditions emerge and are maintained in a dynamic process of creative invention and reinvention as people borrow or adopt new cultural forms. The key issue is not whether a cultural form should change or be utilized to new ends, but who controls that process of change and utilization (Kleymeyer 1994a:325). Thus, conservation or preservation efforts must be coupled with cultural development, which can be defined as "harnessing and promoting all factors which enhance the cultural life of a local population in a geographical area" (Paulias 1991:6).

The idea of "harnessing" cultural resources for development projects is espoused by such bodies as the World Bank, the United Nations, and both governmental and non-governmental organizations. Acknowledging the importance of the cultural dimension of development, the United Nations Educational, Scientific, and Cultural Organization (UNESCO) declared 1988 to 1997 the International Decade for Cultural Development. As part of this initiative, the General Conference of UNESCO at its twenty-sixth session in 1991 adopted a resolution requesting the Director-General, in cooperation with the Secretary-General of the United Nations, to establish an independent World Commission on Culture and Development. The Commission included men and women from all regions of the world who represented diverse disciplines. The task of the Commission was to prepare a World Report on Culture and Development and make proposals for both urgent and long-term action to meet cultural needs in the context of development. The Commission began its work in 1993 and through a series of conferences and specially commissioned studies produced *Our Creative Diversity: The Report of the World Commission on Culture and Development* (1996). Culture, in the Report, is understood in the anthropological sense as the total and distinctive way of life of a people or society. The Report underscores the point that a purely economic approach to development or "development divorced from its human or cultural context is growth without a soul" and that "the ultimate aim of development is the universal physical, mental and social well-being of every human being" (UNESCO 1996:15, 16).

Among its many recommendations, the Report warns against taking an overly "instrumentalist" approach to the role of culture in development, or rather, using culture as a means to an end – in this case economic growth and development. Instead, "the role of culture is a desirable end in itself, giving meaning to existence" (UNESCO 1996:23). It also suggests that culture should not be given an "excessively conservationist" meaning, but should be seen as dynamic and generative. "Once we shift our attention from the purely instrumental view of culture to awarding it a constructive, constitutive and creative role, we have to see development in terms that include cultural growth" (UNESCO 1996:25).

The Commission's Report stresses the need to promote the ideas of "cultural freedom," "cultural rights," and "cultural democracy." Cultural freedom refers to "the right of a group of people to follow or adopt a way of life of their choice" (UNESCO 1996:25). Although this notion of cultural freedom emphasizes the collective cultural freedom of a group, it should also be understood as the protection of every individual within a group. "Cultural freedom properly interpreted is the condition for individual freedom to flourish" (UNESCO 1996:26). The notion of cultural freedom is linked to the idea of cultural rights, which are now widely recognized as deserving the same protection as human rights. Cultural rights are fundamental to achieving cultural democracy. "The core cultural right is that of each person to participate fully in cultural life" (UNESCO 1996:240).

In general, the Report acknowledges the critical importance of cultural diversity as a source of creativity and imagination, fundamental to human survival and

119

well-being. Yet respect for diversity must be coupled with a global ethics that recognizes a core set of shared ethical values and principles. A global ethics is necessary in order to address shared problems and issues. The Report points out that throughout human history, people have survived as a result of cooperation and interdependence, despite their cultural differences, and respect and tolerance of cultural diversity should continue to be promoted.

> Ever since the emergence of Homo Sapiens, human groups have been able to exchange discoveries and innovations, institutional experiences and knowledge. Societies have evolved through co-operation of peoples with contrasting cultures and it is important to promote cultural conviviality through new socio-political agreements that should be negotiated in the framework of global ethics.
>
> (UNESCO 1996:34)

Diversity need not be sacrificed in the search for universal values and ethics. In fact, diversity is the source of such values and ethics. Thus, cultural preservation, through various means, is inherently dedicated to the protection of cultural diversity.

Museums and development

The international professional museum community has also recognized the importance of the cultural dimension of development. On September 5, 1989 the sixteenth General Assembly of the International Council of Museums passed the following Resolution titled "Cultural Dimension of Development." The Resolution acknowledged the significant role culture and museums play in the development process, but also how they are generally a low priority on development agendas.

> Noting that existing and new museums and related institutions in many countries are not accorded their due priority especially in the allocation of funds, the 16th General Assembly of the International Council of Museums meeting in The Hague, The Netherlands, on 5 September 1989, strongly urges all governments, especially those providing development assistance, to give a much higher priority to the cultural dimension of development, in particular to existing and new museums and related institutions.
>
> (Ganslmayr 1990:2)

Museums in developing areas are said to differ from their counterparts in the "developed" world most significantly in their purposes. In many cases, they are seen as instruments of social change and part of the overall development of a society or nation (van Mensch 1988:183). While museums in developing areas still perform conventional museum functions of collection, preservation, display, research, and education, they also work to address and help find solutions to social and economic problems. For example, in North Africa, community-based museums have been used to help combat the devastating environmental, economic, and cultural effects of drought and desertification through the use of displays introducing villagers to new technologies and techniques of resource management (Konare 1985, Vuilleumier 1983). In Mexico, community museums have contributed to indigenous communities' struggles for self-determination and control over their own cultural and economic resources (Erikson 1996). In Irian Jaya, Indonesia, the only library available to people in a remote area is housed in a museum (Kreps 1991). In Colombia, South America, museums have been used to revive and preserve craft traditions that contribute to the socio-economic well-being of traditional societies (Goff 1994). In these contexts, the traditional role of the museum in society is being redefined, restructured, and diversified to address people's specific development needs.

But museums in developing areas have faced a number of challenges in their efforts to contribute to the development process, not in the least of which has been a serious lack of funding, resources, and trained staff. One of their biggest challenges, however, has been overcoming the museum's image (generally held over from colonial era style museums) as a storehouse of relics concerned with the past and an elitist institution dedicated to narrow scholarly interests (see Eoe 1991, Kaplan 1994b, Koffi 1995, Konare 1983 and 1995, Munjeri 1991). Seen from this perspective, museums are luxuries and resources on which government officials, development planners, and aid agencies have been reluctant to spend limited development funds. In the words of Soroi Eoe, Director of the National Museum òf Papua New Guinea: "Why should funds be given to museums if they do not function in the mainstream of the development process?" (1991:2). Museums in developing areas have had to dispel this image and show how museums can be instrumental to development. The museum

> must come down off its pedestal and not only preserve the relics of the past but play an active part in the community, helping people to have more control over their lives . . . It is their [museums'] job to integrate the development strategy into the socio-cultural context.
>
> (Vuilleumier 1983:94–95)

Ardouin and Arinze argue that in development work museums should not limit themselves to their conventional areas of concern. Rather, they should also become involved in other areas critical to the development of society, such as public health problems, the use of new technologies and information, environmental concerns, and the management of natural resources. The museum has a crucial role to play in development, not only as a means of cultural heritage preservation, but also as a source of information and as an instrument of education (Ardouin and Arinze 1995).

Eoe has suggested that museums can also play a critical role in illuminating the cultural implications of development.

> Museums should also serve as development catalysts by assisting governments to forge their development projects in ways that better serve the people of both today and tomorrow. Their privileged view of certain misunderstood development issues should be brought to the attention of the people likely to be affected by development projects.
>
> (1991:3)

121

Eoe goes on to say that

> what is advocated is that museums should play a vigorous part in promoting careful planning and well-designed projects. Their function should be to present factual information on the cultural implications and especially possible penalties of development plans, whether they are the erosion of living cultures or the destruction of the material culture of the past. Indeed, everyone will benefit – the museums, government and people – from such a role.
>
> (1991:3)

The challenge has been to make museums an integral part of people's lives so the museum might better serve in the development process. An important movement in this direction has been the development of the "decentralized museum" concept that began to emerge throughout the world in the 1960s and 1970s. Variants of the concept are the neighborhood museum, ecomuseum, integrated museum, and community museum (see Davis 1999). Fundamental to all of these types of museum is the assumption that the museum should be in service to society and has a primarily social role.

> The decentralized museum places itself at the service of the community in which it is established. Its task is no longer to transmit a universal message to an undefined audience, but to put the local population in contact with their own history, their own traditions, their own values, etc. Through its activities the museum contributes to the community's awareness of its own identity – an identity that has been more or less denied for historical, social, racial or other reasons, or disrupted by centralization, urbanization, etc.
>
> (Maure quoted in van Mensch 1988:183)

Of particular significance is the growth and spread of the ecomuseum idea, which has become particularly popular in developing areas because of its holistic approach to community development and cultural heritage preservation. It is a bottom-up and culture-based approach that places community participation and self-actualization at the core of its mission. It is a dynamic approach to museums and heritage preservation that looks forward rather than just backward. The history of the ecomuseum concept is closely linked to the development of the new museology movement (discussed in Chapter 1). Both the new museology and ecomuseum grew out of a widespread dismay within the museum profession regarding the inability of museums to deal with contemporary social, cultural, environmental, political, and economic changes that confronted people in the post-World War II years (Davis 1999:55, Vergo 1989).

The ecomuseum concept originated in France in the 1970s as part of a movement to decentralize museums and develop museums in historically and environmentally unique regions. Georges Henri Riviere, a French museologist, who emphasized the importance of place, is considered the founding father of the concept. The ecomuseum was created at a time when environmentalism was achieving greater prominence in Europe and was symptomatic of the impact of the green movement throughout society (Davis 1999:59). Subsequently, the ecomuseum idea has been experimented with in a variety of national and cultural settings. Davis estimates that as of 1998, there were some 166 eco-museums in twenty-five countries (1999:76).

The ecomuseum is designed to support the economic vitality of a community and is envisioned as an agent for managing change that links education and culture. It is also seen as a means of empowering a given population through the documentation and preservation of an area's historical, natural, and cultural heritage. The approach is both a framework for examining the nature and structure of cultural institutions and a process for democratizing them. Although the ecomuseum idea is based on a particular set of principles and approaches, one of its unique features is that there is no single definition or model of an eco-museum. Rather, an ecomuseum has "limitless diversity" and can be anything local people or museum professionals want it to be (Davis 1999:68). It is a process whereby people define the museum's meaning and purpose in the process of defining themselves (Fuller 1992). The key concept behind the ecomuseum is creating awareness of the relationships among community, identity, and space (also defined as territory or environment).

Ecomuseums have been described as community learning centers that function to connect the past with the present as a strategy to deal with the future needs of a society. Such a museum begins with what is known by a community of people, or rather, their collective memory, and investigates what events and objects are linked to this memory. The ecomuseum's mission is to:

> develop community autonomy and identity. Rather than serving as a storehouse or temple, both of which isolate objects from ordinary people and require professional assistance for access and understanding, an ecomuseum recognizes the importance of culture in the development of self-identity and its role in helping a community adjust to rapid change. The ecomuseum thus becomes a tool for the economic, social and political growth and development of a society from which it springs.
>
> (Fuller 1992:328)

Ecomuseums differ significantly from conventional museums in their physical forms and collection philosophy. An ecomuseum is defined by the geographical area or audience that it serves, and is not necessarily confined to a single building. Collections are organized around the community's interrelationships with its culture and natural environment and reflect what is important to that community. In addition to objects, collections may consist of photographs, documents, sites, traditional ceremonies, oral histories, flora and fauna, and so forth. Commenting on the ecomuseum's breadth of coverage, van Mensch observed: "It has become increasingly difficult to discern where the museum stops and the real world starts" (van Mensch quoted in Davis 1999:68).

Nancy Fuller, of the Smithsonian Institution Center for Education and Museum Studies, is a leading proponent of the ecomuseum idea and has worked with a number of Native American communities in adapting the concept to their particular needs and purposes. In the essay "The Museum as a Vehicle for

Empowerment: The Ak-Chin Indian Community Ecomuseum Project" (1992), Fuller describes the important role the Ak-Chin Ecomuseum has played in community problem solving. She writes that inherent to the operation of an ecomuseum is a process that teaches people how to investigate an issue and speak out about it. An ecomuseum can provide a place in which to hold discussions and create exhibitions about a problem. It also gives community members actual practice in asking questions, researching facts, communicating ideas, defending positions, and coming to new understandings in ways that are culturally appropriate (1992:332). Thus, the ecomuseum can be a forum for community action. The educational process that takes place in an ecomuseum is "learning through participation," "learning through experience," and "learning through action." The goal is to place a population in the position to answer questions such as where do we come from? Who are we? Where do we want to go? In this respect, an ecomuseum can be a tool for self-determination. According to Rivard, another well-known advocate of the ecomuseum concept, ecomuseums can be a "participatory structure" and "participation of the population is a crucial element of ecomuseology" (Rivard 1984:46).

The Kayan Mentarang People's Museum Development Program[2]

The Kayan Mentarang People's Museum Development Program drew on the principles and philosophies behind the ecomuseum concept as well as those of culture-based approaches to community development. It also grew out of a new paradigm of environmental conservation, which integrates both environmental and cultural conservation into community development. Conventional approaches to conservation, which separated "nature" from "culture" and placed both in opposition to development, are no longer seen as viable. "The connection between culture and development, between culture and nature, and between development and conservation are key to understanding and preserving the natural world today" (Cohn 1988:450, also see Western *et al.* 1994).

It has now become clear that, in many cases, environmental conservation is contingent on the conservation of local cultural resources, especially the knowledge and experiences of people who have lived in a particular ecosystem for generations. Because of their long-standing relationship to and dependence on natural resources, indigenous people often have knowledge and expertise that are missing in approaches to conservation based on western scientific paradigms. Consequently, today, many conservationists are advocating the use of local culture to promote conservation, exploring ways in which cultural resources such as indigenous knowledge and systems of natural resource management can be incorporated into both development and conservation efforts. Concurrent with these views is the movement for community-based conservation, which is dedicated to enlisting the participation of local people to work directly on conservation projects. The goal of community-based conservation is not only to protect natural resources, but also to serve the needs of local communities. "Community-based conservation includes natural resources or biodiversity protection by, for, and with the local community . . . [The] agenda is to regain control over natural resources and, through conservation practices, provide their 'local communities' economic well being" (Western *et al.* 1994:7).

The museum program was one component of the World Wide Fund for Nature (or WWF) Indonesia Programme's Kayan Mentarang Culture and Conservation Project. The project, initiated in 1990, was a collaborative effort on the part of WWF and several Indonesian government agencies. It its initial stage, the project consisted of a series of field studies that examined indigenous systems of land tenure, language, and oral history, and the people's relationships to and use of natural resources. The long-term goal of the project was the development of a conservation management plan for the 1.6 million-hectare Kayan Mentarang National Park located on the border of East Kalimantan, Indonesia and the Malaysian state of Sarawak. The park is the largest block of protected rain forest in Borneo and one of the largest in all Southeast Asia. Central to the project was the participation of local communities in the design and implementation of the park's conservation management plan.

The museum program was proposed in 1995 as part of the Kayan Mentarang Culture and Conservation Project's effort to help preserve the cultural heritage of indigenous people living in the Kayan Mentarang region. A basic tenet of the program was that environmental conservation is inseparable from cultural conservation. The goal of the museum program was to establish community-based museums, or centers for nature and culture, in villages in and adjacent to the Kayan Mentarang National Park. The museums were envisioned as multi-purpose facilities for community education on environmental issues as well as cultural centers devoted to the documentation and preservation of local cultural traditions such as the visual and performing arts, oratory, and customary law.

The Kayan Mentarang region is home to approximately 10,000 Dayaks (see Chapter 2) representing more than a dozen different ethnolinguistic groups. They live in villages averaging in size from 200 to 500 people along the region's many rivers and tributaries. About half are shifting cultivators (predominantly the Kenyah and Kayan) while the rest (Lun Dayeh and Lun Bawang) practice wet-rice cultivation. Most still depend on hunting, fishing, and gathering wild plants to supplement subsistence agriculture. Dayaks also collect forest products such as resins, rattan, wild honey, and *gaharu* (sandalwood) for commercial trade. Thus, Dayaks are highly dependent on the land and its resources for their livelihood.

In 1996, I was hired as a consultant to WWF to carry out a study on the feasibility of setting up the People's Museum Development Program. The study consisted of two field surveys, funded by the WWF Indonesia Programme and the Ford Foundation. The first survey was conducted from July to August 1996 and involved visits to eight villages in the Kayan Mentarang region. The objectives of the survey were to:

- become familiar with the geography, cultures, and people of the targeted area;
- meet with community members to discuss their needs and concerns regarding cultural and environmental conservation issues;
- gather information on existing cultural resources, activities, and facilities.

A primary objective of the first survey was to assess the potential of different communities for creating a museum or cultural center, and then select one community for a pilot project.

Prior to entering the field, I designed a research instrument in collaboration with Kayan Mentarang staff members for organizing and recording field data and for guiding observations. The research instrument was also used to create a socio-economic profile of each community and to make cultural inventories of both tangible and intangible cultural resources. The primary means of collecting data, however, was through informal interviews with community members. Interviews were largely carried out in Bahasa Indonesian (the national language of Indonesia). Over the course of the surveys, I traveled with WWF field staff who served as research assistants, guides, and translators when local languages were used. As natives of the region, field staff also served as informants on local culture.

During the first survey, I interviewed forty-eight individuals who represented various age groups and sectors of society, for example, village leaders, school-teachers, traders, farmers, and members of church and youth groups. Nearly all those interviewed expressed concern over the loss of their traditional culture and lamented the fact that the knowledge and skills related to certain cultural expressions such as dance, music, painting and carving, oratory, and *adat* (customary law and traditions) were not being passed on to the younger generation. Many thought measures should be taken to preserve these aspects of their culture, but few could articulate what these measures might be. Most responded positively to the idea of creating a museum or cultural center in their community as a step toward cultural conservation. However, many also believed their communities lacked the resources and expertise to undertake such a project. In one case, village leaders expressed reservations on the grounds that there were few individuals in the village who possessed the level of education, aptitude, or leisure time to work in a center or museum.

Out of the eight villages I visited only one, Pulau Sapi located on the Mentarang River, already had a facility specifically devoted to cultural activities and cultural heritage preservation. This facility consisted of a newly constructed *rumah adat* (traditional house) fashioned after a Lun Dayeh Dayak longhouse. According to community leaders, the creation of the *rumah adat* was a local initiative and a reflection of elder community members' concern for the preservation of Lun Dayeh traditional culture. Although the community received financial help from the provincial government, support for the building's construction came primarily from local people who donated building materials and labor. The *rumah adat*, at the time of the survey, functioned mostly as a meeting place for special cultural events and activities. Plans were being made, however, for the eight apartments inside the longhouse, including the creation of a small museum as well as rooms that could accommodate tourists. Pulau Sapi was exceptional, within the context of the survey, in the sense that community members (or at least those in influential positions) not only had a high degree of self-awareness regarding the value of their cultural heritage, but also had taken steps to preserve it.

While much traditional culture has been "lost" or is in a state of "decline," according to many interviewed, I observed that much also remained. Of particular importance is the concept of *adat* and especially *hukum adat*, or customary law. Whittier, an anthropologist who conducted field research in the region in the early 1970s, wrote that while the Kenyah concept of *adat* is frequently translated as "custom" or "customary law," its meaning is actually much broader.

> *Adat* and its expression through ritual provides the template for all of Kenyah social organization . . . It includes the whole notion of the proper order and harmony of the cosmos and behavior of its components. *Adat* pertains not just to those aspects of religious life Westerners choose to call 'religion' or 'law,' it underlies all aspects of Kenyah life including relations to other humans as well as the natural and supernatural world. When everything is acting according to its proper *adat* there is harmony and balance. Wrong action, then, leads to imbalance and sickness, death, crop failure and so on. The imbalance may occur in the world of men in which case redress may take the form of a fine or it may occur against the supernatural, in which case a ritual may be required as well.
>
> (1978:117)

At the time of Whittier's writing, Christianity had largely replaced the religious dimensions of *adat*. Its status as a traditional legal system was also diminishing in response to continuing pressure from the government to make *adat* conform to the state ideology and national law (Whittier 1978:118). However, despite these changes, I found that *hukum adat* continued to play a significant role in village society, especially regarding rights and responsibilities related to the use of certain natural resources. A concern for the continued strength and relevance of *hukum adat* was, for instance, demonstrated in 1994 when representatives from nine villages met to document and standardize customary law for the region. Although some see the standardization of *hukum adat* as one more step toward the homogenization and bureaucratization of a diverse cultural form (Sellato n.d.), the fact that customary laws were under discussion and revision exemplified their salience as an adaptive and dynamic cultural form. The fact that most villages still had a *kepala adat* (head of customary law) and a *lembaga adat* (*adat* council) was further evidence of its continued strength and relevance. In many Dayak communities, *adat* is interpreted as traditional or local culture. Therefore, the documentation of *adat* and its ongoing use can be seen as one form of cultural preservation.

Throughout the survey, I encountered many people who lamented the decline in traditional arts, especially the particularly striking and unique styles of Kenyah and Kayan carving and painting (see Sellato 1989 for examples). When I asked what they saw as the source of the decline few could point to any one cause. Most attributed the decline to general forces of culture change, or rather, people's conversion to Christianity, new economic pressures, a break down in or weakening of traditional social structure,[3] and so forth. Thus, many of the motivations for artistic production such as religious beliefs and practices as well as the traditional function of art objects as status markers, no longer exist or are waning in importance (Sellato 1989:24).

127

Figure 5.1 Carved gateway with depictions of dragon jar and the hornbill bird in the village of Long Loreh, East Kalimantan. Photograph by Christina Kreps, 1996.

While carving and painting were conspicuously absent in most of the communities I visited, the village of Long Loreh on the upper Malinau River exhibited an abundance of painting and carving. A large percentage of houses and public structures in the village were decorated with traditional-style carving and painting. When I asked one villager what accounted for this quantity of artistic output, he replied that it was because Long Loreh had participated in the government-sponsored *Lomba Desa*, or village beautification contest in which communities compete for being the most attractive, clean, and orderly. That year, Long Loreh took first place on the district level and second on the provincial. The *Lomba Desa* is one example of how the Indonesian government, through sponsored cultural programs and activities, is becoming the primary impetus behind the production of "traditional" arts (see Acciaioli 1985, Errington 1994 and 1998, Pemberton 1994, Yampolsky 1995).

To summarize the findings of the first survey, I found that people were concerned about cultural preservation issues, even though the level of concern varied from community to community as well as within each community. Not surprisingly, it was the more formally educated, cosmopolitan community members such as schoolteachers, government officials, and village leaders who had a heightened awareness regarding the implications of cultural loss and the value of preservation efforts. I also learned that the majority of cultural activities in villages were government sponsored. These primarily included programs, such as the *Lomba*

Desa, and those that promoted traditional dance and music groups and their participation in regional and national festivals. Most of the people I interviewed were receptive to the idea of creating a cultural center or museum in their community, even though few were familiar with the museum concept or had actually visited a museum. For the most part, the modern museum concept appeared to be a foreign idea to the majority of people I spoke with throughout the survey.

The pilot project and planning process

Based on recommendations from WWF staff and findings from the first survey, the village of Long Pujungan was selected for a second, follow-up survey and site for a possible pilot project (see location on map, Figure 2.2, p. 27). This second survey took place from September to October 1997. Long Pujungan was chosen because the village is located near the border of the Kayan Mentarang National Park, is the seat of the district government, and because community members were well acquainted with WWF since it had been active in the region since 1990. WWF had already established a field post in the village, allowing for more direct support of a potential museum project.

The population of Long Pujungan numbers around 430 and is predominantly composed of Kenyah Dayaks. As the administrative center of the district, the village is also home to a number of civil servants from other Indonesian islands. The village is located at the confluence of the Pujungan and Bahau rivers and can be reached only by small aircraft or boat. During the dry season when the rivers are low, transportation on the rivers slows down. This means supplies such as commercial foodstuffs, fuel, and other goods may diminish in supply until boats can make it up river. Long Pujungan lacked basic services of potable water, a sanitation system, and electricity. A few shops and individual homes were supplied with electricity from privately owned diesel-fueled generators. Despite the limited supply of electricity, several families owned televisions linked to satellite receivers. Television viewing was a common activity at night, providing villagers with an external source of entertainment, information, and cultural influences.

The majority of people in Long Pujungan are Christians, with the exception of a few Muslim families who had moved to the village from Java and Sulawesi. Two Protestant churches and one mosque are located in the village and religious activities tend to be the focus of community life. Little remains of the traditional religion and ritual life owing to the widespread conversion to Christianity beginning in the 1940s.

Unlike some Kenyah Dayak villages, Long Pujungan exhibited few visible signs of traditional artistic or cultural expression. In former times, the Kenyah of Long Pujungan lived in longhouses, but today there are no longhouses in the village and little evidence of the impressive painting and carving that adorned them. Except for the façade of the village meeting house (*balai desa*) and district government office (*kantor camat*), which are both government buildings, I saw

129

very little traditional-style painting or carving (*ukiran*). Family rice barns (*lumbung*) as well as gravesites were also devoid of the elaborate carving and painting for which the Kenyah are well known. In discussions with community members, I was told that there are gifted painters and carvers in the village, but little ukiran is done nowadays because artists need to be paid for their work and few, outside of government agencies, can afford this luxury.

Some forms of traditional handicrafts are still produced in Long Pujungan, for example, beaded baby carriers for which the Kenyah are also famous (see Figure 3.1) as well as some forms of basketry and mat making. Rattan carrying baskets and floor mats are made primarily for local consumption although some women make mats for sale or trade. Today, most families use *karpet*, or linoleum, as a floor covering since it can be less expensive than handmade rattan mats.

Traditional music and dance performances largely take place within the context of government-sponsored events or celebrations such as national and religious holidays, festivals, and on other formal occasions. Although traditional music and dance still take place at weddings, on holidays like Christmas and the New Year, and during festivities around the rice harvest, I was told that dancing is not as common as in the past. Live *sampe* (a four-stringed instrument) playing is considered a dying art due to the increasing popularity of cassette tape and compact disc players.

The main objective of my visit to Long Pujungan was to discuss the idea of creating a cultural center or museum with community members, and if necessary, to help facilitate its planning. During my stay in the village, approximately three weeks, I had the opportunity to speak informally with a number of community members. But the primary forum for discussions was the formal, village meeting organized by the assistant manager of the WWF field post and the *kepala adat*, or chief of customary law and traditions. A total of five meetings took place while I was in Long Pujungan.

The first meeting was held at the WWF field post and was attended mostly by elder men of the community. One woman was present who represented a women's church group. I explained that I had returned to the village to discuss the idea of creating a museum with them as part of WWF's cultural conservation effort. While a few participants had visited the provincial museum of East Kalimantan in the town of Tenggarong down river near the coast, most had never heard of a museum or understood its functions.

In an attempt to make the museum concept less foreign, I explained that a museum is similar to a local cultural form, the *lumbung* or rice barn. In my visits to Kenyah villages during the first survey, I became intrigued by the *lumbung* because they are not only used to store rice, but frequently also house and protect a family's heirlooms. I also learned that *lumbung* embody a number of indigenous, preventive conservation principles and techniques. Here conservation is used in the museological sense as any action taken to protect objects from damage or to control or prevent their deterioration.

For example, *lumbung* are generally located outside the village and on high ground where they can be protected from fires and flooding. A concern for

Figure 5.2 *Lumbung*, or rice barn, with thatched roof and movable awnings for ventilation. Also note the curved planks placed at the base of the structure to prevent pests from entering. Long Pujungan, East Kalimantan. Photograph by Christina Kreps, 1997.

conservation can also be seen in the *lumbung*'s design and architectural features, such as movable awnings and vents, which are used to control interior temperatures and airflow. Such "climate control" measures are essential for the protection of rice and other goods in the hot and humid tropical climate of the region. The use of traditional-style thatched roofing also aids ventilation and is considered to be a particularly adaptive architectural feature in tropical climates. It is also thought to be superior to modern building materials such as zinc roofing, which has become particularly popular (see Waterson 1990:87). Today, many *lumbung* are covered with zinc roofing. This is probably due to the fact that its installation is less labor intensive than thatching, and zinc is often seen as a prestige item. But zinc rusts quickly, provides no insulation, and generates heat. The climatically maladaptive quality of zinc was pointed out to me when a villager explained how one *lumbung* with zinc roofing exploded several years ago. He surmised that the roofing had generated an excessive amount of heat in the *lumbung*, creating gases that caused the explosion. Sadly, precious heirloom jars and the family's rice supply were destroyed in the explosion. Consequently, in this man's opinion, traditional thatch roofing was preferable to zinc.

Indigenous techniques for "pest management" are also evident in the *lumbung*. Particularly ingenious is the placement of curved wooden planks or disks at the

131

Figure 5.3 *Lumbung*, or rice barn, with zinc roofing and circular disks placed at the base to prevent pests from entering. Notice the inverted heirloom jars on the veranda to the front. Photograph by Christina Kreps, 1996.

top of piles that support the structure, which is an effective means of preventing rodents from entering. I was told that sometimes the skin of a weasel-like animal[4] was also hung inside the *lumbung* to deter pests. The pungent smell of the skin is said to repel pests like mice and rats. Because this animal, when alive, feeds on mice and rats, villagers say the rodents are afraid to enter the *lumbung*. Natural fumigants, such as the smoke of burning peppers, are also used inside the *lumbung* to eradicate insects and slow the growth of mold. Interestingly, recent scientific research has shown that certain chemical properties in the capsicum of peppers contain antifungal and antibacterial properties.[5] Obviously, the Dayaks have known this for some time.

In general, I saw the *lumbung* as functionally analogous to the museum both in terms of a place to store and protect valuable property and a structure that embodied conservation principles and techniques. Of course, there are many ways in which the *lumbung* is not like a museum, but my point was to create a conceptual link between the museum and a local "conservation structure," or a structure that embodies both a conservation ethos and actual conservation methods. The *lumbung* could also be seen as an example of "appropriate technology," particularly suited to its environment.

After our initial discussion, meeting participants concluded that they liked the *lumbung*/museum idea. They saw how it could be used to revitalize and preserve certain aspects of traditional Kenyah culture and help ensure that future generations "know what it means to be a Kenyah Dayak." They also recognized a museum's potential for educating visitors about Kenyah culture.[6] The *kepala adat* announced that he would call a meeting of the *lembaga adat*, or council of customary law, to discuss the idea further. After this initial meeting at the WWF field post, discussions regarding the museum project took place within the *lembaga adat* and in the home of the *kepala adat*.

Over the course of the next few weeks, four additional meetings were held at the *kepala adat*'s home. It was only after the second meeting that the council decided to create a museum and began making plans for its construction, including its architectural design, which they believed should be modeled after a traditional-style *lumbung*. The council also began discussing what kinds of activities should take place in their museum as well as the sorts of objects that would be stored in it. They saw the project not only as a way of conserving important cultural property, but also as a means of reviving arts such as traditional architecture, painting and carving, dance, and music. We also discussed how the museum could function as a community archives or repository for important documents recording village history, customary law, and cultural knowledge. During my stay I discovered that several community members act as "village historians" or "ethnographers," recording in written documents significant historical events, decisions made by the *lembaga adat*, oral history, and cultural traditions.[7] The council appointed a committee to oversee the museum's construction and its further planning. Construction was to begin the following month after the rice fields were weeded and when people had more leisure time.

Lessons and outcomes

The people of Long Pujungan had to postpone the construction of their museum due to hardships brought on by the drought and fires of late 1997 and the economic and political upheavals that began taking place in Indonesia in early 1998. However, according to a Kayan Mentarang staff member I spoke with in 2000, the people of Long Pujungan eventually hope to create a museum in their community. Despite these setbacks, the planning phase of the museum project provided valuable lessons in methodology and had a number of positive outcomes.

For instance, the use of the *lumbung* proved to be an effective strategy for making the museum concept less foreign in the local context. By drawing a functional analogy between the museum and the *lumbung*, I hoped to conceptually link the museum idea with existing concepts of cultural conservation. The approach is based on the common pedagogical technique of starting with the familiar and proceeding to the unfamiliar. It is also commensurate with development and environmental conservation strategies that acknowledge and build on local concepts and practices in an attempt to make interventions compatible to local circumstances.

I saw the *lumbung* concept as a starting point for further discussions on the form, functions, and role of the museum in the community. While in Long Pujungan, I learned that although today each family owns its own individual *lumbung*, in former times the village maintained a *lumbung desa* or one that belonged to the whole village. This *lumbung* was used to store communal property such as ritual regalia and goods received for payment of fines when customary laws were broken. Through the process of talking about the old *lumbung desa*, community members began to question why they no longer had a *lumbung desa*, which in turn, stimulated reflections on the sources and consequences of culture change. In short, the *lumbung desa* became a catalyst for consciousness raising about cultural loss as well as revitalization as the *lumbung desa* became their model for a museum, in terms of both architectural features and functions. The *lumbung* analogy was effective because it was a familiar cultural form, or indigenous model of a museum, that had long been a part of Kenyah culture. Unlike a museum, the people knew how to make a *lumbung* and did not see it as something beyond their capabilities.

Although I had devised a work plan before setting off to Long Pujungan, I did not go there with a predetermined idea of how the work process should unfold or what its outcome should be. Rather, once I was in the field, the work process became one of creative dialogue, exchange, and interaction. And even though I tried to explain the basic functions and purposes of a museum, I did not present the people of Long Punjungan with a predetermined idea of what a museum is or should be. The aim was to let the community define for itself the museum's meaning and purposes, as well as form and functions.

The bottom-up participatory approach to the project also brought encouraging results. The community's decision to create a museum on its own was exceptional in the Indonesian context where community development projects, until recently, seldom took place outside the top-down, highly centralized government bureaucracy. To underscore this point, the assistant manager of the WWF field post told me that community members initially had been confused by the approach to the project and decision-making process, which they described as *terbalik*, or reversed from the way in which projects were usually presented to them by outsiders. They were far more accustomed to outsiders, such as government officials or representatives of non-governmental organizations, coming to the village and telling them what to do and how to do it in addition to providing outside funding for projects. Rarely were they given the opportunity to make decisions on their own regarding community development projects. Because WWF could not provide funding for the construction of a museum, the *lembaga adat* had to decide how they would fund the project. The council concluded that a museum would be a good use of village development funds, and since most of the materials and labor would be free, the museum should not require a large outlay of funds. Thus, although I had introduced the idea of creating a museum in Long Pujungan, the project became a community-based endeavor, executed through a local, traditional institution – the *lembaga adat*.

My experience with the Kayan Mentarang People's Museum Development Program reinforces Kleymeyer's assertion that cultural energy generated through cultural activities can serve as a motivational force in a community. Cultural energy can have an empowering effect that serves not only the particular concerns of a project, in this case environmental and cultural conservation, but also those directly affected by and involved in a project.

According to several people I spoke with in Long Pujungan, there was a great deal of frustration and despair in the community. As an indicator of these feelings, some pointed to the recent emergence of alcohol and drug abuse in the community as well as increased violence. Many felt discouraged by what they perceived as being "left behind" in the development process, and by unfulfilled promises on the part of government officials. Too many disappointments had left people with a sense of skepticism about what they could expect from outside help. The museum project may have been embraced so enthusiastically because the community members saw it as something they could do, to a certain degree, for and by themselves. Indeed, the assistant manager of the WWF field post, a native and resident of Long Pujungan, said it had been a long time since he had seen people so excited about a community project. In short, the museum planning process had an empowering effect on the community as villagers became increasingly aware of their power to act on their own behalf.

Perhaps of equal or greater importance is how the project helped renew the community's sense of pride in their cultural heritage and identity. This outcome was particularly powerful in light of the fact that historically Dayaks have been perceived as backward, uncivilized "primitives." Over the past century or more Dayaks have been looked down upon for their pagan religions and former headhunting traditions. Portrayals of Dayaks as savage headhunters and examples of their "primitive" culture still appear in the national print media (see Schiller 1997). In recent years, Dayaks also have come under attack for their "primitive agricultural practices" said to "destroy the environment." As Sellato, an anthropologist who has worked among the Dayaks of Kalimantan for some twenty years, has observed:

> Dayak cultures have been deeply destabilized. The successive overlords never attempted to replace what they wanted to discard with new, positively-seen elements that would help the Dayak refocus their cultural pride and identity . . . Today's Dayak do not have a high sense of self-esteem, they feel inferior, even convincing themselves that they are backward primitives.
>
> (n.d.)

Although I considered my initial work in Long Pujungan a success in terms of generating cultural energy and creating awareness about cultural heritage preservation, there were several aspects of the methodological approach to the project that can be seen as problematic. Of special concern is the short period of time, twenty-five days, devoted to assessing Long Pujungan's cultural life. From an anthropological perspective, it is impossible to present a valid account of a people's culture without the benefit of long-term fieldwork.

135

We can also question if cultural resources can be adequately identified by outsiders and then used to "measure" degrees of "cultural loss" or "cultural integrity." This approach is especially problematic if too much attention is focused on so-called "traditional" cultural resources. In searching for evidence of "traditional culture," one can overlook new cultural expressions or how earlier forms have evolved in response to changing social conditions. As previously noted, an excessively conservative approach denies the creative, generative quality of culture and its role in people's further cultural development. The presence or absence of any cultural form and the degree to which it conforms or diverges from some presumed traditional state should not necessarily be seen as an indicator of a community's cultural vitality. Indeed, community members themselves should set the criteria for determining what constitutes cultural resources, their significance, and how they should be treated. Once again, the critical issue is who decides what should be valued and supported, and who controls the decision-making process.

Despite these methodological concerns and the fact that plans for the museum have yet to be realized, the Kayan Mentarang People's Museum Development Program may be seen as an alternative model of museum development in Indonesia. As previously discussed in Chapter 2, museum development in Indonesia, until recently, largely has been orchestrated through a highly centralized national museum system in a decidedly top-down fashion. Furthermore, state funds for museum development have been primarily devoted to national and provincial museums rather than community-based initiatives. This structure is in keeping with the Indonesian government's general approach to cultural development, which also has been highly centralized and top down. According to some Indonesian museologists, these factors have prevented museums from contributing more fully to the Indonesian people's sociocultural development.

Bambang Sumadio, a former director of the Directorate of Museums, in an interview in 1992, told me that provincial museums had not become what he had originally envisioned them to be, that is, popular culture centers that reflect local culture and inspire the people. Instead, they had become "administrative offices" mired in bureaucracy and political interests. Encumbered by these factors, museums were not serving the cultural needs of their communities nor contributing to their development.

Sumadio's vision for provincial museums embodied many of the concepts and principles behind the ecomuseum as well as culture-based approaches to development. To Sumadio, museums should be a local point of cultural reference "so as the people develop they don't get lost." Museums should provide the "roots to come back to for consultation." He stated that people should not necessarily "stick to old ways, but if they develop into something it has to be something that fits them; so they do not become strangers in their own country and own culture. Museums should give them points of reference." Sumadio believed the ethnography of the local people should be well represented in museums to serve as a "point of reference." Museums should "look for what cultural conditions exist in order to keep them alive." For this reason, ethnography should not just be in the form of objects, "but also other things that go along with them." For example, if a boat is displayed then the museum must also display the technology for making the boat. And not just the tools, but also the technical engineering or know-how involved in boat making. Sumadio added that when local knowledge is incorporated into museum exhibits, it is important also to show how local knowledge systems have modern scientific principles behind them. "The people just call them something else." He stressed that museums should look for the positive and inventive aspects of local culture and demonstrate how they can contribute to development. This is an example of how museums can help sustain local culture while functioning in the development process. In Sumadio's opinion, museums can also contribute to local economic development by helping people develop and market their arts and crafts. This not only aids them economically, but also helps keep artistic traditions alive.

According to Sumadio, government officials see museums primarily as an economic resource in the form of a tourist attraction. However, he believed tourism should be of secondary importance to museum development. In his view, "culture and education should come first." Although museums can serve economic purposes, they are first and foremost cultural and educational institutions. The museum "should be a place that inspires local people, not a place to consciously indoctrinate them."

Sumadio observed that it was unfortunate that government bureaucracy dictated museum operations, but he hoped the situation would improve in the future. This problem was not created by museums themselves, but was a result of the fact that museums are part of the larger government bureaucracy. One solution to this problem, he suggested, was the establishment of more private museums in Indonesia. These museums could serve as a training ground for museum workers and provide them with models of good museum management. He also stressed that museums should work to gain support from non-governmental organizations, which are more independent, and to a certain degree, can work outside government bureaucratic restrictions. Sumadio asserted that some sectors of society need control, but "culture needs freedom of movement." In the future, he hoped museums would be less dependent on the government and develop in such a way that "society will trust them."

Sumadio's vision for museums in Indonesia may yet be realized. Since 1998, Indonesia's new governments have been instituting significant democratic reforms, which in turn have been influencing the national museum system. When I visited the Directorate of Museums' office in August 2000, I was told that one of its current directives was to decentralize the national museum system, and to explore private funding possibilities for museums. The staff hoped these initiatives would inspire greater community participation in museums and support for their further development.

Traditional conservation methods as "appropriate technology"

In an essay titled "Developing or Traditional Area Museums" (1980), David Baradas, former Director of the Museum of Philippine Life, observes that there is a basic difference between museums in technologically developed areas and developing or traditional area museums.

> In technologically developed areas we have museums which are artefact-focused. The main activity has been to collect artefacts . . . Museums which are artefact-focused should logically be conservation-conscious . . . There is no choice. By alienating an artefact from its context, one is suddenly saddled with the responsibilites of conservation. Not to conserve is tantamount to a criminal act.
>
> (1980:79)

On the other hand, "developing or traditional area museums . . . are and should be context-focused. The main thrust of the activity is direct relevance to the lives of the people where the museum is located" (1980:79).

For Baradas, this difference in format has presented problems for museums in developing areas. "Having copied the artifact-focused format of the technologically developed area, one is confronted with the same responsibility – conservation – which is a tedious and expensive process beyond the reach of most museums in developing areas" (1980:79). Because of the strain on resources posed by the conservation of objects, especially under tropical conditions, it is better to channel scarce resources toward preserving the skills of people who make the objects. "The emphasis should be on preserving skills rather than making the artefact the end product of our attention" (Baradas 1980:79). In Baradas' opinion, funds should be given to social activities that result in the production of artifacts, especially arts and crafts. Thus, museums can support the continuing vitality of traditional arts and crafts or support their revitalization in areas where they have begun to wane.

Baradas' remarks point to one of the greatest challenges for museums in developing areas, that is, the conservation of their collections. Modern conservation techniques related to storage, climate control, and pest management used in western museums are generally too costly for museums in developing areas. Furthermore, the museum staff often does not have the opportunity to acquire adequate training in professional museum conservation. One solution to this problem, as Baradas suggests, is for museums to focus on preserving skills related to the production of objects. But another solution is the preservation and application of traditional conservation materials and methods.

Agrawal, in *Appropriate Technologies for the Conservation of Museum Collections* (1981), writes, "the use of sophisticated imported technology has not given the results which were desired and sought after. This is because research efforts have not been directed towards the development of technologies which fit the needs and possibilities of these countries" (1981:69). The author points out that there are traditional techniques that could take care of many conservation needs, but are not pressed into service "because modern techniques are always considered superior or because the traditional techniques have been forgotten and are not known to curators" (1981:69). Agrawal presents examples of traditional techniques that have been used in Indian households for storage and maintenance of materials. The author suggests that "by suitably adapting these technologies the problems of advanced technology can be avoided, and the non-availability of resources within the country can also be countered to a great extent" (1981:70). Agrawal stresses that greater research needs to be done in the field, however, to ascertain the efficacy of many of these methods. Agrawal describes natural products commonly used as insecticides for the protection of books, manuscripts, and textiles as well as methods of climate control and storage techniques.

Chemical products normally used as fumigants are often not available to museums in developing areas and are generally too costly to use on a regular basis. There is, therefore, a great need for research into alternative natural products. In India, as well as in other countries, several natural products have been used for protecting household goods, such as books, religious manuscripts, and textiles from insect attack. Some of the most commonly used natural insect repellents are *neem* leaves from the margosa tree, camphor, tobacco, black cumin seeds, tumeric, sandalwood, and peacock feathers. In addition to insecticidal properties, many of these products also contain disinfectant and medicinal properties and thus have been used in traditional medicine.

Agrawal describes in detail how each substance is prepared and used. For example, camphor (*Cinnamomum*) is packed in small bags, which are then placed in cupboards where valuable documents and papers are stored (1981:72). Black cumin seeds are sometimes mixed with powdered camphor and then sprinkled between the folds of textiles, particularly woolens, to prevent insect attack. Cumin seeds contain a volatile oil, which, according to Agrawal, probably accounts for their insect repellent property (1981:72–73). Sandalwood is one of the oldest perfumes in India, and in many traditional households it is placed inside cupboards or boxes to protect textiles. It also has been long used for medicinal purposes (1981:74). Peacock feathers are commonly believed to have beneficial effects when placed between book pages. "It has been observed, for reasons yet unknown, that paper materials that have peacock feathers placed between their leaves do not ordinarily attract bookworms" (1981:74).

The importance of climate control for the preservation of museum objects is widely recognized. Too dry or too humid conditions can be extremely damaging to objects, particularly those made of organic materials. Air-conditioning in buildings is the optimal method of regulating temperature and humidity. However, air-conditioning is a costly proposition for museums in developing areas. Additionally, it requires a constant supply of electricity, which is not always assured in these areas. In view of these factors, alternative means of climate control need to be adopted.

Agrawal describes how in northern India, people have traditionally used curtains or screens made of *khas*, or the roots of a perennial grass, *Vetiveria bory*

139

(*Gramineae*). Khas screens are hung like curtains on windows and doors in houses. One of the principal properties of khas is that it can retain water for long periods of time. Water is sprinkled on the curtains and slowly evaporates, thus humidifying the air. At the same time, a fragrance is emitted from the khas.[8] The custom of making screens from the roots of the grass goes back to ancient times. Khas grows wild throughout India and is also cultivated in some areas. It is also believed to possess antifungal and antibacterial properties. Agrawal recommends that museums that cannot afford air-conditioning use khas screens on their doors and windows. "In the National Museum in New Delhi, khas screens are in fact fixed on the main entrances doors, as well as on some windows every summer" (1981:77).

Several traditional practices have been used for the storage of manuscripts and books. Palm-leaf manuscripts, for example, are always kept between two strong boards around which a cord is securely tied. This practice helps prevent the palm leaf from curling. To a certain extent, it also helps retain humidity. Wood from the margosa (neem) tree or *Michelia champaca* is preferred for the preparation of the boards. The wood of this tree is known to be insect proof (1981:78).

Books and manuscripts of either palm leaf or paper traditionally were wrapped in a square of cotton cloth. This practice helped retain humidity and kept out dust. The color of cloth used was almost always red. Why red cloth was always chosen is not fully known, but Agrawal suggests that it is possible that the red color deflects damaging ultraviolet and near ultraviolet rays of light. "Here, again, however, the unconscious scientific wisdom of this practice is yet to be proved scientifically" (1981:79).

This is just a sampling of the many materials and traditional conservation techniques Agrawal describes. The author stresses that intensive surveys are needed of these materials and techniques in order that "these practices, which are now disappearing fast as a result of the growth of industries and adoption of modern chemicals and dyes, do not become completely lost" (1981:82). While Agrawal's work concentrates on the application of appropriate conservation technology in Indian museums, the author encourages museums elsewhere to explore this approach as a possible solution to conservation problems.

The conservation of collections is a serious concern in most Indonesian museums. They face many of the problems Agrawal describes, such as a lack of supplies, equipment, and professional training in conservation. For example, at the Provincial Museum of Central Kalimantan, Museum Balanga (discussed in Chapter 2), one staff member (the museum's conservator) had received basic training in professional conservation practices. However, he often complained that he could not properly care for the collections because the museum did not have the necessary equipment and supplies, despite the fact that the museum had a conservation laboratory. Manuals on conservation techniques, distributed by the Directorate of Museums, were of little use because they tended to be written for highly trained professional conservators. He told me that, as an alternative solution to conservation problems, he often resorted to using traditional products commonly used in Indonesian households for cleaning and protecting objects. For instance, tamarind paste and citrus juice were used for cleaning brassware and other metals. Citronella and other oils were applied to wooden objects to seal the wood and keep it from cracking. Citronella oil also acted as an insecticide. Interestingly, Agrawal writes that these same products are used for similar purposes in India (1981:81). The museum's conservator hoped that the museum would be able to acquire more "modern technology" in the future to better deal with conservation problems. But in the meantime, these products and methods seemed to be relatively effective.

Another possible solution for the protection and preservation of valuable cultural resources is the promotion of "community-based conservation." This bottom-up, participatory approach combines the knowledge and skills of professional curators with those of local people on preservation projects, such as the restoration of buildings or sites. According to Munzenrider, Chief Conservator in the Conservation Department of the Museum of New Mexico, community-based conservation can "reinforce cultural traditions as well as offer exposure to current conservation approaches and concerns" (1998:2). Munzenrider worked with community members in the village of Arroyo Seco in northern New Mexico in the restoration of an adobe church built in 1834. Adobe churches in New Mexico represent, in both their structure and contents, centuries-old traditions of architecture, building methods, religious art, and restoration practices. The churches are generally located in the heart of the community and play a central role in village life. The church in Arroyo Seco was abandoned in the 1960s for a more modern church built adjacent to it, but remained an important historical and cultural landmark.

Through the cooperative efforts of Father Vincent Chavez of the Archdiocese of Santa Fe, Munzenrider, and community members, the church was restored using local materials and techniques such as traditional mud and straw hand-plastered adobe. Community members provided labor and expertise in traditional building and restoration methods. An altarscreen, painted in the 1860s by a well-known colonial artist, was also restored. Munzenrider observes that

> because restoration of the church was a community effort, the community is more invested in the long-term preservation of the church and its alter-screen. The dedicated efforts of the community resulted in a renewed sense of pride in their collective history as represented in the church.
>
> (1998:2)

In a visit to a village upriver in Central Kalimantan, Indonesia in 2000, I saw the results of a similar community-based conservation project. A traditional Dayak longhouse, or *rumah bentang*, had been designated a *caga budaya* (cultural preserve) and restored through the efforts of the provincial-level Department of Education and Culture and local community members. The structure was approximately eighty years old. There were some twenty-five people living in the house at the time of my visit, who were descendants of its original builders and inhabitants. Prominently displayed on one wall was a genealogy chart, recounting the family's lineage. The head of the family, an elder

141

Figure 5.4 Restored *bentang*, or longhouse, in Central Kalimantan designated as a "cultural preserve." Photograph by Christina Kreps, 2000.

man, proudly recited how the house had been restored using traditional building materials and techniques. Newly carved wooden figures, executed in traditional style, stood guard at the entrance, protecting the house and its inhabitants from evil spirits and misfortune. The family was responsible for the upkeep of the house, and received a yearly stipend from the government for this purpose. A sign was posted in front of the house, which notified the public of its status as a protected site, and how any vandalism of the site would result in a fine or imprisonment. The restoration of the house was an extremely important project because few examples of Dayak longhouses still exist in Central Kalimantan.[9] The villagers were obviously very proud of the house and dedicated to its preservation. The provincial government had initiated the project,but it was now in the hands of the community.

The designation of the house and its surrounding examples of traditional Dayak art as a "cultural preserve" protected by law was also a very important development. The theft of traditional art, such as carvings, is a serious problem throughout Kalimantan. Dayak carvings have become popular items on the international "primitive art" market, and the high prices they can bring are a strong inducement for looting. Thus, protective measures such as fines or threat of imprisonment are a needed deterrent. Traditionally, social sanctions and taboos functioned to dissuade vandalism or theft, and served as a means of

Figure 5.5 Alfrid Kunen, head of family residing in restored *bentang*, or longhouse.
Photograph by Christina Kreps, 2000.

protecting sites or objects. But conversion to Christianity and Islam has weakened these traditional institutions in most Dayak communities. The fact that a large percentage of the inhabitants in this village still adhere to their traditional religion, Kaharingan, may account for the abundance of traditional art that can still be seen in this village.[10] The Kaharingan religion serves as an impetus for the production of traditional art and provides a moral structure for its protection.

Community-based conservation is an example of how museum functions and concerns are being decentralized and adapted to local needs. It also offers a possible solution to conservation problems faced in developing area museums. But such approaches are not only applicable in developing areas. They are also relevant in other contexts, as shown in previous discussions on the growing importance of Native American methods of traditional care in both mainstream American and Native American museums. Traditional conservation practices are yet another example of indigenous curatorial practices, and as such, contribute to our further understanding of approaches to curation and cultural heritage preservation cross-culturally.

As museums throughout the world continue to be decentralized and democractized in their efforts to become more socially relevant, such practices will continue to grow in importance. Of critical concern is how people in varying national and cultural contexts are gaining greater control over the protection and management of their cultural heritage. What is occurring is the liberation of culture from the management regimes of western museology, science, and development models, which have placed all human development on a single trajectory. At stake is nothing less than the preservation of cultural diversity and its endless potential.

6

Comparative museology and cross-cultural heritage management: emerging paradigms for museological practice

I have argued, throughout this book, that while the museum is generally construed as a uniquely western, modern invention, museological behavior is a long-standing cross-cultural phenomenon. To support this argument, I provided examples of non-western models of museums and curatorial practices from a number of cultures. I also showed how, in many cases, contemporary examples of indigenous museums and cultural centers are extensions of earlier traditions, demonstrating that museum-like structures and museological-type behavior are not new in many indigenous societies.

I have also challenged assertions that non-western peoples are not concerned with the care and preservation of their material culture by offering examples of indigenous concepts of cultural preservation as well as actual conservation practices. This evidence is of critical importance because such claims often have been used to justify the collection and retention of non-western people's cultural property in museums. I have also shown how certain forms of cultural property, such as sacred and ceremonial objects, have been essential means of cultural transmission and thus necessary for the perpetuation of cultural traditions, and in turn, cultural heritage preservation. A deeper understanding of the power and meaning certain objects hold for their cultures of origin bolsters native peoples' requests for the repatriation of these materials.

In presenting these arguments and supporting evidence, my goal has been to help liberate culture, and its collection, curation, interpretation, and preservation in museums, from the management regimes of Eurocentric museology. The liberation of culture is not only about giving back or restoring a people's right to and control over the management of their cultural heritage. It is also about liberating our thinking from the Eurocentric view of what constitutes a museum, artifact, and museological practice so that we might better recognize alternative forms. The liberation of culture allows for the emergence of a new museological discourse in which points of reference are no longer solely determined and defined by the west. The aim is to open the field to include multiple voices, which represent a wide range of experiences and perspectives, and to give credence to bodies of knowledge and practice that have been historically overlooked or devalued. This "new inclusiveness" acknowledges that those who have been marginalized as "the others" are central to the creation of new museological paradigms.

Indigenous museum models and curatorial practices have much to contribute to our understanding of museological behavior cross-culturally, or rather, of how people in varying cultural contexts perceive, value, care for, and preserve cultural resources. Ironically, while anthropologists have been concerned with the collection and study of non-western material culture, until recently they were rarely concerned with the systematic study and documentation of the ways in which people care for and preserve their material culture. However, these practices, as cultural expressions in themselves, deserve the same attention given to other aspects of culture such as language, religion, social organization, and so forth. If one of the principle purposes of anthropology is to try to understand humans in all their variety, as well as the ways in which they are alike, then we must not overlook potential sites for the investigation of difference and similarity.

One of the aims of this book is to contribute to the further development of comparative museology, or the cross-cultural study of museological forms and practices. If museology "puts practice in context and gives meaning to what museums do in society" (Kaplan 1992:49), then comparative museology potentially allows us to do this cross-culturally. In this concluding chapter I discuss how comparative museology provides a conceptual framework for exploring museological forms and practices in diverse national and cultural settings as well as for putting theory into practice. In this respect, comparative museology contributes to the further liberation of culture by opening avenues for the ongoing development of more inclusive, cross-cultural approaches to cultural heritage management.

The comparative approach and cross-cultural analysis

As noted in Chapter 1, my approach to the study of non-western models of museums and curatorial practices is grounded in the comparative approach and cross-cultural analysis of cultural anthropology. These research methods have been cultural anthropology's main tools for examining the similarities and differences in cultures, and for arriving at what may be universal as well as variable about human cultures (Ember and Ember 2001:1–2). A basic assumption of the comparative approach is that the phenomena in question are of like kind, and that comparison is possible because patterns (kinds of phenomena that occur repeatedly) can be identified (Ember and Ember 2001:5). To compare cultures, or particular cultural phenomena, is not to deny their individual uniqueness or specific qualities. Rather, similarity and uniqueness can be present simultaneously and seen as part of a "continuum of variation." "The important point here is that similarities cannot be seen or recognized until we think in terms of variables, qualities or quantities that vary along specified dimensions . . . Once researchers perceive and specify similarity, they can perceive and recognize difference" (Ember and Ember 2001:4).

Throughout the book, I have attempted to show how western and indigenous models of museums and curatorial practices are both similar and different as well as similarities and differences in how objects are perceived, valued, and treated. In doing so, I have also tried to show how we can come to some general conclusions on what constitutes museological behavior cross-culturally. As Ember and Ember suggest, "cross-cultural comparison tells us about what is general, what is true for some or many or even all human cultures" (2001:1).

The most obvious point of convergence lies in the fact that museum-like structures have been present in many societies since ancient times. Although these structures possess their own distinct features, as expressions of a particular culture, they can be identified as falling along a continuum of variation in the degree to which they function as structures for the collection, storage, and display of valued objects. The role of curator is also present in many cultures. If we think of a curator as a "caretaker" or "keeper," as the term has been used in some contexts, then we can see how certain individuals or specific groups in many societies, such as priests, shamans, spiritual leaders, royal functionaries, and so on are indeed curators. These traditional curators generally possess specialized knowledge and skills acquired through lengthy training or apprenticeship, not unlike that required of western professional curators. Furthermore, many societies have developed elaborate means of conserving objects, using conservation techniques that have been shown to be relatively effective over time. These techniques also reflect a concern for preserving the tangible evidence of cultural heritage.

In addition to observing these general characteristics of museological structures and behavior, I have also pointed out differences, especially between western and indigenous models of museums and curatorial practices. One of the most distinctive differences is how objects are perceived and treated. For example, as discussed in previous chapters, in many societies some objects are perceived as being animated with a living force or life energy. This is especially true of objects of sacred or ceremonial value, which reflect a society's distinct cosmology, religious beliefs, and practices. Objects, which embody or represent ancestors, may also be empowered with a spirit or force. For example, to the Maori, ancestor images are not just representations of an ancestor but are that ancestor and its living spirit. Mead reinforces this perspective in his remarks on Maori *taonga*, or cultural treasures, and their *mauri* (living force). "For the living relatives the *taonga* is more than a representation of their ancestors; the figure is their ancestor and woe betide anyone who acts indifferently to their *tipuna* (ancestor)" (Mead 1990:166). Similarly, for many Native American people, objects are alive and thus need to breathe and be treated in such a manner that allows their vital energies to be expressed. Furthermore, while some objects are preserved through various conservation techniques, others must be allowed to live out their life cycle, such as the Zuni "War Gods," whose powers are generated only through their physical disintegration (Ladd 2001). Spirits may also inhabit certain objects. As discussed previously, in Borneo, offerings or sacrifices are often made to the spirits that inhabit heirloom jars to solicit their support or appease their potentially volatile nature. These views of objects as sacred,

147

alive, and animated by vital forces and spirits stand in stark contrast to how objects are viewed and thus treated in western museums. In such contexts, objects are largely seen as static, inanimate entities valued on the basis of their material properties.

We have also seen in the *haus tambaran* of Papua New Guinea, Australian Aboriginal "Keeping Places," and for many Native American tribes, how knowledge about objects as well as access to them is generally not part of the public domain. But rather, knowledge and access is restricted to certain members of a society, such as males or females, elders, initiated individuals, and so on. Taboos or other social restrictions may also serve to limit access and use. Such taboos, in turn, have functioned to protect objects from theft, vandalism, or destruction.

Additionally, objects or collections housed in indigenous museum models are typically not owned by an abstract "public" or held in "public trust" in the sense they are in western-style museums. They often remain the property of certain families, clans, ritual organizations, or other corporate units, which frequently continue to exercise proprietary rights over particular objects or collections. For instance, in the Kwagiulth Museum and Cultural Centre in British Columbia, objects are not considered the property of the museum or even communal, tribal property, but rather individual or family property. Objects, such as masks and ritual regalia, are displayed with labels identifying an object's owner, generally a chief and his family. "The objects belong to specific families since, traditionally, there is no such thing as tribal property" (Clifford 1991:227). Thus, displays reflect traditional rights to the ownership of property as well as systems of kinship and social organization. Similarly, at the Hoopa Tribal Museum in California, a large percentage of the museum's collection is not owned by the museum, but simply on loan from individual tribal members or families. Family collections are also physically kept together in museum exhibits. Some objects such as ritual regalia may also be removed from the museum for use in ceremonies and on other special occasions (Davis 1989).

What becomes clear when looking at how objects are perceived and treated in indigenous museums is that they are not decontextualized to the degree they are in western museums. Objects remain ensconced in their larger cultural contexts, and in direct relationship to people's lives as part of ongoing cultural traditions. In indigenous museum-like models, "most of the objects continue to fulfill their original function, and indeed, are frequently still in regular usage" (Simpson 1996:113). They retain their singular meanings and specificity as family heirlooms and treasures, as sacred objects necessary for the perpetration of religious beliefs and practices, or as documents of a community's history and heritage.

Cross-cultural comparison enables us to identify the differences and similarities in how objects are perceived, valued, and treated as well as the forms museums take and the purposes they serve in various cultural settings. This type of comparison also reveals the epistemological biases and assumptions embedded in our own professional museum culture. As Karp and Lavine suggest, we begin to discover the artifice of our practices when we look at them in comparison with those in other cultural contexts (1991:1). Through comparison, we also begin to see more clearly how western museological paradigms have been imposed on other cultures and the consequences of this imposition.

However, as shown throughout the book, museums have been undergoing radical changes as they have been made increasingly aware of the meanings their collections hold for their cultures of origin. Greater recognition of alternative perspectives and approaches has led to a critical reassessment of some of the most fundamental concepts underpinning the interpretation and representation of objects in museums. In turn, museology has been undergoing a dramatic transformation, and in the process, new paradigms of thought and action have begun to emerge. Museum practices are now being reassessed and redefined within a new framework of greater cultural sensitivity and awareness. The balance of power in the collection, preservation, and representation of culture is shifting as indigenous communities are making their voices heard and taking greater control over the management of their cultural heritage. As Richard West has asserted, the "rules of the road" have changed, and museums are increasingly responding to these changes. "Museums can no longer set the rules and determine the playing field" (Haas 1996:4).

Rethinking the decontextualized object and culture

One issue that has become of critical concern is the overarching problem of decontextualization, or the act of detaching objects from their original cultural contexts. In contrast to indigenous museums, objects in western-style ethnographic museums have been extracted from their original cultural contexts and recontextualized through the lens of western scientific and aesthetic interpretative frameworks (Stocking 1985). Within these frameworks, objects are assigned new generalized meanings and values as objects of "ethnography" or "art." In the words of Kirshenblatt-Gimblett, "ethnographic artifacts are objects of ethnography. They are artifacts created by ethnographers. Such objects become ethnographic by virtue of being defined, segmented, detached, and carried away by ethnographers" (1991:387). The "in context" exhibition strategy, so often employed in ethnographic museums, is an attempt to recreate an absent cultural whole for the decontextualized object, drawing on the ethnographer's own interpretative frames. "Just as the ethnographic object is the creation of the ethnographer, so, too, are the putative wholes of which they are part" (1991:389). The aim of in context display strategies is "to bring . . . dead specimens 'to life' through the theater of installation" (Kirshenslatt-Gimblett 1998:165).

Today, there is a rethinking of the role of the object in museological theory. The "object [is] losing (some would say simply changing) its place in the theory of the museum" (Clavir 1994:53). As museums are becoming more people- and community-centered (rather than object-centered), and concerned with people's living culture and not just their past, they are being liberated from "the romanticism . . . of the decontextualized object" (Galla 1997:155).

Decontextualization is now called into question with increasing recognition of how it has contributed to a "distancing" between museums and the cultures their collections represent: a distancing both in spatial and temporal terms through the act of physically removing objects from their cultures of origin and their consignment to a "traditional" past, and a conceptual distancing through the imposition of western systems of cultural interpretation and representation. The cultural divides created through decontextualization are beginning to narrow through greater interaction between museums and indigenous people as well as through the increasing presence of the "native voice" in museological discourse. The perspectives, values, and cultural concerns of Native peoples regarding objects originating in their communities are increasingly being represented in museums.

> Museums usually define the "unique character and significance" of an object according to the meaning researched by curators for that object and its place in the museum system of values (rarity, condition, attribution, authenticity, etc.). The postmodern "living" museum may attempt to give priority to the originating culture's system of values (e.g. following cultural protocols for sacred or sensitive objects). It follows that in these museums, cultural needs to use an object and culturally appropriate maintenance of an object may take precedence over standard museum . . . procedures.
>
> (Clavir 1996:101–102)

The conceptual barriers that have historically divided museums and indigenous communities are now being put on the table for open discussion. Both the terms and style of engagement are being reconfigured, leading to new levels of understanding and approaches to practice. Miriam Clavir, a conservator at the University of British Columbia Museum of Anthropology, comments on the value of "face-to-face" discussions in negotiating conceptual terrain.

> Challenges to fundamental conceptual frameworks are often received as adversarial by those who believe in the value of the framework. Indeed, they may well be presented as such by a challenger who perceives an entrenched and hostile system. Core emotions as well as core beliefs and intellectual arguments may be involved for all participants. This is one reason why it is valuable for conservators to take part in face-to-face discussions with indigenous peoples from different cultures on conservation issues: the whole person is involved, and points of view can be appreciated as well as understood.
>
> (1996:103)

Museum professionals and anthropologists are now recognizing that Native people's perspectives on the material in museum collections differ, often profoundly, from their own, and that other people's cultural truths, although different, also have value. As Richard West observes: "Museums interpreting Indian collections, many of which are based in a science tradition, often have been reticent to embrace the notion of multiple or relative culture truths" (West 1994:55). Members of the museum and scientific community are now obliged to listen to other people's narratives of cultural truth, and acknowledge their legitimacy within particular frameworks of understanding. "The notion of the free and open museum dedicated to revealing the truth about humankind is as obsolete as the notion of 'value free' science" (Haas 1996:6).

In West's view, it is not so much that the anthropological enterprise has been wrong as that it is incomplete.

> I do not believe anthropology has ever achieved its full potential in expli-cating and defining Indian cultures . . . I think anthropology has fallen short of its potential [because] it has not allowed Indians, in any system-atic way, to tell their own story. The scholarly result is not so much wrong as incomplete.
>
> (1993:7)

In this respect, what Rosaldo has said for the remaking of social analysis in anthropology and its relationship to its subjects is equally applicable to muse-ology.

> Social thinkers must take other people's narrative analyses nearly as seri-ously as "we" take our own. Both the content and idiom of "their" moral and political assertions will be more subversive than supportive of business as usual. They will neither reinforce nor map onto the terrain of inquiry as "we" have known it. Narrative analyses told or written from divergent perspectives . . . will not fit together into a unified master summation. A source at once of insight and discomfort, the dilemma of "incommensura-bility," or lack of fit among diverse narratives, makes it imperative to attend with care to what other people are saying, especially if they use unfamiliar idioms and speak to us from socially subordinate positions. Taking account of subordinate forms of knowledge provides an opportu-nity to learn and productively change "our" forms of social analysis. It should broaden, complicate, and perhaps revise, but in no way inhibit, "our" own ethical, political and analytical insights.
>
> (1989:147–148)

Anthropologists and museologists are beginning to show greater respect and appreciation not only of other people's cultural truths, but also for how these truths are grounded in how people *feel* about objects and their power to evoke intense emotions. The emotional power of objects and their meaning to their originating cultures has been brought to light, for example, in the course of NAGPRA consultations and repatriation ceremonies. In the following passage, one author describes the atmosphere of a repatriation ceremony, and the emotional and deeply personal nature of people's relationships to objects.

> The elders spoke of the importance for young people to know and touch their past if they are to have an identity in the future . . . As soon as the formalities were over, a crowd gathered around the table where the arti-facts lay. Looking, touching, admiring, shedding tears, they clearly felt empowered by their very presence.
>
> (Morrison quoted in Clavir 1994:54)

On the one hand, recognizing and showing greater respect for how people feel about objects is tantamount to showing greater respect for their human and cultural rights. But on the other hand, it also can contribute to a better under-standing of how feelings and emotions are part of the cultural milieu in which objects exist and are given meaning and value. The emotional force of objects and the cultural force of emotions can be another basis of cross-cultural compar-ison since all humans have the capacity to feel emotions and express them through various mediums, including objects.

Attention to the emotional and personal dimension of objects moves us closer to overcoming the problem of the decontextualized and alienated object and culture in museums. It also opens new paths to cross-cultural understanding and appreciation, which, ideally, is one of the primary goals of anthropology and museum work.

Cross-cultural heritage management

> Museums evolved as European institutions, preserving European culture and displaying other cultures as curiosities. Now they are attempting to incorporate those other cultures in their structures. Doing so will remake them as institutions.
>
> (Glaser and Zenetou 1996:233)

Mainstream ethnographic museums are in the process of being remade as indige-nous concepts of and approaches to cultural heritage interpretation, representa-tion, and preservation are increasingly taking their place beside western approaches. This movement signals a new era in which museums can no longer avoid the consequences of their colonial pasts. Today, they are meeting them head-on and using them as an opportunity to break new ground in their rela-tionships with indigenous people and the representation of their cultures. "A new generation of museum professionals is proactively addressing the steward-ship of cultural property, its presentation and interpretation in museums" (Kirshenblatt-Gimblett 1998:165). What is occurring is a shift from a "colonial" to a "cooperative" museology (Clifford 1991:224). In this new era of inclusive-ness, museums, perhaps more than ever, have the opportunity to use their collec-tions and resources for promoting cross-cultural awareness and appreciation. But such efforts, as Galla contends, take substantial reflexivity.

> It is essential to address questions of displacement, dispossession and colo-nization as an integral part of the history of indigenous people and, in doing so, the positive side of cultural adaptation, resilience and survival should be included in cultural presentation. It is within this context that museums, as centres of excellence for cultural education, have an impor-tant role in raising the cross-cultural awareness of the wider society.
>
> In the realization of such an objective and frameworks for consciousness raising in-house cross-cultural training are a priority. This requires clarity of concepts, policies, perspectives and a considerable amount of individual and institutional introspection.
>
> (1996:86)

In the remaking of museums, Galla advocates the development of "cross-cultural heritage management" strategies. For Galla, cross-cultural heritage management entails systematic research on the nature and function of heritage management systems, for example, through studies in comparative museology. It also involves collaboration among the various stakeholders. "The discourse of cross-cultural heritage requires systematic research, consultation and negotiation with a range of stakeholders" (1996:89). Cross-cultural heritage management is not just about formulating new museological theory, but also about translating theory into practice. Cross-cultural heritage management strategies bring together diverse concepts and approaches in a spirit of cooperation and collaboration.

> The ultimate roles and responsibilities of the museum will be determined by how well they listen to the voices and values of the many indigenous people whose cultural heritage they represent. The challenges should be met with strategies that are reflective, revealing, confronting and amenable to reconciliation of community of all cultural backgrounds.
>
> (Galla 1996:94)

Cross-cultural heritage management can be seen as a form of cultural hybridization in the sense that it draws on and integrates diverse concepts and approaches. However, cross-cultural heritage management strategies are not just a matter of simply mixing or merging concepts and approaches. Rather, they acknowledge the right of each to be understood and exist on its own terms. Cross-cultural heritage management implies a mutual "give and take" in which diverse concepts and approaches are acknowledged and respected. Contrary to conventional approaches to heritage management, the particular is not masked for the sake of generality. But rather, diverse concepts and approaches coalesce around unified goals.

The integration of Native people's traditional care practices into mainstream American museums is one example of a cross-cultural heritage management strategy. More and more, museums are working with representatives of Native communities to devise more culturally sensitive and appropriate methods for the storage, conservation, and display of indigenous materials (Rosoff 1998, Flynn and Hull-Walski 2001). Such cross-cultural collaborations are leading to new insights as well as approaches to the care and treatment of objects in museum collections. In her conservation work with First Nations of Canada, Clavir has found that: "Traditional 'conservation care' may be able to bring together different concepts to create a new and mutually satisfactory program for preservation" (1994:56).

Negotiations over repatriation can also lead to arrangements whereby museums and Native communities become partners in the custodianship of certain objects, each accommodating the other's approaches for the safekeeping and preservation of objects. For example, in some cases, museums are being seen as "way stations" or "safehouses" for certain objects that cannot be returned to Native communities for various reasons. As Clavir describes:

> In certain cases, the originating people do not want the object back at this time. This may be, for example, because there are no cultural mechanisms in place to accept such a sacred or powerful object back home after being so long without traditional use. It may be because the appropriate guardian of the object is no longer alive or the appropriate ritual is not known. It may be that the tribe has elected, for whatever period of time, to leave the object in the safekeeping of the museum, in a "stewardship" relation in which the museum takes museum-type care of the object and allows access to appropriate tribal members for traditional care.
>
> (1994:54)

Cross-cultural heritage management strategies are also being worked out for what Clavir terms "appropriate access" to collections. As previously discussed, many Native peoples are requesting restricted access to and use of collections, especially those of a sacred or ceremonial nature, based on traditional values and customs.

> In terms of collections, which are housed in urban museums, it may be appropriate access which is being requested. Appropriate access, however, may challenge the norms of standard museum and western cultural practice. For example, certain objects in both Makah and Zuni societies should not be seen or handled by women, including museum staff if these objects are in a museum. Certain objects from the US Southwest should not be seen outside of their religious context. Many medicine bundles from the Plains should not be opened and the contents seen, except by the person who has the ceremonial right to open and use that bundle. Some objects should not be seen by people from the community who are uninitiated; this may affect objects on display or in Visible Storage, which might be seen by school groups. Navaho museum staff members need to know in advance if they will be exposed to objects associated with the dead, including archeological objects. In addition, there are often rituals, which must be performed when certain objects are accessed.
>
> (Clavir 1994:55)

Requests for restricted access may run contrary to the trend toward democratization in museums (Ames 1992), but for museologists, what is viewed as appropriate access will depend on how cultural sensitivity is conceived and balanced with public access. As is true in all cross-cultural heritage management strategies, determining what constitutes appropriate access requires dialogue and collaboration between museums and Native communities.

As a collaborative and inclusive framework for museological practice, cross-cultural heritage management strategies invariably approach curation as a social process, and are based on the premise that people's relationships to objects are primarily social and cultural ones (Cash Cash 2001). By looking at how curation is embedded in larger social and cultural contexts beyond the museum, we can better appreciate how objects, despite their enclosure and isolation in museums, are still "things in motion" and have "social lives." The human and social contexts of things are illuminated when we examine them in motion. We have to trace the movement of things themselves "for their meanings are inscribed in their forms, their uses, their trajectories. It is only through the analysis of these trajectories that we can interpret the human transactions and calculations that enliven things" (Appadurai 1994:77). Seeing how objects possess social lives and function as part of the larger, dynamic flow of culture liberates them from their static positioning in museums. It also illuminates how objects are linked to whole systems of cultural expression and are not always what outsiders perceive them to be. For instance, among some Northern Californian Indian tribes, a basket is not just a utilitarian object made of plant fibers or an example of fine craftsmanship. It is also a song made visible. The point is to look beyond the physical and readily apparent dimensions of an object to discover those other cultural dimensions that lie behind it (Toelken 1982:10).

Cross-cultural heritage management is also about sharing curatorial authority and power in the interpretation and representation of culture. Sharing authority is perhaps one of the greatest challenges for museologists because it runs counter to the trend toward specialization and professionalization in museums.

> One of the consequences of the increasing professionalization of museum work is that members of this developing profession begin to consider it their special responsibility and privilege to control and structure the relations between collections and the public. Curatorial staff who hold this view present themselves as the necessary agents not only for the care but also for the interpretation of heritage, just as teachers consider the curricula a necessary condition for learning.
>
> (Ames 1992:97)

Sharing authority and power should not diminish the role of professionalism in museums. Instead, it should widen the field and make room for the inclusion of other forms of knowledge and expertise.

> In the face of demands to include more voices in decisions about exhibits and research, museums have the opportunity to gain strength by giving up power. They give up power in the sense of granting authority to Native people in making decisions about the use and accessibility of relevant collections, and they become stronger through the support and insights of the people represented in their collections and exhibits.
>
> (Haas 1996:7)

In some cases, museums must not only share power and authority, but also cede it by letting people "speak for themselves" and tell their own stories from their own perspectives.

> One way of recapturing one's culture is to take control of the language and definitions and descriptions and to have members of the culture speak for themselves, present their culture such as their music, their dances and their various art forms in a manner they consider appropriate to them.
>
> (Mead 1990:165)

155

HuupuKawanum Tupaat: Out of the Mist. Treasures of the Nuu-chah-nulth Chiefs is an example of a recent exhibit in which curatorial authority was not only shared with the people whose culture was on display, but also relinquished, to a certain degree. The exhibit was a collaborative effort, organized by the Nuu-chah-nulth Tribal Council and curators Martha Black and Alan Hoover of the Royal British Columbia Museum (RBCM) in Victoria, British Columbia. It opened at the RBCM in July 1999 and then traveled to the Denver Museum of Nature and Science where it was on display from October 2000 to January 2001.

A unique feature of the exhibit was its inclusion of three Nuu-chah-nulth "hosts" who traveled with the exhibit and served as cultural interpreters. The Nuu-chah-nulth Tribal Council paid the hosts' salaries while the exhibition was at the RBCM. But one of the conditions for the exhibition traveling to other venues was that each institution had to agree to support three hosts for the duration of the show. This support included funding for salaries, housing, and transportation.

According to Willard Gallic, Protocol Officer of the Tribal Council, the purpose of having hosts present in the exhibit was to bring "life into the exhibit" and life to the objects by putting visitors into direct contact with representatives of Nuu-chah-nulth culture. As Sinclair comments in her review of the exhibit:

> The objects require a level of personal representation that far exceeds the static nature of an exhibition, especially considering the significance of storytelling and oral traditions within the cultural groups that comprise the Nuu-chah-nulth Nation. For many Nuu-chah-nulth peoples, the objects on view in *Out of the Mist* function as a mnemonic device for handing stories down from one generation to the next.
>
> (2001:49)

Underscoring their responsibility as ambassadors of their culture, each host had to undergo training and be approved by the elders of the Tribal Council in order to become an exhibit host.[1]

In addition to the hosts, the exhibit also included videos of Nuu-chah-nulth people discussing contemporary life and culture. The presence of the hosts in the exhibit and videos depicting aspects of contemporary Nuu-chah-nulth life helped reinforce the point that the objects on display were part of living, dynamic cultural traditions.

> More often than not, museums display objects in a setting devoid of true cultural context . . . But *Out of the Mist* challenges the established museum approaches for both presentation and interpretation. This exhibition excels at identifying Nu-chah-nulth peoples as part of a living tradition through a multitude of cultural contexts.
>
> (Sinclair 2001:48)

Out of the Mist allowed the Nuu-chah-nulth people to speak for themselves and present their culture more completely through their participation in all aspects of the exhibition, i.e. its planning, development, and presentation. This high level of participation reflects considerable institutional commitment to the collaborative process. The exhibit also stands as an example of how museums, Native communities, as well as museum audiences all can benefit from collaboration and the sharing of curatorial authority. Exit interviews, conducted by the Denver Museum of Nature and Science staff, confirmed the effectiveness of this strategy. Visitors reported that contact with the Nuu-chah-nulth hosts created a greater sense of "intimacy" and "truly enhanced [their] experience." And for some, the presence of the hosts was "the best part of the exhibition" (Sinclair 2001:50). In short, *Out of the Mist* demonstrates how "in relinquishing power and authority in representing cultural diversity, museums can become common meeting grounds for all cultures and forums for cross-cultural understanding to a wide public audience" (Haas 1996:1).

Museums can not only serve as forums for cross-cultural understanding, but also as models of positive and productive intercultural relationships in their display of cross-cultural approaches to heritage management. "Museums have a crucial role not only in preserving, continuing and managing cultural heritage, but also in modeling community relations strategies" (Galla 1996:94). This role is especially important at a time when issues of diversity and multiculturalism figure prominently in public discourse. "Museums, as institutions that represent, display and interpret cultures, should assume a leadership role in shaping awareness of and attitudes toward . . . cultural diversity" (Glaser and Zenetou 1995:233). At the same time museums are striving to promote awareness of the value of cultural diversity, they are also "looking for ways to illustrate, through cultural diversity, our common humanity" (Glaser and Zenetou 1995:234). As "laboratories for experimenting with new cultural combinations and encounters" (Nederveen Pieterse 1997:140), museums can demonstrate how respect and tolerance of diversity are not incompatible with the aims and purposes of unity, but in fact, are necessary to achieving real cultural democracy. "It is because museums have a formative as well as reflective role in social relations that they are potentially of such influence" (Macdonald 1996:4).

The critical approach

The critical approach is imperative to the further development of comparative museology and cross-cultural heritage management for it is only through sustained critique and reflexivity that practice can be continually transformed. Museology, like other forms of social practice, is an ongoing process and museums are laboratories for testing museological theory. As such, museums should be concerned with not only "best practice," but practice that is continually reassessed in light of new approaches as well as changing social conditions and concerns.

> Museums are socially and historically located; and as such, they inevitably bear the imprint of social relations beyond their walls and beyond the present. Yet museums are never just spaces for the playing out of wider

157

> social relationships; a museum is a process as well as a structure, it is a creative agency as well as "contested terrain."
>
> (Karp and Lavine 1991:1)

The critical analysis of museums in diverse national and cultural settings is important for revealing how

> museums not only exist within a particular time and space, [but] also help articulate particular temporal and spatial orders. It is in this respect that we can see them as not just existing within a context but also as themselves creating cultural contexts.
>
> (Macdonald 1996:8)

Because culture is constructed it is always open to challenge, debate, and negotiation. Thus, museums are sites for examining how a community's structures and relations of power are played out in the creation of its cultural context. Here it is important to keep in mind that no community is homogenous, and that communities are composed of various segments that have overlapping, but sometimes different interests and perspectives (Karp 1992:28). In this regard, museums can be seen as a "zone of contestation," or a zone where different groups with diverse interests debate what culture is, and how it should be constructed and represented (Appadurai and Breckenridge 1992:38). The Provincial Museum of Central Kalimantan, Museum Balanga, discussed in Chapter 2, serves as a case in point.

Museum Balanga, like other Indonesian provincial museums, is supposed to represent the cultural heritage of all ethnic groups in the province. Today, the province of Central Kalimantan is culturally diverse, comprised of ethnic groups from throughout the archipelago. However, despite this diversity, the museum is primarily devoted to collecting, preserving, and displaying "Dayak" cultural heritage. This is largely due to the fact that Dayaks comprise approximately two-thirds of the 1.5 million total population of the province. In fact, Central Kalimantan has been referred to as the "Dayak Heartland" due to the predominance of Dayak peoples. And even though there are a number of different Dayak groups living in the province, the museum, for the most part, focuses on the representation of Ngaju-Dayak culture. This is because the Ngaju are the most numerous and have been historically the most economically and politically powerful Dayak group in Central Kalimantan (Ave and King 1986, Miles 1976, Schiller 1997). Consequently, in Museum Balanga, Ngaju-Dayak culture is represented as "Dayak culture" and the culture of the province.[2]

Museum Balanga's lack of diversity does not go unchallenged, however. Non-Dayaks criticize the museum for focusing on Dayak culture, and some Ngaju as well as other Dayak groups contest the museum's tendency to highlight select aspects of Dayak culture. What actually constitutes Ngaju-Dayak culture is debated among community members, but many believe everything "Dayak" originates in the ethic of Kaharingan, and Kaharingan is the basis of traditional Dayak culture (Schiller 1997). (Kaharingan is the traditional religion of several Dayak groups in Kalimantan, including Ngaju, Ot Danum, Ma'anyan, and

Luangan.) Schiller estimates that some 30 percent of the peoples known as Ngaju embrace Kaharingan (1997:23). Despite the fact that the majority of Dayaks are now Muslims or Christians, Kaharingan rituals and associated objects serve to represent "Dayak culture" in Museum Balanga.

By concentrating on Ngaju-Dayak culture, Museum Balanga is not representing the cultural diversity of the province, or even that of the Dayak people in general. Consequently, it is not adhering to the principle of "representational proportionality," or rather, that "the cultures of different groups should be equally represented within the museum, and represented on their own terms" (Bennett 1992:30). Museum Balanga is not unique in its lack of representational proportionality, but rather, illustrates a general tendency in museums. As Bourdieu has observed, "museums betray in the tiniest of details of their morphology and organization, their true function which is to reinforce for some the feeling of belonging and for others the feeling of being excluded" (Bourdieu quoted in Price and Price 1992:20).

Museum Balanga exemplifies the complexities behind the museum's role in the construction of cultural contexts in diverse communities as well as the challenges museums face in achieving the ideal of cultural democracy. It also underscores the need to interrogate what constitutes a community, local, regional, or national cultural context as a site for cultural construction. What are the boundaries of such contexts, and who decides what falls within these boundaries? Who and what is included or excluded and why? In theorizing museums in our own as well as other societies we need to be concerned with "museums as sites in which socially and culturally embedded theories are performed. The interest here is in the stories museums tell . . . and the relation those stories have to those of other sites" (Macdonald 1996:3).

Studies in comparative museology can contribute to the growing body of literature on the critical theory of museums. Such studies not only broaden our scope of inquiry, but also reveal new sites for exploration and explication. Through comparative analysis we discover that there is not one museology, but a world full of museologies. Just as museums are as diverse as the communities they represent, so too are the ways in which people perceive, care for, and preserve their cultural heritage.

In calling for a more diverse and inclusive museology, we must guard against imposing "a new, reverse exclusivity to replace the old exclusivity" (West 1993:7), or succumbing to extreme cultural relativism. We must remain wary and critical of all cultural practices that work against the principle of human equality and dignity. Konare addresses this concern in a set of questions related to the creation of community-based museums in Mali. In Konare's opinion, these museums, on the one hand, should be based on each community's own "conservation structures" and cultural traditions, but on the other hand, they should not reinforce exclusive, undemocratic cultural traditions.

> How can the hierarchization, specialization and separatism prevalent in most traditional societies be reconciled with the need to democratize and

popularize culture? How can taboos existing for certain categories of persons (women in particular) be lifted in order to allow them to view the masks, statuettes and other objects of male initiation societies? How can we enable those outside the caste to perform specialized activities? Can a museum be considered as such if access to it is limited? Should museums be designed according to social categories? Segregation of this type, based on the intangible principle of the community's right to control its own culture, must be condemned, however, on the basis of the principle of equality of all peoples.

(1983:147)

The challenge is to reconcile our respect and need for diversity with the need to acknowledge and respect the principles of universal human rights and cultural democracy.

Critical comparative museology provides a framework for identifying and examining the similar problems and challenges museums face across cultures, time, and space. Such analysis leads to a better understanding of the problematic nature of museums and systems of cultural heritage preservation in general, regardless of their context. It also provides alternative perspectives on how museological dilemmas can be addressed, and possibly resolved. The aim is to continually problematicize museums and museological practices cross-culturally rather than take them for granted or accept them uncritically. Critical analysis is the first step toward liberating culture and for transforming practice.

Notes

1 Introduction

1 For discussions on the problematic nature of the term "cultural property" and how it reflects western concepts regarding property and its ownership, especially within western legal systems, see articles by Handler, Tsosie, Welsh and Berman in *Museum Anthropology* 1997, 21(3).
2 For further critiques of conventional approaches to cultural heritage management see Handler (1987, 1988) and Kirshenblatt-Gimblett (1998).

2 The Eurocentric museum model in the non-European world

1 Information on Indonesian museum development is based on field research conducted on the Provincial Museum of Central Kalimantan over an eighteen-month period from 1991 to 1992 and in a subsequent visit in 2000. It should be noted here, however, that much of the data presented on government policies related to museum and cultural development, and their ideological underpinnings, pertains to policies and programs instituted by the Suharto "New Order" government, which was in power from 1965 to 1998. Since the collapse of the Suharto regime in 1998, the Indonesian government has been undergoing restructuring with its movement toward greater democratization and decentralization. Consequently, government policies on museums and cultural development are currently in a state of transition on both bureaucratic and ideological levels.
2 For a more extensive treatment of the issues addressed in this chapter see Kreps (1994).
3 Not surprisingly, the Dutch have been especially active in Indonesian museum development, sponsoring training programs for Indonesians in both Indonesia and the Netherlands. During my period of fieldwork in Indonesia I attended two museum-training workshops sponsored by the Dutch government's Ministry of International Development Cooperation. Instructors from the Reinwardt Academy, a higher vocational school for museum training formerly located in Leiden and now part of the Amsterdam School of Fine Arts, organized and taught workshop courses.
4 Interview with Bambang Sumadio, January 1991.
5 The role of the museum in helping create a "modern" and "civilized" citizenry has been thoroughly interrogated by Bennett (1994, 1995) and Duncan (1995).
6 See essays in Kaplan (1994) for examples of how museums have been enlisted to promote national development and help forge national identities.
7 In August 1999, the province of East Timor succeeded from the Republic of Indonesia. Consequently, the country is now composed of twenty-six provinces.
8 As part of its effort to advance professional museum training in Indonesia, the Directorate initiated the Indonesian Museum Training Program in 1990, co-sponsored by the Jakarta-

based Yayasan Nusantara Foundation, the Ford Foundation, and Asian Cultural Council. The program has involved sending museum workers (primarily from provincial museums) to the United States for training in museums. Since 1995, approximately ten individuals have participated in this program.

9 The island of Borneo is divided among the states of Malaysia, Brunei, and Indonesia. Indonesian Borneo, known collectively as Kalimantan, is comprised of the provinces of East, West, South, and Central Kalimantan.

10 Between 1991 and 1992, several Museum Balanga workers participated in the previously mentioned Dutch-sponsored museum training workshops. One worker was selected for participation in the Indonesian Museum Training Program, and in 1994, studied museology at the Burke Memorial Museum at the University of Washington in Seattle for six months.

11 When I visited Museum Balanga in 2000 I met a new staff member who was trained in anthropology. While conducting research at the museum in 1991 and 1992, the Director of the museum told me that the Directorate of Museums was trying to place an anthropologist in the museum. Thus, the Directorate was finally successful in meeting this objective.

12 One of Basir Muka's *hampatung karuhei* is in the collection of Museum Balanga. This piece is featured in Sellato's book, *Hornbill and Dragon* (1989: 226).

13 Parts of the following section were first published in Kreps (1998).

14 See Schiller (1997:44, 101) for examples of the contemporary use of jars in wedding ceremonies and death rituals among the Ngaju.

15 See Sellato (1989:232, no. 397) for a photograph showing village elders discussing a fine for adultery being paid in jars. The photograph was taken in a village on the upper Kapuas River in Central Kalimantan in the 1980s.

16 For a review of the historical development of national museums in Africa and their colonial roots see Kaplan (1994b) and Munjeri (1991).

3 Indigenous models of museums, curation, and concepts of cultural heritage preservation

1 As Clifford points out: "Every appropriation of culture, whether by insiders or outsiders, implies a specific temporal position and form of historical narration . . . The Western practice of culture collecting has its own logical genealogy, enmeshed in distinct European notions of temporality and order" (1997:232).

2 Handler also highlights the social dimension of curatorship in his definition of the museum as a social arena. The museum is "an institution in which social relationships are oriented in terms of a collection of objects which are made meaningful by those relationships – though these objects are often understood by museum natives to be meaningful independently of those social relationships" (1993:36).

3 Here one recalls Kopytoff's idea of a "cultural biography of things" because each *pusaka* object is a "culturally constructed entity endowed with culturally specific meanings and classified into culturally constituted categories" (1986:68).

4 During my own field research among the Kenyah of East Kalimantan in 1996 and 1997, I observed how heirlooms such as jars and gongs were stored inside the house or in the family *lumbung*. This practice will be discussed further in Chapter 5.

5 The Dayak, Christian family that I lived with in Palangka Raya referred to their large collection of gongs, jars, and brassware as "antiques."

6 See Taylor (1994) for discussions on the loss of Indonesian art and antiquities to the international art market.

7 During my period of field work at Museum Balanga I noted several instances in which Museum Balanga was the recipient of objects that had been recovered or confiscated by authorities.

8 It was unclear whether the villagers thought the museum workers were "commercial" collectors, which frequently visited villages, or whether or not they had had negative experiences with museum representatives in the past. One museum staff member told me that villagers (particularly those living in more remote areas) were often suspicious of anyone wearing the requisite blue civil servant shirt – a symbol of the government.

9 Burton in the book *Museums and Cultural Centres in the Pacific* (1991: 66–69) refers to this center as the Romunga Haus Tumbuna.

10 This differs from previously described practices in Indonesia where "foreign" objects were collected and preserved as part of *pusaka*. In addition to the Chinese jars as well as European cannons and weapons, examples of European technology were also coveted as *pusaka*. In my travels throughout Kalimantan I often saw items such as old sewing machines and World War II airplane parts kept as *pusaka*.

11 See Simpson (1996) for an extensive and detailed description of specific Keeping Places and Australian Aboriginal museums and cultural centers. Simpson also discusses how various government agencies and non-governmental organizations support these facilities.

12 New Zealand, or Aotearoa, is officially a "bicultural" nation composed of Maori and *Pakeha* (people of European descent). The government acknowledges and supports this partnership through various policies and programs that promote biculturalism (Clavir 2002:218).

13 As spaces to store and protect precious items and food supplies with great symbolic significance, the Maori *pataka* is similar to the Indonesian *lumbung*.

14 For a detailed description of the Oron Museum, its history, and collection of *Ekpu* figures see Nicklin (1999).

4 Reclaiming the spirit of culture

1 The literature on the politics of cultural representation in museums is now extensive. See for example, Clifford (1988, 1997), Karp and Lavine (1991), and Macdonald and Fyfe (1996). On the representation of Native American and First Nations peoples specifically see Ames (1992), King (1998) and McLoughlin (1999).

2 Debates over the final wording of the Declaration on the Rights of Indigenous Peoples largely rest on whether or not a definition of indigenous peoples should be included in the draft. Leaving the term undefined has raised a number of State concerns, among them the political implications of the link between the term "peoples" and the principle of self-determination. According to Quesenberry, " if the determination of indigenous status is solely a matter of self-identification, some States argue that any stateless group, including ethnic and national minorities, would be in a position to claim such status and with it the right to self-determination. Indigenous representatives, on the other hand, argue that the definition is a concern of the indigenous themselves and should not be subject to a State's concept of which groups or persons are included in the term" (Quesenberry 1999:106).

3 Other legislation that addressed the rights of Native Americans prior to NAGPRA includes the Indian Civil Rights Act of 1968, the Indian Self-Determination and Education Assistance Act of 1975, and the American Indian Religious Freedom Act of 1978 (Simpson 1996:136).

4 Perhaps some of the earliest and most renowned repatriation cases were those concerning the return of wampum belts to the Iroquois Confederacy. See Abrams (1994) and Simpson (1996) for descriptions of how the Confederacy negotiated their return from various museums.

5 It would be misleading to represent the repatriation of the "War Gods" from the museum to the Zuni as a seamless transaction without contestation. For a more detailed account of the debates surrounding both the Denver Art Museum and Smithsonian cases see Merrill *et al.* (1993).

6 On the Zuni "War God" case also see Simpson (1996:191–209).

7 Also see Clavir (2002:56–61) for a more extended discussion on and different interpretations of "culturally sensitive objects."

8 See Flynn and Hull-Walski (2001) for examples of how the Department of Anthropology
of the National Museum of Natural History has accommodated requests from non-Native
American constituencies.

9 Also see Clavir (2002) and Rose's paper, "Ethical and Practical Considerations in
Conserving Ethnographic Museum Objects" (1988).

10 The Smithsonian Institution was specifically exempted from NAGPRA because provisions
for repatriation were provided for it in the NMAI Act.

11 See Williamson (1997) for further details on conservation practices at the NMAI.

12 According to Joyce Herold of the Denver Museum of Nature and Science, not all tribes
object to having pipes and their stems joined while on display or in storage. This is an
example of why it is important to consult tribes individually to obtain information on
object care and handling. Generalizations cannot be made about appropriate care and
treatment since each tribe has its own protocols. Personal communication with Joyce
Herold, October 3, 2001.

13 See Simpson (1996) for a detailed discussion on the history and development of Native
American museums and cultural centers. Also Hanson (1980).

14 Also so Lee (1998) for a description of the Yup'ik Piciryarait Museum in Bethel, Alaska.

15 For a similar example from British Columbia see Clifford (1991).

16 See Clavir (2002) for other examples of the practice of loaning objects for ceremonial use
to community members as well as different interpretations of the meaning of "use" from
the perspectives of both museum professionals and Native peoples.

17 Also see Clavir (2002:176) on traditional care practices among the Makah.

18 Personal communication with Karen Cooper, Training Program Manager, Smithsonian
Center for Education and Museum Studies, July 30, 2001.

19 Hanson, in an article written in 1980, presents a different point of view on relations
between tribal museums and the mainstream professional museum community. Hanson
writes: "The museum community generally has been extremely supportive of Native
American museums, and some have made a genuine commitment to assist them"
(1980:49).

5 Museums, culture, and development

1 Appropriate technology also has had its critics. It has been described as sentimental, conservative, and paternalistic. Some claim it is merely a new form of colonialism, designed
to keep poor people poor by denying them the benefits of modern technology and by offering them only cheap, second-rate products and processes (Burkey 1993:197). I use the concept as a means of arguing how museums and museum practices, as cultural technologies,
should be adapted to local cultural contexts by drawing on people's own knowledge,
skills, and resources.

2 Parts of this section were first published in the article 'Environmental Conservation and
Cultural Action', *Practicing Anthropology* (2002) 24(2):28–32.

3 Both the Kenyah and Kayan are traditionally ranked societies, stratified into noble, com-
moner, and slave classes. Although the importance of class and the power of aristocrats
have diminished over the past decades due to processes of democratization (e.g. the out-
lawing of slavery, state-sponsored education, formal government institutions, new economic opportunities, etc.), social class can still be an influential factor in village life (see
Whittier 1978 on traditional social organization).

4 My informant gave me three Kenyah names for this animal: *sengagang*, *atui*, and *bilut* and
said it resembled a large *tikus* or rat. An ethnobotanist I spoke with who was doing
research in the area at the time of my research identified the animal as either a Malay
weasel (*Mustela nudipes*) or a giant squirrel (*Ratufu affinis*). She explained that the animal, among the Kenyah, is thought to have "magical" powers due not only to its strong
odor, but also to its bright yellow coloring and its being difficult to capture. She also

described how the hair of the animal is mixed with *damar* (resin) and coconut oil for use as a traditional medicine.

5 Andy Vuong, "Study Peppered with Promise." *The Denver Post*, February 2, 2001, column C-1.

6 At the time of my research Long Punjungan did not attract a lot of outside visitors and was not a tourist destination. But villagers and WWF staff hoped it would become one in the future as "eco-tourists" are increasingly drawn to the newly established Kayan Mentarang National Park.

7 Over the years, I have found this to be a common practice among the Dayaks. I have met many "informal scholars" who have taken it upon themselves to be the chroniclers of their people's culture and history. Having been the subject of ethnographic accounts for a century or more, Dayaks are well acquainted with the work of anthropologists and have produced texts remarkably similar to those written by anthropologists. In some cases, these texts are created for the authors' own personal satisfaction or the benefit of their community. But more often than not, they are created out of a desire to teach others about their culture and history. In this light, these texts can be seen as examples of what literary scholar Mary Louise Pratt refers to as "autoethnography" or cultural expressions in which "colonized subjects undertake to represent themselves in ways that *engage* with the colonizers' own terms" (1992:7, italics in the original). Produced by those who have themselves been the subjects of ethnographies, autoethnographies are verbal or visual texts that have been used by indigenous people to represent themselves to others (Dobkins 2001:25).

8 Agrawal points out that the distilled oil of khas has been historically highly prized as a perfume.

9 Government-sponsored efforts to renovate and preserve Dayak longhouses are somewhat ironic considering that the Indonesian government was largely responsible for their demise in the first place. During the Indonesian anti-communist fervor of the 1960s, longhouses were seen as "seeds of communism" and thus dismantled (Sellato n.d.). Interests in developing longhouses as tourist attractions largely motivate today's preservation efforts. However, the village under discussion here is not a tourist destination at the present time, and it not likely to become one in the near future due to its geographical isolation.

10 The name of the village is intentionally omitted here in order to protect it from potential looting. For an example of how scholarship on traditional art and publication of its sources has contributed to the loss of materials on some Indonesian islands see Barnes (1994).

6 Comparative museology and cross-cultural heritage management

1 In exhibition strategies that emphasize self-representation it is important to remember that: "cultural self-representation as a principle . . . does not settle the question of representation and power but shifts it from the intercultural to the intracultural sphere. More precisely, cultural insiders can contest the ways in which culture is constructed and represented interculturally" (Nederveen Pieterse 1997:134).

2 In this respect, Museum Balanga is similar to other Indonesian provincial museums in its tendency to highlight the culture of the dominant ethnic group in the province (see Taylor 1994).

Bibliography

Abrams, G. (1994) "The Case for Wampum: Repatriation from the Museum of the American Indian to the Six Nations Confederacy, Brantford, Ontario, Canada" in F. Kaplan (ed.) *Museums and the Making of "Ourselves": The Role of Objects in National Identity*, London and New York: Leicester University Press, pp. 351–384.

Acciaioli, G. (1985) "Culture as Art: From Practice to Spectacle in Indonesia," *Canberra Anthropology*, 8(1,2):148–172.

Adhyatman, S. and A. Rhido (1982) *Martavans in Indonesia.* [*Tempayan di Indonesia*], Jakarta: The Ceramic Society of Indonesia.

Agrawal, O. (1981) *Appropriate Technologies in the Conservation of Cultural Property*, Paris: UNESCO.

Alasuutari, P. (1995) *Researching Culture: Qualitative Method and Cultural Studies*, London: Sage Publications.

Alexander, J. (1993) "The Lahanan Longhouse" in J. Fox (ed.) *Inside the Austronesian House: Perspectives on Domestic Designs for Living*, Canberra: Australian National University, pp. 30–43.

Ames, M. (1992) *Cannibal Tours and Glass Boxes: The Anthropology of Museums*, Vancouver, BC: University of British Columbia Press.

Anyon, R., T.J. Ferguson and J. Welch (2000) "Heritage Management by American Indian Tribes in the Southwestern United States" in F. McManamon and A. Hatton (eds) *Cultural Resource Management in Contemporary Society: Perspectives on Managing and Presenting the Past*, New York and London: Routledge, pp. 120–141.

Appadurai, A. (1994) "Commodities and the Politics of Value" in S. Pearce (ed.) *Interpreting Objects and Collections*, New York and London: Routledge, pp. 76–91.

Appadurai, A. and C. Breckenridge (1988) "Why Public Culture?" *Public Culture Bulletin*, 1(1):1–9.

—— (1992) "Museums Are Good to Think: Heritage on View in India" in Ivan Karp, Christine Mullen-Kreamer and Steven Lavine (eds) *Museums and Communities: The Politics of Public Culture*, Washington, DC: Smithsonian Institution Press, pp. 34–55.

Appell, G. (1988) "Costing Social Change" in M. Dove (ed.) *The Real and Imagined Role of Culture in Development: Case Studies from Indonesia*, Honolulu: University of Hawai'i Press, pp. 271–284.

Aragon, L. (1994) "Multiculturalism: Some Lessons from Indonesia," *Cultural Survival Quarterly*, 18(2,3):72–76.

Ardouin, C. and E. Arinze (eds) (1995) *Museums and the Community in West Africa*, Washington, DC: The West Africa Museums Program and the Smithsonian Institution Press.

Arinze, E. and A. Cummins (eds) (1996) *Curatorship: Indigenous Perspectives in Post-Colonial Societies. Proceedings. Mercury Series, Directorate Paper 8*, Canadian Museum of Civilization with the Commonwealth Association of Museums and the University of Victoria, British Columbia.

Arnoldi, M. and K. Hardin (1996) "Introduction: Efficacy and Objects" in M.J. Arnoldi, C. Geary and K. Hardin (eds) *African Material Culture*, Bloomington: Indiana University Press, pp. 1–28.

Asad, T. (1973) *Anthropology and the Colonial Encounter*, London: Ithaca Press.

Ave, J. and V. King (1986) *Borneo: People of the Weeping Forest*, Leiden: National Museum of Ethnography.

Baradas, D. (1980) "Developing or Traditional Area Museums" in R. Edwards and J. Stewart (eds) *Preserving Indigenous Cultures: A New Role for Museums*, Canberra: Australian Government Publishing Service, pp. 79–80.

Barley, N. (1994) *Smashing Pots: Works of Clay from Africa*, Washington, DC: Smithsonian Institution Press.

Barnes, R. (1994) " 'Without Cloth We Cannot Marry': The Textiles of Lamaholot in Transition" in P. Taylor (ed.) *Fragile Traditions: Indonesian Art in Jeopardy*, Honolulu: University of Hawai'i Press, pp. 13–27.

Barreiro, R. (1994) "The Way South: Latin American Indigenous Encounters" in *Native American Expressive Culture*, New York: Akwe:kon Press and National Museum of the American Indian, xi(3–4):68–74.

Barringer, T. and T. Flynn (eds) (1998) *Colonialism and the Object. Empire, Material Culture and the Museum*, London and New York: Routledge.

Barth, F. (1989) "The Analysis of Culture in Complex Societies," *Ethnos*, 54(3–4):120–142.

Bazin, G. (1967) *The Museum Age*, trans. Jane van Nuis Cahill, New York: Universe Books.

Bennett, T. (1992) "Putting Policy into Cultural Studies" in L. Grossberg, C. Nelson and P. Treichler (eds) *Cultural Studies*, London and New York: Routledge, pp. 23–37.

—— (1994) "The Exhibitionary Complex" in N. Dirks, G. Eley and S. Ortner (eds) *Culture, Power, History: A Reader in Contemporary Social Theory*, Princeton: Princeton University Press, pp. 123–154.

—— (1995) *The Birth of the Museum: History, Theory, Politics*, London and New York: Routledge.

Berman, T. (1997) "Beyond the Museum: The Politics of Representation in Asserting Rights to Cultural Property," *Museum Anthropology*, 21(3):19–28.

Bock, C. (1988[1881]) *The Headhunters of Borneo*, Singapore: Graham Bash.

Boswell, D. and J. Evans (eds) (1999) *Representing the Nation: A Reader. Histories, Heritage, and Museums*, London and New York: Routledge.

Bouquet, M. (ed.) (2001) *Academic Anthropology and the Museum*, New York and Oxford: Berghahn Books.

Boylan, P. (1996) "ICOM at Fifty," *Museum*, 191(43):47–53.

Bray, T. (ed.) (2001) *The Future of the Past: Archeologists, Native Americans, and Repatriation*, New York and London: Garland Publishing.

Burcaw, G. (1975) *Introduction to Museum Work*, Nashville: American Association for State and Local History.

Burkey, S. (1993) *People First: A Guide to Self-Reliant, Participatory Rural Development*, London and New Jersey: Zed Books.

Burton, J. (1991) "The Romunga Haus Tumbuna, Western Highlands Province, PNG" in S. Eoe and P. Swadling (eds) *Museums and Cultural Centres in the Pacific*, Port Moresby: Papua New Guinea National Museum, pp. 66–70.

Canclini, N. (1995) *Hybrid Cultures: Stategies for Entering and Leaving Modernity*, trans. C. Chippari, Minneapolis: University of Minnesota Press.

Cannon-Brookes, P. (1984) "The Nature of Museum Collections" in J. Thompson (ed.) *Manual of Curatorship: A Guide to Museum Practices*, London: Butterworths, pp. 115–126.

Cash Cash (2001) "Medicine Bundles: An Indigenous Approach" in T. Bray (ed.) *The Future of the Past: Archeologists, Native Americans, and Repatriation*, New York and London: Garland Publishing, pp. 139–145.

Chambers, R. (1993) *Challenging the Professions: Frontiers for Rural Development*, London: Intermediate Technology Institute Publications.

Childs, E. (1980) "Museums and the American Indian: Legal Aspects of Repatriation," *Council for Museum Anthropology Newsletter*, 4(4):4–29.

Chin, L. (1988) "Trade Objects: Their Impact on the Cultures of the Indigenous Peoples of Sarawak, Borneo," *Expedition*, 30(1):59–64.

Clark, S. (1997) "Representing Native Identity: The Trail of Tears and the Cherokee Heritage Center in Oklahoma," *Cultural Survival Quarterly*, 21(1):36–40.

Clavir, M. (1994) "Preserving Conceptual Integrity: Ethics and Theory in Preventive Conservation" in R. Ashok and P. Smith (eds), *Preventive Conservation: Practice, Theory, and Research, Preprints of the Contributions to the 15th Ottawa IIC Congress, 12–16 September, 1994*, Ottawa: Canada.

—— (1996) "Reflections on Changes in Museums and the Conservation of Collections from Indigenous Peoples," *Journal for the American Institute of Conservation*, 35:99–107.

—— (2002) *Preserving What is Valued: Museums, Conservation, and First Nations*, Vancouver: University of British Columbia Press.

Clifford, J. (1987) "Of Other Peoples: Beyond the Salvage Paradigm" in Hal Foster (ed.) *Discussions in Contemporary Culture*, Seattle: Bay Press, pp. 121–150.

—— (1988) *The Predicament of Culture: Twentieth Century Literature, Ethnography, and Art*, Cambridge: Harvard University Press.

—— (1991) "Four Northwest Coast Museums: Travel Reflections" in Ivan Karp and Steven Lavine (eds) *Exhibiting Cultures: The Poetics and Politics of Museum Display*, Washington, DC: Smithsonian Institution Press, pp. 212–254.

—— (1997) *Routes: Travel and Translation in the Late Twentieth Century*, Cambridge: Harvard University Press.

Cohn, J. (1988) "Culture and Conservation," *BioScience*, 38(7):450–453.

Cole, D. (1986) *Captured Heritage: The Scramble for Northwest Coast Artifacts*, Seattle: University of Washington Press.

Craig, B. (1990) "Relic and Trophy Arrays as Art Among the Mountain-Ok, Central New Guinea" in A. Hanson and L. Hanson (eds) *Art and Identity in Oceania*, Honolulu: University of Hawai'i Press, pp. 196–210.

Cruikshank, J. (1995) "Imperfect Translations: Rethinking Objects of Ethnographic Collections," *Museum Anthropology*, 19(1):25–38.

Damais, A. (1992) "Pusaka in Times of Change" in H. Soebadio (ed.) *Pusaka: Art of Indonesia*, Singapore: Archipelago Press, pp. 205–208.

Dark, P. (1990) "Tomorrow's Heritage is Today's Art, and Yesteryear's Identity" in A. Hanson and L. Hanson (eds) *Art and Identity in Oceania*, Honolulu: University of Hawai'i Press, pp. 244–268.

Davenport, W. (1990) "The Figurative Sculpture of Santa Cruz Island" in A. Hanson and L. Hanson (eds) *Art and Identity in Oceania*, Honolulu: University of Hawai'i Press, pp. 98–110.

Davis, L. (1989) "Locating the Live Museum," *News from Native California*, 4(1):4–9.

Davis, P. (1999) *Ecomuseums: A Sense of Place*, London and New York: Leicester University Press.

Denyer, S. (1978) *African Traditional Architecture*, New York: Africana Publishing Company.

Departemen Pendidikan dan Kebudayaan (1986) *Direktori Museum-Museum di Indonesia. Volumes 1 and 2*, Jakarta: Proyek Pengembangan Permuseuman.

—— (1987) *Sejarah Direktorat Permuseuman*, Jakarta: Proyek Pengembangan Permuseuman.

Directorate of Museums (1999) *Directory of Museums in Indonesia*, Jakarta: Department of Education and Culture, Directorate General for Culture.

Directorate Permuseuman (1989) *Pembangunan Permuseuman di Indonesia Sampai Akhir Pelita IV*, Jakarta: Direktorate Jenderal Kebudayaan dan Pendidikan, Proyek Pengembangan Permuseuman.

Dobkins, R. (2001) "Art and Autoethnography: Frank Day and the Uses of Anthropology," *Museum Anthropology*, 24(2/3):22–29.

Dove, M. (1988) "Introduction: Traditional Culture and Development in Contemporary Indonesia" in M. Dove (ed.) *The Real and Imagined Role of Culture in Development: Case Studies from Indonesia*, Honolulu: University of Hawai'i Press, pp. 1–37.

Duncan, C. (1995) *Civilizing Rituals: Inside Public Art Museums*, London and New York: Routledge.

Durrans, B. (1992) "Behind the Scenes: Museums and Selective Criticism," *Anthropology Today*, 8(4):11–15.

Edson, G. (ed.) (1997) *Museum Ethics*, London and New York: Routledge.

Edson, G. and D. Dean (1994) *The Handbook for Museums*, New York and London: Routledge.

Edwards, R. and J. Stewart (1980) *Preserving Indigenous Cultures: A New Role for Museums*, Canberra: Australian Government Publishing Service.

Ember, C. and M. Ember (2001) *Cross-Cultural Research Methods*, Walnut Creek: Altamira Press.

Eoe, S. and P. Swadling (eds) (1991) *Museums and Cultural Centres in the Pacific*, Port Moresby: Papua New Guinea National Museum.

Erikson, P. (1996) " 'So My Children Can Stay in the Pueblo': Indigenous Community Museums and Self-Determination in Oaxaca, Mexico," *Museum Anthropology*, 20(1): 37–46.

Errington, S. (1994) "Unraveling Narratives" in P. Taylor (ed.) *Fragile Traditions: Indonesian Arts in Jeopardy*, Honolulu: University of Hawai'i Press, pp. 139–165.

—— (1998) *The Death of Authentic Primitive Art and Other Tales of Progress*, Berkeley: University of California Press.

Escobar, A. (1995) *Encountering Development: The Making and Unmaking of the Third World*, Princeton: Princeton University Press.

Evans, R. (1999) "Tribal Involvement in Exhibition Planning and Conservation Treatment: A New Institutional Approach," *ICOM Ethnographic Conservation Newsletter*, 19:13–16.

Fabian, J. (1983) *Time and the Other: How Anthropology Makes Its Object*, New York: Columbia University Press.

Featherstone, M., S. Lash, and R. Robertson (1995) *Global Modernities*, London: Sage Publications.

Flynn, G. and D. Hull-Walski (2001) "Merging Traditional Indigenous Curation Methods with Modern Museum Standards of Care," *Museum Anthropology*, 25(1):31–40.

Foster, R. (1991) "Making National Cultures in the Global Ecumene," *Annual Review of Anthropology*, 20:235–260.

Foulcher, K. (1990) "The Construction of an Indonesian National Culture: Patterns in Hegemony and Resistance" in A. Budiman (ed.) *State and Civil Society in Indonesia*, Victoria, Australia: Centre for Southeast Asian Studies, Monash University, pp. 301–320.

Friedman, J. (1990) "Being in the World: Globalization and Localization" in M. Featherstone (ed.) *Global Culture: Nationalization, Globalization, and Modernity*, London: Sage Publications, pp. 311–328.

Fuller, N. (1992) "The Museum as a Vehicle for Community Empowerment: The Ak-chin Indian Community Ecomuseum Project" in I. Karp, C. Mullen-Kreamer, and S. Lavine (eds) *Museums and Communities: The Politics of Public Culture*, Washington, DC: Smithsonian Institution Press, pp. 327–365.

Galla, A. (1996) "Indigenous Peoples, Museums and Frameworks for Effective Change" in E. Arinze and A. Cummins (eds) *Curatorship: Indigenous Perspectives in Post-Colonial Societies. Proceedings. Mercury Series, Directorate Paper 8*, Canadian Museum of Civilization with the Commonwealth Association of Museums and the University of Victoria, British Columbia, pp. 82–95.

—— (1997) "Indigenous Peoples, Museums and Ethics" in G. Edson (ed.) *Museum Ethics*, London and New York: Routledge, pp. 140–155.

Ganslmayr, H. (1990) "Cultural Dimension of Development Resolution," *ICME News*, 16:2–3.

Garza, C. and S. Powell (2001) "Ethics and the Past: Reburial and Repatriation in American Archeology" in T. Bray (ed.) *The Future of the Past: Archeologists, Native Americans, and Repatriation*, New York and London: Garland Publishing, pp. 37–56.

Glaser, J. and A. Zenetou (1996) *Museums: A Place to Work*, London and New York: Routledge.

Goff, B. (1994) "Reviving Crafts and Affirming Culture: From Grassroots Development to National Policy" in C. Kleymeyer (ed.) *Cultural Expressions and Grassroots Development: Cases from Latin America and the Caribbean*, Boulder and London: Lynne Reiner Publishers, pp. 121–134.

Gulliford, A. (2000) *Sacred Objects and Sacred Places: Preserving Tribal Traditions*, Boulder: University of Colorado Press.

Haas, J. (1996) "Power, Objects, and a Voice for Anthropology," *Current Anthropology*, 37 Supplement:S1–S22.

—— (2001) "Sacred Under the Law: Repatriation and Religion Under the Native American Graves Protection and Repatriation Act (NAGPRA)" in T. Bray (ed.) *The Future of the Past: Archeologists, Native Americans, and Repatriation*, New York and London: Garland Publishing, pp. 117–126.

Hakiwai, A. (1999) "Kaitiakitanga-Looking After Culture: Insights from 'Within' – Two Curatorial Perspectives," *ICOM Ethnographic Conservation Newsletter*, 19:10–12.

Handler, R. (1987) "Heritage and Hegemony: Recent Works on Historic Preservation and Interpretation," *Anthropological Quarterly*, 60(3):137–141.

—— (1988) *Nationalism and the Politics of Culture in Quebec*, Madison: University of Wisconsin Press.

—— (1992) "On the Valuing of Museum Objects," *Museum Anthropology*, 17(1):33–36.

—— (1993) "An Anthropological Definition of the Museum," *Museum Anthropology*, 17(1):33–36.

—— (1997) "Cultural Property, Culture Theory and Museum Anthropology," *Museum Anthropology*, 21(3):3–4.

Hannerz, U. (1989) "Culture Between Center and Periphery: Toward a Macroanthropology," *Ethnos*, 54(3–4):200–216.

Hanson, A. and L. Hanson (1990) *Art and Identity in Oceania*, Honolulu: University of Hawai'i Press.

Hanson, J. (1980) "The Reappearing Vanishing American," *Museum News*, 59(2):44–51.

Harjo, S. (1996) "Introduction" in *Mending the Circle: A Native American Repatriation Guide*, New York: American Indian Ritual Object and Repatriation Foundation.

Harris, N. (1981) "Cultural Institutions and American Modernization," *Journal of Library History*, 16(1):28–47.

—— (1990) *Cultural Excursions: Marketing Appetites and Cultural Tastes in Modern America*, Chicago: University of Chicago Press.

Harrisson, B. (1990) *Pusaka: Heirloom Jars of Borneo*, Singapore: Oxford University Press.

Harth, M. (1999) "Learning from Museums with Indigenous Collections: Beyond Repatriation," *Curator*, 42(4):274–284.

Hauenschild, A. (1998) *Claims and Reality of New Museology: Case Studies in Canada, the United States and Mexico*, Ph.D. dissertation. Hamburg: University of Hamburg. English edition published by the Center for Museum Studies, Washington, DC: Smithsonian Institution.

Hazeltine, B. and C. Bull (1999) *Appropriate Technology: Tools, Choices, and Implications*, San Diego and London: Academic Press.

Healy, K. (1994) "The Recovery of Cultural Resources for Development" in *1994 Festival of American Folklife Program*, Washington, DC: Smithsonian Institution and National Park Service, pp. 14–19.

Herold, J. (2001) "The Spirit of Repatriation: Ten Years of NAGPRA at the DMNS," *Denver Museum of Nature and Science Members' Monthly*, 2(5):6.

Heryanto, A. (1988) "The Development of 'Development'," *Indonesia*, 46:1–24.

Hinsley, C. (1981) *Savages and Scientists: The Smithsonian Institution and the Development of American Anthropology, 1840–1910*, Washington, DC: Smithsonian Institution Press.

Hooper-Greenhill, E. (1989) "The Museum in the Disciplinary Society" in S. Pearce (ed.) *Museum Studies in Material Culture*, London: Leicester University Press, pp. 41–72.

—— (1992) *Museums and the Shaping of Knowledge*, London and New York: Routledge.

—— (2000) *Museums and the Interpretation of Visual Culture*, London and New York: Routledge.

Hose, C. and W. MacDougall (1966) *The Pagan Tribes of Borneo*, Vols 1 and 2, London: Frank Cass and Company.

Hoskins, J. (1998) *Biographical Objects: How Things Tell the Stories of People's Lives*, New York and London: Routledge.

House, C. (1994) "The Art of Balance" in *All Roads are Good: Native Voices on Life and Culture*, Washington, DC: National Museum of the American Indian, Smithsonian Institution, pp. 91–101.

Hudson, K. (1977) *Museums for the 1980s: A Survey of World Trends*, Paris: UNESCO.

—— (1987) *Museums of Influence*, Cambridge: Cambridge University Press.

Hufford, M. (1994) *Conserving Culture: A New Discourse on Heritage*, Urbana and Chicago: University of Illinois Press, pp. 1–14.

Huizer, G. and B. Mannheim (eds) (1979) *The Politics of Anthropology: From Colonialism and Sexism Toward a View from Below*, The Hague: Mouton Publishers.

Hunt, M. and P. Seitel (1985) "Cultural Conservation" in *1985 Festival of American Folklife Program*, Washington, DC: Smithsonian Institution and National Park Service.

Hymes, D. (ed.) (1972) *Reinventing Anthropology*, New York: Pantheon.

Jessup, H. (1990) *Court Arts of Java*, New York: The Asia Society and Harry N. Abrams.

Jones, A.L. (1993) "Exploding Canons: The Anthropology of Museums," *Annual Review of Anthropology*, 22:201–220.

Joseph, O. (1980) "Cook Islands" in R. Edwards and J. Stewart (eds) *Preserving Indigenous Cultures: A New Role for Museums*, Canberra: Australian Government Publishing Service, pp. 141–143.

Kaeppler, A. (1992) "Ali'I and Maka'ainana: The Representation of Hawaiians in Museums at Home and Abroad" in I. Karp, C. Mullen-Kreamer and S. Lavine (eds) *Museums and Communities: The Politics of Public Culture*, Washington, DC: Smithsonian Institution Press, pp. 458–475.

—— (1994) "Paradise Regained: The Role of Pacific Museums in Forging National Identity" in F. Kaplan (ed.) *Museums and the Making of "Ourselves.": The Role of Objects in National Identity*, London and New York: Leicester University Press, pp. 19–44.

Kahn, M. (2000) "Not Really Pacific Voices: Politics of Representation in Collaborative Museum Exhibits," *Museum Anthropology*, 24(1):57–74.

Kapferer, B. (1988) *Legends of the People, Myths of the State: Violence, Intolerance, and Political Change in Sri Lanka and Australia*, Washington, DC: Smithsonian Institution Press.

Kaplan, F. (1992) "Growing Pains," *Museum News*, 71(1):49–51.

—— (1994) "Nigerian Museums: Envisaging Culture as National Identity" in F. Kaplan (ed.) *Museums and the Making of "Ourselves": The Role of Objects in National Identity*, London and New York: Leicester University Press.

Karp, I. (1992) "Introduction: Museums and Communities: The Politics of Public Culture" in I. Karp, C. Mullen-Kreamer and S. Lavine (eds) *Museums and Communities: The Politics of Public Culture*, Washington, DC: Smithsonian Institution Press, pp. 1–17.

Karp, I. and S. Lavine (eds) (1991) *Exhibiting Cultures: The Poetics and Politics of Museum Display*, Washington, DC: Smithsonian Institution Press.

Karp, I., C. Mullen-Kreamer and S. Lavine (eds) (1992) *Museums and Communities: The Politics of Public Culture*, Washington, DC: Smithsonian Institution Press.

Kartiwa, S. (1992) "Pusaka and the Palaces of Java" in H. Soebadio (ed.) *Pusaka: Art of Indonesia*, Singapore: Archipelago Press, pp. 159–164.

King, C.R. (1998) *Colonial Discourses, Collective Memories, and the Exhibition of Native American Cultures and Histories in the Contemporary United States*, New York and London: Garland Publishing.

Kipp, R. (1993) *Dissociated Identities: Ethnicity, Religion, and Class in an Indonesian Society*, Ann Arbor: University of Michigan Press.

Kirshenblatt-Gimblett, B. (1991) "Objects of Ethnography" in I. Karp and S. Lavine (eds) *Exhibiting Cultures. The Poetics and Politics of Museum Display*, Washington, DC: Smithsonian Institution Press, pp. 386–443.

—— (1998) *Destination Culture: Tourism, Museums, and Heritage*, Berkeley: University of California Press.

Kleymeyer, C. (1994a) "Cultural Traditions and Community-Based Conservation" in D. Western, R. Wright and S. Strum (eds) *Natural Connections: Perspectives in Community-Based Conservation*, Washington, DC: Island Press, pp. 323–346.

—— (1994b) "Introduction" and "The Uses and Functions of Cultural Expression in Grassroots Development" in C. Kleymeyer (ed.) *Cultural Expressions and Grassroots Development: Cases from Latin America and the Caribbean*, Boulder and London: Lynne Reiner Publishers, pp. 1–13, 17–36.

Koffi, A. (1995) "Socio-Historical Factors for Improved Integration of Local Museums: at Boundiali, Cote d'Ivoire" in C. Ardouin and E. Arinze (eds) *Museums and the Community in West Africa*, Washington, DC: The West African Museums Program and Smithsonian Institution Press, pp. 87–94.

Konare, A. (1983) "Towards a New Type of Ethnographic Museum in Africa," *Museum*, 35(3):146–149.

—— (1995) "The Creation and Survival of Local Museums" in C. Ardouin and E. Arinze (eds) *Museums and the Community in West Africa*, Washington, DC: The West African Museums Program and Smithsonian Institution Press, pp. 5–10.

Kopytoff, I. (1986) "The Cultural Biography of Things: Commoditization as Process" in A. Appadurai (ed.) *The Social Life of Things*, Cambridge: Cambridge University Press, pp. 64–91.

Kreps, C. (1991) *Report to the Ford Foundation on Survey Trip to the Museum Siwalima, Ambon, Maluku, and the Museum for Culture and Progress, Agats, Irian Jaya, 22 May to 4 June 1991.*

—— (1994) "*On Becoming 'Museum-Minded': A Study of Museum Development and the Politics of Culture in Indonesia*," Ph.D. dissertation, Eugene: University of Oregon.

—— (1997) "Participatory Approaches to Museum Development," *Smithsonian Center for Museum Studies Bulletin*, 5(3):1–12.

—— (1998) "Museum-Making and Indigenous Curation in Central Kalimantan, Indonesia," *Museum Anthropology*, 22(1):5–17.

—— (2002) "Environmental Conservation and Cultural Action," *Practicing Anthropology*, 24(2):28–32.

Kurin, R. (1989) "Why We Do the Festival" in *1989 Festival of American Folklife Program*, Washington, DC: Smithsonian Institution and National Park Service, pp. 8–21.

Ladd, A. (2001) "A Zuni Perspective on Repatriation" in T. Bray (ed.) *The Future of the Past: Archeologists, Native Americans, and Repatriation*, New York and London: Garland Publishing, pp. 107–116.

Lavine, S. (1992) "Audience, Ownership, and Authority: Designing Relations between Museums and Communities" in I. Karp, C. Mullen-Kreamer and S. Lavine (eds) *Museums and Communities: The Politics of Public Culture*, Washington, DC: Smithsonian Institution Press, pp. 137–157.

Lee, M. (1998) "The Ugtarvik and the Yup'ik Piciryarait Museums: A Case Study in Comparative Anthropological Museology," *Museum Anthropology*, 22(1):43–48.

Leibrick, F. (1989) "The Power of Objects: Material Culture's Strategic Importance to Orang Ulu Ethnicity and the Processes of Change," *Sarawak Museum Journal*, 61(4): 198–213.

Lewis, P. (1990) "Tourist Art, Traditional Art and the Museum in Papua New Guinea" in A. Hanson and L. Hanson (eds) *Art and Identity in Oceania*, Honolulu: University of Hawai'i Press, pp. 149–163.

MacClancy, J. (1997) "Anthropology, Art and Contest" in J. MacClancy (ed.) *Contesting Art: Art, Politics and Identity in the Modern World*, Oxford and New York: Berg, pp. 1–26.

Macdonald, S. (1996) "Theorizing Museums: An Introduction" in S. Macdonald and G. Fyfe (eds) *Theorizing Museums: Representing Identity and Diversity in a Changing World*, Oxford: Blackwell Publishers.

Macdonald, S. and G. Fyfe (eds) (1996) *Theorizing Museums: Identity and Diversity in a Changing World*, Oxford: Blackwell Publishers.

Marcus, G. (1995) "Ethnography in/of the World System: The Emergence of Multi-Sited Ethnography," *Annual Review of Anthropology*, 24:95–117.

Marcus, G. and M. Fischer (eds) (1986) *Anthropology and Cultural Critique: An Experimental Movement in Human Sciences*, Chicago: University of Chicago Press.

Martowikrido, W. (1992) "Heirlooms of the Outer Islands" in H. Soebadio (ed.) *Pusaka: Art of Indonesia*, Singapore: Archipelago Press.

Mauger, J. and J. Bowechop (n.d.) *Tribal Collections Management at the Makah Cultural and Research Center*, Washington, DC: American Indian Museum Studies Program, Office of Museum Programs, Smithsonian Institution.

Mayberry-Lewis, D. (1994) "Forward: Culture and Development" in C. Kleymeyer (ed.) *Cultural Expressions and Grassroots Development: Cases from Latin American and the Caribbean*, Boulder and London: Lynne Reiner Publishers, pp. ix–xv.

Maynard, P. (1985) "The New Museology Proclaimed," *Museum*, 37(148):200–201.

McLoughlin, M. (1999) *Museums and the Representation of Native Canadians*, New York and London: Garland Publishing.

Mead, S. (1983) "Indigenous Models of Museums in Oceania," *Museum*, 35(139):98–101.

—— (1990) "The Nature of Taonga" in *Taonga Maori Conference Papers*, Wellington, New Zealand: Cultural Conservation Advisory Council, Department of Internal Affairs.

Meister, N. (1999) "Exploring Representations of the Pacific in Majority and Minority Museums," unpublished M.Sc. thesis, Boulder, CO: University of Colorado.

Merrill, W., E. Ladd and T.J. Ferguson (1993) "The Return of the Ahayu:da: Lessons for Repatriation from Zuni Pueblo and the Smithsonian Institution," *Current Anthropology*, 34(5):523–568.

Messenger, P. (ed.) (1989) *The Ethics of Collecting Cultural Property*, Albuquerque: University of New Mexico Press.

Metcalf, P. (1982) *A Borneo Journey Into Death: Berawan Eschatology from Its Rituals*, Philadelphia: University of Pennsylvania Press.

Mibach, L. (n.d.) "The Native North American Approach to Conservation" in *Symposium 86 Proceedings*, Canadian Conservation Institute, Ottawa, Ontario.

Mibach, L. and S. Wolf Green (1989) "Sacred Objects and Museum Conservation: Kill or Cure?" in G. Horse Capture (ed.) *The Concept of Sacred Materials and Their Place in the World*, Cody, Wyoming: The Plains Indian Museum Buffalo Bill Historical Center, pp. 57–66.

Mihesuah, D. (ed.) (2000) *Repatriation Reader: Who Owns American Indian Remains?*, Lincoln and London: University of Nebraska Press.

Mihing, T. (1989) *Sekelumit Koleksi Museum Negeri Kalimantan Tengah*, Palangka Raya: Departemen Pendidikan dan Kebudayaan Kantor Wilayah Propinsi Kalimantan Tengah.

Miles, D. (1976) *Cutlass and Crescent Moon: A Case Study of Social and Political Change in Outer Indonesia*, Sydney: Center for Southeast Asian Studies.

Mula, B. (1991) "The Gogodala Cultural Centre, Balimo, Western Province, PNG" in S. Eoe and P. Swadling (eds) *Museums and Cultural Centres in the Pacific*, Port Moresby: Papua New Guinea National Museum, pp. 70–74.

Munjeri, D. (1991) "Refocusing or Reorientation: The Exhibit or the Populace: Zimbabwe on the Threshold" in I. Karp and S. Lavine (eds) *Exhibiting Cultures: The Poetics and Politics of Museum Display*, Washington, DC: Smithsonian Institution Press, pp. 444–456.

Munzenrider, C. (1998) "Report on a Community-Based Conservation Project," *ICOM Ethnographic Conservation Newsletter*, 18:1–2.

Nason, J. (2000) " 'Our' Indians: The Unidimensional Indian in the Disembodied Local Past" in A. Kawasaki (ed.) *The Changing Presentation of the American Indian: Museums and Native Cultures*, Washington, DC: National Museum of the American Indian, Smithsonian Institution, pp. 29–46.

Nederveen Pieterse, J. (1995) "Globalization and Hybridization" in M. Featherstone, S. Lash and R. Robertson (eds) *Global Modernities*, London: Sage Publications, pp. 45–68.

—— (1997) "Multiculturalism and Museums: Discourse about Others in the Age of Globalization," *Theory, Culture, and Society*, 14(4):123–146

Nero, K. and N. Graburn (1978) "The Institutional Context of the Arts of Oceania with Special Reference to Micronesia," Berkeley: *Kroeber Anthropological Society Papers* nos. 57 and 58.

Newton, D. (1994) "Old Wine in New Bottles, and the Reverse" in F. Kaplan (ed.) *Museums and the Making of "Ourselves": The Role of Objects in National Identity*, London and New York: Leicester University Press, pp. 269–290.

Nicklin, K. (1983) "Traditional Preservation Methods: Some African Practices Observed," *Museum*, 35(138):123–127.

—— (1999) *Ekpu: The Oron Ancestor Figures of South Eastern Nigeria*, London: The Horniman Museum and Gardens.

O'Connor, S. (1983) "Art Critics, Connoisseurs, and Collectors in the Southeast Asian Rain Forest: A Study in Cross-Cultural Art Theory," *Journal of Southeast Asian Studies*, 15(2):400–408.

Okita, S. (1982) "Museums as Agents for Cultural Transmission," *Nigeria Magazine*, 143:2–20.

Parker, P. (1990) *Keepers of the Treasures: Protecting Historic Properties and Cultural Traditions on Indian Lands*, Washington DC: National Park Service, United States Department of the Interior.

Paulias, N. (1991) "The Cultural Heritage of the Pacific: Preservation, Development, and Promotion" in S. Eoe and P. Swadling (eds) *Museums and Cultural Centres in the Pacific*, Port Moresby: Papua New Guinea National Museum, pp. 5–10.

Pearce, S. (ed.) (1991) *Museum Studies in Material Culture*, London and Washington, DC: Leicester University Press and Smithsonian Institution Press.

—— (1992) *Museums, Objects, and Collections: A Cultural Study*, Washington, DC: Smithsonian Institution Press.

Pemberton, J. (1994) *On the Subject of "Java,"* Ithaca: Cornell University Press.

Pomian, K. (1994) "The Collection: Between the Visible and Invisible" in S. Pearce (ed.) *Interpreting Objects and Collections*, London and New York: Routledge, pp. 160–174.

Pratt, M.L. (1992) *Imperial Eyes: Travel Writing and Transculturation*, London: Routledge Press.

Price, R. and S. Price (1992) *Equatoria*, London and New York: Routledge.

Quesenberry, S. (1999) "Recent United Nations Initiatives Concerning the Rights of Indigenous Peoples" in T. Johnson (ed.) *Contemporary Native American Political Issues*, Walnut Creek and London: Altamira Press, pp. 103–118.

Rahman, A. (1993) *People's Self Development: Perspectives on Participatory Action Research*, London and New Jersey: Zed Books.

Richter, A. (1994) *Arts and Crafts of Indonesia*, San Francisco: Chronicle Books.

Rivard, R. (1984) "Opening Up the Museum". Unpublished manuscript.

Robb, K. (1992) *Museums and Nation Building: The Role of the Museums in the National Development of Costa Rica. A Contribution in the Study of Culture and Development*, Ph.D. dissertation, Indiana University.

Roberts, C. (1994) "Object, Subject, Practitioner: Native Americans and Cultural Institutions," in *Native American Expressive Culture*, New York: Akwe:kon Press and National Museum of the American Indian, xi(3–4):22–29.

Rosaldo, R. (1989) *Culture and Truth: The Remaking of Social Analysis*, Boston: Beacon Press.

Rose, C. (1988) "Ethical and Practical Considerations in Conserving Ethnographic Museum Objects" in T. Morita and C. Pearson (eds) *The Museum Conservation of Ethnographic Objects*, Senri Ethnological Studies 23, Osaka, Japan: National Museum of Ethnography.

Rosoff, N. (1998) "Integrating Native Views into Museum Procedures: Hope and Practice at the National Museum of the American Indian," *Museum Anthropology*, 22(1):33–42.

Ryan, F. and F. Vivekananada (1993) *Finding New Routs in Old Paths: Linking Cultural Needs to Technical Knowledge Appropriate Technology Inspires Developing Societies Concept, Controversy and Clarification*, Stockholm: Bethany Books.

Sahlins, M. (1994) "Goodbye to Tristes Tropes: Ethnography in the Context of Modern World History" in R. Borofsky (ed.) *Assessing Cultural Anthropology*, New York: McGraw-Hill, pp. 377–395.

Said, E. (1978) *Orientalism*, New York: Vintage Books.

Scharer, H. (1963) *Ngaju Religion: The Conception of God Among a South Borneo People*, trans. R. Needham, The Hague: Nijhof.

Schech, S. and J. Haggis (2000) *Culture and Development: A Critical Introduction*, Oxford: Blackwell Publishers.

Schildkrout, E. (1999) "Royal Treasury, Historic House, or Just a Museum? Transforming Manhyia Palace, Ghana, into a Site of Cultural Tourism," *Museum Anthropology*, 22(3): 14–27.

Schiller, A. (1986) "A Ngaju Ritual Specialist and the Rationalization of Hindu-Kaharingan," *Sarawak Museum Journal*, 36 (new series):231–242.

—— (1997) *Small Sacrifices: Religious Change and Cultural Identity among the Ngaju of Indonesia*, New York and Oxford: Oxford University Press.

Schneebaum, T. (1982) "The Asmat Museum of Culture and Progress," *Cultural Survival Quarterly*, 6(4):36–37.

Schultz, E. (1994) "Notes on the History of Collecting and Museums" in S. Pearce (ed.) *Interpreting Objects and Collections*, London and New York: Routledge, pp. 175–187.

Sellato, B. (1989) *Hornbill and Dragon*, Jakarta: Elf Aquitaine Indonesie.

—— (n.d.) "Culture, History, Politics and the Emergence of Provincial Identities in Kalimantan". Unpublished manuscript.

Sharma, B. (1999) "Cultural Preservation Reconsidered: The Case of Canadian Aboriginal Art," *Critique of Anthropology*, 19(1):53–62.

Simpson, M. (1996) *Making Representations: Museums in the Post-Colonial Era*, London and New York: Routledge.

Sinclair, J. (2001) "HuupuKwanum Tupaat: Out of the Mist: Treasures of the Nuu-chah-nulth Chiefs at the Denver Museum of Nature and Science," *Museum Anthropology*, 25(1):48–53.

Smidt, D. and N. McGuigan (1993) "An Emic and Etic Role for Abelam Art (Papua New Guinea): The Context of a Collecting Trip on Behalf of the Rijksmuseum voor Volkenkunde, Leiden" in P. Dark and R. Rose (eds) *Artistic Heritage in a Changing Pacific*, Honolulu: University of Hawai'i Press, pp. 121–142.

Soebadio, H. (1985) *Cultural Policy in Indonesia*, Paris: UNESCO.

—— (1992) "Introduction" in H. Soebadio (ed.) *Pusaka: Art of Indonesia*, Singapore: Archipelago Press, pp. 15–16.

Stanley, N. (1998) *Being Ourselves for You: The Global Display of Cultures*, London: Middlesex University Press.

Stocking, G. (1985) "Introduction: Objects and Others: Essays on Museums and Material Culture" in G. Stocking (ed.) *Objects and Others: Essays on Museums and Material Culture*, Madison: University of Wisconsin Press, pp. 3–14.

Sumadio, B. (1985) "Future-Oriented Cultural Policies and Development Programs," *Museografia*, 15(1):5–10.

—— (1987) "Provincial Museums in Indonesia: Their Role in National Development". Paper presented at the International Council of Museums Committee on Museums of Ethnography Meeting "The Presentation of Culture," Leiden, the Netherlands, August 31 to September 5.

Sutaarga, A. (1987) *Introduction to Museums in Indonesia*, The International Council of Museums National Committee in Indonesia. A Special Issue Multiplied by ICOM-Indonesia. Jakarta: Direktorate of Museums.

175

Suyati (1990) *Collection Classification for Provincial Museums*, Jakarta: Direktorate Permuseuman.

Tamarapa, A. (1996) "Museum Kaitiaki: Maori Perspectives on the Presentation and Management of Maori Treasures and Relationships with Museums" in E. Arinze and A. Cummins (eds) *Curatorship: Indigenous Perspectives in Post-Colonial Societies. Proceedings. Mercury Series, Directorate Paper 8*, Canadian Museum of Civilization with the Commonwealth Association of Museums and the University of Victoria, British Columbia, pp. 160–177.

Taylor, P. (1994) "The Nusantara Concept of Culture: Local Traditions and National Identity as Expressed in Indonesia's Museums" in P. Taylor (ed.) *Fragile Traditions: Indonesian Art in Jeopardy*, Honolulu: University of Hawai'i Press, pp. 71–90.

Taylor, P. and L. Aragon (1991) *Beyond the Java Sea*, Washington and New York: National Museum of Natural History and Harry N. Abrams.

Toelken, B. (1982) "Seeing with Both Eyes" in *Native Arts Issues 81/82*, Juneau: Alaska State Council on the Arts.

Trope, J. and W. Echo-Hawk (2000) "The Native American Graves Protection and Repatriation Act" in D. Mihesuah (ed.) *Repatriation Reader: Who Owns Native American Remains?*, Lincoln and London: University of Nebraska Press, pp. 123–168.

Tsosie, R. (1997) "Indigenous Peoples' Claims to Cultural Property: A Legal Perspective," *Museum Anthropology*, 21(3):5–11.

Tutai, V. (1991) "The National Museum of the Cook Islands" in S. Eoe and P. Swadling (eds) *Museums and Cultural Centres in the Pacific*, Port Moresby: Papua New Guinea National Museum, pp. 201–204.

UNESCO (1995) *The Cultural Dimension of Development: Towards a Practical Approach*, Paris: UNESCO.

UNESCO (1996) *Our Creative Diversity: The Report of the World Commission on Culture and Development*, 2nd edn, Paris: UNESCO.

Van Beek, G. (1990) "The Rites of Things: A Critical View of Museums, Objects and Metaphors," *Etnofoor*, 3(1):26–44.

Van Mensch, P. (1988) "What Contributions has Museology to Offer to the Developing Countries?" in *Museology and Developing Countries: Help or Manipulation*, International Committee for Museology Study Series 14.

Vergo, P. (ed.) (1989) *The New Museology*, London: Reaktion Books.

Vuilleumier, J. (1983) "Museum Programming and Development Policy," *Museum*, 35(138): 94–97.

Wagner, F. (1988) *Art of Indonesia*, Singapore: Graham Brash.

Walsh, K. (1992) *The Representation of the Past: Museums and Heritage in the Post-Modern World*, London and New York: Routledge.

Warren, L., J. Slikkerveer and D. Brokensha (eds) (1995) *The Cultural Dimensions of Development: Indigenous Knowledge Systems*, London: Intermediate Technology Publications.

Waterson, R. (1990) *The Living House: An Anthropology of Architecture in South-East Asia*, London: Thames and Hudson.

Watson, R. (1997) "Museums and Indigenous Cultures: The Power of Local Knowledge," *Cultural Survival Quarterly*, 21(1):24–25.

Welsh, P. (1997) "The Power of Possessions: The Case Against Cultural Property," *Museum Anthropology*, 21(3):12–18.

West, R. (1993) "Research and Scholarship at the National Museum of the American Indian: The New 'Inclusiveness'," *Museum Anthropology*, 17(1):5–8.

—— (1994) "The National Museum of the American Indian Perspectives on Museums in the 21st Century," *Museum Anthropology*, 18(3):53–58.

—— (2000) "Introduction: A New Idea of Ourselves: The Changing Presentation of the American Indian" in A. Kawasaki (ed.) *The Changing Presentation of the American Indian: Museums and Native Cultures*, Washington, DC: National Museum of the American Indian, Smithsonian Institution, pp. 7–14.

Western, D., M. Wright and S. Sturm (eds) (1994) *Natural Connections: Perspectives in Community-Based Conservation*, Washington, DC: Island Press, pp. 92–122.

Whittier, H. (1978) "The Kenyah" in V. King (ed.) *Essays on Borneo Societies*, Hull Monographs on Southeast Asia no. 7, Oxford: Oxford University Press.

Williams, R. (1960) *Culture and Society: 1780–1950*, New York: Anchor Books.

Williamson, L. (1997) "Pest Management at the National Museum of the American Indian," *ICOM Ethnographic Conservation Newsletter*, 15:2–3.

Wolfe, S. and L. Mibach (1983) "Ethical Considerations in the Conservation of Native American Sacred Objects," *Journal for the American Institute of Conservation*, 23:1–6.

World Bank (1996) *The World Bank Participation Sourcebook*, Washington, DC: The World Bank.

Yampolsky, P. (1995) "Forces for Change in the Regional Performing Arts of Indonesia," *Bijdragen tot de Taal-, Land-en Volkenkunde*, 151:700–725.

Watson, D. M. S., *Paleontology and Modern Biology*. New Haven:
Yale University Press, 19—.

Wheeler, W. M., *Social Life Among the Insects*. New York: Harcourt, Brace and Company, 19—.

Whitehead, A. N., *Science and the Modern World*. New York: The Macmillan Company, 19—.

Wieman, H. N., *The Wrestle of Religion with Truth*. New York: The Macmillan Company, 19—.

Wright, S., "Evolution in Mendelian Populations," *Genetics*, 19—.

Index